The Fantasy
Economy

Neil Kraus

The Fantasy Economy

Neoliberalism, Inequality, and
the Education Reform Movement

TEMPLE UNIVERSITY PRESS
Philadelphia • *Rome* • *Tokyo*

TEMPLE UNIVERSITY PRESS
Philadelphia, Pennsylvania 19122
tupress.temple.edu

Library of Congress Cataloging-in-Publication Data

Names: Kraus, Neil, 1968– author.
Title: The fantasy economy : neoliberalism, inequality, and the education
reform movement / Neil Kraus.
Description: Philadelphia : Temple University Press, 2023. | Includes
bibliographical references and index. | Summary: "This book offers a new
perspective on wage stagnation, growing inequality, and the current
education reform agenda. The author argues that education must be
understood as a necessary public service providing critical benefits,
many of which are not strictly economic yet are essential for democratic
society"— Provided by publisher.
Identifiers: LCCN 2023001594 (print) | LCCN 2023001595 (ebook) | ISBN
9781439923702 (cloth) | ISBN 9781439923719 (paperback) | ISBN
9781439923726 (pdf)
Subjects: LCSH: Education—Economic aspects—United States. | Labor
supply—Effect of education on—United States. | Income distribution—
United States. | Educational change—United States. | Business and
education—United States. | Education—United States—Public opinion. |
Education—Political aspects—United States.
Classification: LCC LC66 .K73 2023 (print) | LCC LC66 (ebook) | DDC
370.973—dc23/eng/20230426
LC record available at https://lccn.loc.gov/2023001594
LC ebook record available at https://lccn.loc.gov/2023001595

Printed in the United States of America

9 8 7 6 5 4 3 2 1

For all teachers and students.

Contents

Tables and Illustrations

Preface and Acknowledgments

I have been thinking about the issues raised in this book since I was a child in the 1970s, the youngest of three siblings growing up in a suburb of Syracuse, New York. It was a time of major economic upheaval, and the loss of industry and decline of labor unions significantly changed the structure of economic opportunity. Service-sector jobs requiring minimal education and paying low wages proliferated, and the notion that one had to go to college to enter the middle class was becoming increasingly accepted.

But I learned at a young age that higher education attainment did not automatically create employment security. My parents went to college in the 1950s, when few Americans pursued higher education, and both received degrees from Le Moyne College in 1954. They were outstanding students, winning many honors in both high school and college. I recall one summer evening in the mid-1970s, when I was about seven or eight years old, my father came home from work and looked very upset. We quickly learned that he had lost his job that day. A few minutes later, a police officer parked outside our house on our dead-end street. For several minutes, we watched the officer sit in his car and wondered why he was outside our house. Then he came to the door, and my father answered. He asked my dad if he had just gotten gas at a particular station that he often stopped at on his way home, and my father answered yes. This was in the 1970s, when in Syracuse (and presumably in most of the country) you could pump your gas first and then pay after. But that night, my dad was so upset about losing his job that he left the gas station without paying. My father apologized profusely, telling the officer the story of losing his job that day. The officer was also apologetic, and he accepted money from my dad for the gas and left. My father lost not only that job but several other jobs during my childhood. To be clear, we never lived in poverty, nor were we ever close. My parents' frugality, and the relatively low cost of living in Syracuse, meant that periodic unemployment, while extremely stressful, did not affect our family the way it does so many others. But I saw firsthand that my dad's college degree and many academic honors, which included being named valedictorian of his high school class, were not guarantees of employment stability in a changing political economy.

As a young child, I also contemplated the economic trajectory of people with less formal education, such as my maternal grandparents, who were Irish immigrants. My grandmother passed away when I was a toddler, but I visited my grandfather throughout my youth, and I recall him telling me about the many years he worked as a custodian for the Syracuse City Schools. He was employed by the district for most of his working life, and my grandmother cleaned houses for employment. After arriving in the United States with virtually nothing, they raised three daughters, and their jobs afforded them economic stability and modest upward mobility. My grandfather's pension from the school district allowed him to live for several years in nursing homes after my grandmother's passing. Like so many other Americans with minimal formal education, they shared in the prosperity of the postwar years. Learning of their experiences showed me that in an earlier time, one's economic livelihood did not depend on one's formal education.

When I was in middle school in the early 1980s, I also remember the emerging national obsession with the nation's schools. My parents subscribed to multiple news magazines and the daily newspaper, and although I didn't like reading much at that age, I could not help but notice the extensive negative media coverage that the schools received. In high school, I entered the labor force for the first time. Like most middle-class youth, I used my family connections to get nearly all my part-time jobs, which provided another key lesson in the nation's structure of opportunity. I also became very interested in political and economic issues, and I thought a lot about poverty and economic opportunity. I was a good student, even if I did not particularly enjoy most of school. But with two high-achieving older siblings—both of whom attended college—as well as two parents who were college graduates, my family took going to college as a given. Besides, it seemed like I had no choice if I wanted any economic security. While I was nervous about college, I was also excited about the prospect. I enrolled at my parents' alma mater, Le Moyne College, in the fall of 1986.

The night before I started classes, a family friend enthusiastically told me, "The sky's the limit, Neil." And I believed him. College meant learning about all kinds of things that I had never learned about before. And despite my father's occasional hard luck with employment, I also believed that I could enjoy middle-class stability if I got a college degree. I did not feel that I had to select a major on the basis of the wages offered in the jobs associated with it. I majored in history and took a variety of courses in political science, philosophy, religion, and English with many excellent professors in small classes. For me, college was a great experience. During and after college, I worked for Catholic Charities in Syracuse in several different jobs with elementary-age schoolchildren. I had no experience with children and no formal training or education in a related field, but my mother worked for the organization, and she helped me get employment there. In one of those jobs, almost all the kids I worked with were Black and in poverty, and I got to know them and their families well. The experience was life changing and further refined my thinking about economic opportunity, which seemed to be about much more than education.

In graduate school, I wrote a dissertation on urban politics and policy, which developed into my first book, about the role of racism in local decision-making affecting the formation of segregated, high-poverty neighborhoods in Buffalo, New York. In that book and my second, which focused on local politics and inequality through case studies of Gary and Minneapolis, I examined urban school districts in some depth. I was not very familiar with human capital theory at the time, but looking back now, I realize that I implicitly attached far too much significance to policies such as racial and economic desegregation of urban schools as prescriptions for reducing inequality. I still support these policies, which have been shown to improve educational outcomes for disadvantaged students. But poverty is about a lack of income, and no education policies can change the factors that shape the labor market.

This book started out very differently from the finished product. Many years ago, I began researching a book on K–12 education reform. At the time, I was involved in several committees on my campus, the University of Wisconsin, River Falls (UWRF), yet the political dynamics of education made no sense to me. Despite possessing something that everyone ostensibly needs—education itself—both the K–12 and especially the higher education systems operate from a position of permanent political weakness. Austerity budgeting was a given, and public higher education had to continuously defend its mere existence. If everyone needs higher education, how could this be? While much of the opposition to education seemed to be rooted in the larger hostility toward government, there appeared to be something else going on that made education particularly vulnerable to political attacks.

The more I looked at official labor market data, however, the less confusing this was to me. In data provided by public agencies and much scholarly work, I discovered the misleading nature of so much of the conventional wisdom regarding the economy and education system. In sum, I learned that the country was far better educated than ever before but that the labor market was dominated by low-wage, low-education jobs. The labor market was not becoming more specialized or dominated by technical fields, and wages for most workers, including many working in jobs requiring bachelor's and advanced degrees, had stagnated for decades. Despite these realities—or because of them—neoliberalism had deliberately assigned the education system the impossible task of providing economic opportunity for all. But because education cannot create jobs for graduates or set wage rates, public opposition or indifference to education was easy to mobilize. In sum, the real economy explained everything.

This book grew out of my frustration that so many education reforms are being led by institutions and individuals who advance a version of the economy and education system that is, at its core, an interest group campaign to continuously frame the debate about economic opportunity and inequality as solely a discussion about education. This has been a remarkably successful project, so much so that most educators and citizens believe the tenets of what I call the fantasy economy. Therefore, getting beyond the fantasy economy is a formidable task indeed. At the same time, because we live in the real economy, perhaps it is not as difficult as it might appear.

Numerous people have been extremely helpful in making this book a reality. First and foremost, I would like to thank Temple University Press. Aaron Javsicas showed interest in this project from the time I first spoke to him at a conference several years ago, and his detailed feedback on the manuscript, along with those of two anonymous reviewers, significantly improved the final product. And Gary Kramer's assistance was also much appreciated. UWRF provided me with a sabbatical during the spring 2020 semester, which, despite being cut short by COVID-19, allowed me significant time to work on the project. Many current and former colleagues offered me encouragement along the way, including Eoin Breadon, Tricia Davis, Matt Dooley, Sandy Ellis, Connie Foster, Greta

Gaard, Brett Kallusky, Jim Madsen, John Mazis, Karl Peterson, Kiril Petkov, Chris Simer, Kris Tjornehoj, John Walker, John Wheeler, Jim White, Walter Wietzke, Jennifer Willis-Rivera, Zhiguo Yang, and Dean Yohnk. Since arriving at UWRF in 2005, Davida Alperin has been an outstanding colleague, and her support of my work is much appreciated. The support of John Heppen, Doug Margolis, Mialisa Moline, and Alex Tupan has been especially helpful, and their leadership over many years on UWRF's Faculty Senate has been critical. Several individuals, including Ryan Fischer, Victoria Houseman, Chad Goldberg, Moira Lynch, Lissa Schneider, and Aaron Weinschenk, also read drafts of chapters, and their comments were extremely helpful. Katie Possehl also provided critical assistance with technical aspects of the manuscript, and her help is much appreciated.

Two colleagues deserve particular thanks—Jon Shelton and Cyndi Kernahan. Jon, a noted labor historian at UW Green Bay, read several drafts of chapters, and our many conversations over the years helped me clarify my arguments. His work on human capital, exemplified in his book *The Education Myth: How Human Capital Trumped Social Democracy* (2023), provides the necessary historical context for how what I call the fantasy economy developed. Jon's support for my work has been critical. Cyndi, director of the Center for Excellence in Teaching and Learning and professor of Psychological Sciences at UWRF as well as an accomplished scholar of race and teaching and learning, also read drafts of many chapters and provided essential feedback. Her extensive knowledge of higher education issues provided me with important insights into my arguments, and she also introduced me to the work of teaching- and learning-scholar Kevin Gannon. Cyndi's continuous support and encouragement has been extraordinarily valuable.

Three former students deserve thanks as well: Nick Carrow, Isaac Russell, and Richard Simones. I had many conversations with Nick, Isaac, and Richard about the issues raised here, and their insights have informed my thinking in many ways. Other longtime friends deserve thanks, including Scott Bornkessel, Charlie Machabee, Martin Markowitz, Kevin Ryan, and Eric Ziegelmayer. Scott's knowledge of technology was extremely helpful; Kevin and Eric provided insightful feedback on my ideas and arguments. Steve Yoch's encouragement was also much appreciated. Political scientists and Le Moyne College emeriti faculty John Freie and Sue Behuniak have always been supportive of my work and remain good friends. Le Moyne College history professor Doug Egerton also deserves thanks. Two friends also from my Le Moyne days, Marc Cassidy and Ron Resetarits, have informed my thinking on many of these issues, and Marc educated me on nonprofit organizations as well. Thanks also go to Dara Orenstein. My graduate school adviser at the State University of New York (SUNY) at Albany, Todd Swanstrom, also deserves mention. Our many conversations over the years have been very helpful in shaping my thinking on a variety of issues, and his support of my work is much appreciated.

Several educators have had lasting impacts on me and my family and deserve thanks, including my sixth-grade teacher, Helene Reiben, as well as Pete Dymit, Angie Elliott, and Sandy Katkov, all of the Minnetonka School District in Minnesota. Helene, Pete, Angie, and Sandy represent the millions of educators whose concern for their students knows no bounds. Two Catholic priests taught me courage, compassion, and the importance of humor, especially during difficult times: Vincent Kilpatrick and Stephen O'Gara.

I would also like to thank my brother and sister, David Kraus and Eileen Lynch, for their many years of support and encouragement, as well as my sister- and brother-in-law, Connie Campanaro and Bill Lynch. In addition, I acknowledge my deceased parents, Donald and Noreen Kraus, without whom I would never have developed an interest in these issues. They believed in me, even when I doubted myself, and I still feel their presence, every day. Finally, it takes a great deal of time to write a book, and much of that is time away from family. Most of all, then, I would like to thank my family, Jennifer, Ben, and Alex, and recognize that completing the book would not have been possible without their love and support.

The Fantasy
Economy

Introduction

Change the mission of K–12 schools to take educational
responsibility for the economic futures of all students.
—Sue E. Berryman and Thomas R. Bailey,
The Double Helix of Education and the Economy

The United States has been underproducing college-going
workers since 1980. Supply has failed to keep pace with
growing demand, and as a result, income inequality has
grown precipitously.
—Anthony P. Carnevale and Stephen J. Rose,
The Undereducated American

Over the last several decades, wage stagnation and growing inequality have become the defining characteristics of American society. While inequality increased significantly in the late nineteenth and early twentieth centuries, by the middle twentieth century, the gap between the lowest and highest earners had shrunk. During this period, the United States was characterized by the mixed economy that resulted from the New Deal, in which markets "play the dominant role in producing and allocating goods and innovating to meet consumer demand" but "government plays a dominant or vital role in the many places where markets fall short" (J. Hacker and Pierson 2016, 3). But beginning in the late 1970s, a new political economy, neoliberalism, emerged, "[suggesting] that governments, or 'the state,' should interfere as little as possible with the market, instead allowing its 'invisible hand' to guide economic, political and social relationships" (Stuesse 2016, 9). By the time President Ronald Reagan took office in 1981, the contours of neoliberalism were firmly in place, and free market supremacy became further entrenched with the fall of the Soviet Union several years later.

As neoliberalism became ascendent, domestic manufacturing employment and union membership began a steady decline. As a result, the real economy became increasingly dominated by low-education, low-wage jobs, even as educational attainment rates reached all-time highs. Because of the disconnect between the labor market and the educational attainment of the population, then, millions of Americans were underemployed—working in jobs that typically required less formal education than they had received and being paid less as a result. But wages also stagnated for millions more bachelor's and advanced degree holders working in jobs commensurate with their education levels. Despite these trends, Americans were consistently told the opposite: that K–12 schools and higher education were failing, creating a permanent shortage of skilled workers. U.S. students had fallen well behind students around the world, and the citizenry was poorly prepared for the new labor market, which had an abundance of high-education, high-technology, high-wage jobs. According to this view, then, wage stagnation, growing inequality, and even poverty itself were caused by the education system, not by the larger political economy. This is what I call the fantasy economy.

The fantasy economy is a misleading articulation of the economy and education system rooted in the economic self-interests of corporations and the wealthy. While its intellectual origins go back much further, I argue that it has been the product of a political campaign that was aggressively initiated during the Reagan administration in the 1980s to justify the neoliberal transformation of the U.S. political economy. Reflecting its roots in human capital theory, the fantasy economy defines education as the exclusive mechanism providing the citizenry with economic opportunity and intentionally reduces the role of the state in mitigating the effects of the market. Thus, when confronted with the reality of stagnating wages and widening inequality, economic elites inevitably turn the discussion back to education and the qualifications of the workforce.

As an interest group campaign and the foundation of the education reform movement, the fantasy economy rests on two major empirical claims: both the education system and the workforce are chronically deficient. These claims, continually echoed by corporate interests, are reinforced by funded researchers, university policy centers, and think tanks. And because they have become conventional wisdom, it is not surprising that such claims are repeated unwittingly by major media, the education establishment, and any number of scholars. Rather than viewed as shaped by public policies and business practices, growing inequality and wage stagnation are deliberately framed as *educational problems with educational solutions*. Yet as I will show, these claims are not born out by the evidence.

As in the "education gospel" (Grubb and Lazerson 2004) narrative, in the fantasy economy, the education system is deeply flawed. More specifically, reformers argue that K–12 schooling has declined over time and that American students are perpetually inferior to those of numerous other nations, especially in math and science, which has led to the significant emphasis on STEM (science, technology, engineering, and math) education. While critics have advocated market-based K–12 reforms for several decades, in recent years higher education has come under increasing attack to shore up the fantasy economy's second major assumption of a permanently inadequate labor force. No matter what the conditions of the macroeconomy, or the number of associate's, bachelor's, and advanced degrees awarded, leading institutions and thought leaders of the fantasy economy continually remind us that both the quantity and quality of the labor force are always lacking. The public is further warned that in the longer term, a substandard educational system and deficient workforce could lead to the supplanting of the United States as the world's dominant economic and military power. Arguments claiming education and workforce weaknesses, then, are ultimately two sides of the same coin and mutually reinforcing. In a seemingly endless rhetorical loop, a failing education system is cited as the cause of an inferior workforce, which, in turn, is held up as evidence for the necessity of further education reform.

I choose to label this campaign a fantasy because it is a distortion of and distraction from reality. The image of a labor market full of jobs requiring highly educated, highly paid knowledge workers is far more desirable—especially for an increasingly educated population—than the real economy dominated by low-wage, service-sector jobs typically requiring little formal education. In the fantasy economy, then, the assumption of the unambiguously positive economic effects of obtaining more formal education and training is foundational. In terms of average or median wage levels, it is certainly true that bachelor's and advanced degree holders earn more than those with less formal education. But when significant numbers of college graduates fail to secure gainful employment and take jobs below their education level, or when graduates struggle financially in jobs requiring college degrees, the fantasy economy's focus goes back to the education system time and again, while promoting research that distorts or ignores these structural labor market realities. And the tens of millions of individuals working in low-wage jobs requiring a high school degree or no formal credential are told that because of an increasingly complex labor market, more education and training are the only ticket to economic stability. Indexing the minimum wage to inflation, limiting the use of contract workers or noncompete agreements, facilitating workers' ability to join a labor union, or simply pressuring employers to raise the wages of workers are noticeably not part of this discussion, which focuses exclusively on formal education's role in economic uplift. Constructed by the interests that have benefited disproportionately from the economic growth of the last several decades, the fantasy economy leaves existing political and economic arrangements untouched and focuses all attention on the education system.

In creating the concept of the fantasy economy, I build on pioneering works addressing many popular myths associated with education and the economy, including Berliner and Biddle's *The Manufactured Crisis* (1995) and Grubb and Lazerson's seminal *The Education Gospel* (2004). Berliner and Biddle carefully documented the many flaws of using aggregate testing data as an indicator of U.S. student achievement. Publishing in 1995, before the term STEM was even coined, they also successfully challenged claims about the inferiority of American scientific education and the alleged shortages of scientists and engineers. Grubb and Lazerson's work showed the extent to which current critiques of education had deep historical roots. They correctly pointed out the disconnect between education reformers' repeated claims of a high-education labor market and the realities of a low-education labor market and courageously affirmed that "the notion of an overwhelming surge in education requirements for jobs is absurd, and the promotion of college for all is in some ways dishonest" (Ibid., 19). They also maintained that a disproportionate emphasis on education fails to adequately consider the many ways that society should meaningfully address inequality.

But while these and many other education scholars have correctly questioned the assumption of a failing school system, few have systematically questioned elites' depiction of the current and future labor market and economy. Nor have scholars adequately addressed the funded research of the K–12 and higher education reform movements. I argue that, as a political campaign, the fantasy economy represents economic elites' effort to justify the new political economy by attributing wage stagnation and increasing inequality solely to the education system. Thus, economic self-interest drives the fantasy economy. Therefore, I follow the reasoning of James Madison, one of the most important figures in the shaping of our constitutional system. In Federalist #10, Madison argued that the "most common and durable source of factions has been the various and unequal distribution of property. Those who hold and those who are without property have ever formed distinct interests in society. Those who are creditors, and those who are debtors, fall under a like discrimination. A landed interest, a manufacturing interest, a mercantile interest, a moneyed interest, with many lesser interests, grow up of necessity in civilized nations, and divide them into different classes, actuated by different sentiments and views." For Madison, the causes of faction were "sown in the nature of man." Different economic classes have different economic interests.

The economic self-interest of corporations and the wealthy is manifest in the fantasy economy campaign in several distinct ways. First, as analysts like Diane Ravitch have forcefully argued (2010, 2013, 2020), the immediate economic interests of a large and growing number of firms are a fundamental component of the education reform movement. Numerous firms profit from the universal implementation of standardized tests, the sale of myriad educational services and products, and the proliferation of charter schools, for example. The educational consulting industry has become the primary beneficiary of the permanent crisis model—in both K–12 and higher education—upon which the fantasy economy is premised. And the leaders of numerous education reform organizations frequently earn high salaries to advocate for education reform policies.

But I also argue that the fantasy economy's depiction of the labor market is very much a reflection of the economic self-interests of corporations as employers. In most political discussion, business interests' advocacy for tax breaks and deregulation are appropriately seen as self-interested. Yet the power of the fantasy economy paradigm has allowed business interests' characterizations of the needs of the labor market to be viewed as disinterested, enabling claims of worker shortages and skills gaps to remain effective decades after they were first introduced. Yet as Michael Teitelbaum (2014a) has shown, efforts to shape the public perception of a chronic shortage of scientists and engineers have their origins in the middle twentieth century and have had a significant impact on public policies in recent years, including the continuous growth in STEM education at all levels and the expansion of the H-1B visa program. I argue that the fantasy economy is as much driven by firms' desire to keep labor costs down as by the desire for expanding markets for educational products and services and by the high incomes earned by many education reformers.

Although these links between the economic self-interest of elites and the core ideas of the fantasy economy are clear, such arguments are often caricatured. For example, in the *New York Times* review of Diane Ravitch's 2020 book *Slaying Goliath*, Annie Murphy Paul writes that Ravitch "often seems more interested in settling scores and in calling out by name the 'predatory billionaires' behind 'the corporate assault on public education'" (Paul 2020). Moreover, when the debate is focused only on the profits of companies selling educational products and services, the firms employing engineers and technology workers, or many education reformers' high incomes, the role of foundations—arguably the biggest players in education reform—is neglected. Because charitable foundations do not sell any products and employ relatively few individuals, the argument presumably goes, they cannot benefit economically from the education policies they advocate. Thus, in most mainstream discussion, to even inquire about the economic interests of foundations or their preferences regarding other policies or practices affecting the economic livelihoods of workers is out of bounds.

But this view of foundation interests as distinct from the interests of corporations and the wealthy is a relatively recent historical development. In one of philanthropy's founding documents, "The Gospel of Wealth," first published in 1889, Andrew Carnegie maintained that the economic interests of the rich were a driving force in the burgeoning philanthropic system and argued forcefully against changing the fundamentals of American capitalism that produced extreme inequality: "We start, then, with a condition of affairs under which the best interests of the race are promoted, but which inevitably gives wealth to the few. Thus far, accepting conditions as they exist, the situation can be surveyed and pronounced good" (Carnegie 1901, 17). According to Carnegie, the wealthy individual, after providing "moderately for the legitimate wants of those dependent upon him," should "consider all surplus revenues which come to him simply as trust funds, which he is called upon to administer, and strictly bound as a matter of duty to administer in the manner which, in his judgment, is best calculated to produce the most beneficial results for the community—the man of wealth thus becoming the mere trustee and agent for his poorer brethren, bringing to their service his superior wisdom, experience, and ability to administer, doing for them better than they would or could do for themselves" (Ibid., 21–22).

In the ensuing decades, then, it was understood that the economic interests of businesses were part of the motivation for corporate charitable giving. For example, in 1955, Standard Oil of New Jersey and a group of affiliated companies, including Esso Standard Oil, Esso Shipping, Esso Research and Engineering, Esso Export, and Interstate Oil Pipe Line, created the Esso Education Foundation to "continue and coordinate their programs of financial assistance to privately supported colleges and universities" (American Chemical Society 1955, 4398). The new foundation received initial pledges of $1.5 million from participating companies (equivalent to over $16 million in 2022 dollars). For many years before the creation of its foundation, Standard Oil and its affiliates had "assisted education by providing grants, fellowships, and scholarships for specific projects and studies of basic interest to their business" (Ibid.). When describing the creation of the foundation, an industry newsletter reported that Standard Oil "believes that companies, both as good citizens and in their own interests, should give positive support to colleges and universities" (Ibid.). The Esso Education Foundation went on to give millions of dollars to hundreds of private colleges and universities throughout the 1950s and 1960s, a period when public higher education was expanding all over the country. In 1966, when describing a grant to the University of Dayton for hospital construction, the foundation's chairman stated: "Increased private assistance, including corporate support, will help to encourage growth in initiative and independence. In seeking the most effective use of its available funds, the Esso Education Foundation will continue to study the changing needs of higher education and to adjust the emphasis of its grant programs to help meet them" (University of Dayton 1966). In acknowledging the gift, the university's president used similar language, implicitly equating corporate and foundation giving: "The generous educational support of business and industry, of which this is an outstanding example, is a never-ending source of encouragement" (Ibid.). Further, in partnering with the Black power movement in the 1960s, the Ford Foundation sought to incorporate Black people into the mainstream, and leaders at Ford and other organizations would "determine and oversee the process by which this incorporation would happen to best serve the interests of corporate capitalism" (Ferguson 2013, 83). Corporate interests were reflected in foundation giving, and there was no illusion to the contrary.

But in the years that followed, corporate leaders became increasingly dismayed by striking schoolteachers and political activities on college campuses. I argue that therefore, to advance their interests in both K–12 and higher education, elites began a campaign to create the belief that foundation giving was totally distinct from corporate interests, and this perception was facilitated by the creation of institutions such as the American Association for Higher Education and *Change* magazine. And after decades of extensive foundation giving to education, these efforts have been largely successful, particularly in higher education. However, the prevalence of teachers' unions remains a barrier to the completion of this project in K–12 schooling. As a result, foundations are periodically asked about their motivations for their extensive K–12 activities while rarely having to address similar questions regarding their higher education philanthropy.

Yet foundation leaders bristle when asked whether their economic self-interests might influence their education-related giving. For example, when Bill Gates was asked in a 2014 interview whether his or Microsoft's economic interests were a motivating factor in the Gates Foundation's philanthropy with respect to advancing the Common Core, he vigorously denied any such personal economic motivation (Layton 2014a). Gates was also asked about his foundation's significant financial influence on the development of the Common Core, and he downplayed the Gates Foundation's total giving, equating it with a "rounding error" three times in the same brief response. For Gates, funding education reform was not political: "We don't fund political groups. . . . These are not political things. . . . We fund people to look into things" (Ibid.). Yet given the existence of public K–12 and higher education systems, compulsory schooling laws, and the multitude of other federal, state, and local regulations touching on every aspect of schooling, I maintain that all education policy is inherently political. And placing such disproportionate emphasis on education's role in creating economic opportunity to the exclusion of other public policies and employer practices necessarily represents a political agenda.

Moreover, the business press appears far less hesitant to equate foundations with corporate interests, the significance of which is underscored when taking into account higher education's lack of consideration of the motives of foundations. In the aftermath of the attempted insurrection at the Capitol by supporters of President Donald Trump on January 6, 2021, the *New York Times* outlined the business community's reckoning with its support for the president. The first individual quoted in the article was Darren Walker, president of the Ford Foundation: "This is what happens when we subordinate our moral principles for what we perceive to be business interests. . . . It is ultimately bad for business and bad for society" (Gelles 2021). The leader of one of the nation's leading foundations spoke about the negative impact of the events of January 6 on business.

Therefore, to fully incorporate the role of foundations in education reform, I argue that the conception of economic self-interest should be expanded to include the very terms of debate established by the fantasy economy regarding economic opportunity. A leading political science text on interest groups affirms: "Frequently, interest groups struggle to *frame* political issues. Public policy issues can be considered in different ways, each invoking different values" (Berry and Wilcox 2018, 8, emphasis in original). Further, an "inherent trait of interest groups is that they present only their side of an issue to the public, offering facts and interpretations most favorable to their positions" (Ibid.). While growing economic inequality and long-term wage stagnation are not typically questioned, these issues can be framed very differently with respect to causation and prescription. As political activity driven by self-interest, the fantasy economy's framing of economic inequality therefore focuses exclusively on education and intentionally deflects attention away from decades of public policies and changing business practices that have directly and indirectly contributed to stagnating wages for most while simultaneously producing extraordinary income and wealth gains for a small minority.

As Anand Giridharadas has argued, "For whoever treats a disease recasts it—with their own diagnosis, prescription, and prognosis. To take on a problem is to make it your own, and to gain the right to decide what it is not and how it doesn't need to be solved" (Giridharadas 2018, 33). I argue that elites place such an emphasis on education's role in providing economic opportunity because this conversation deflects attention from the larger political economy that has allowed a small minority to prosper in recent decades. I maintain that this, then, is the all-encompassing motivation for the extensive coalition perpetuating the fantasy economy: to define the terms of public debate and set parameters for acceptable policy discussion.

In *The Education Gospel*, Grubb and Lazerson identify what they call the Education Coalition, a wide-ranging group that has traditionally supported vocationalism in both K–12 and higher education, including economic reformers, parents and their children, social reformers, educators, and business interests (Grubb and Lazerson 2004, 12). The coalition echoing the tenets of the fantasy economy is similarly vast, going well beyond firms involved in educational services and employing scientists and engineers to include foundations, the business community, financial institutions, funded researchers, and think tanks. Because this narrative is considered common knowledge, major media and the education establishment also reflexively echo its core claims. Parents, students, and the major media have implicitly endorsed the fantasy economy primarily because it is, far and away, the dominant narrative regarding economic opportunity, and the realities of neoliberalism have compelled them to do so. When education is at the center of discussion, questions about what appear to be settled issues within the neoliberal framework, including labor law and the role of unions, minimum wage laws, deregulation, taxation, antitrust, privatization, and trade, are not up for consideration. Routine business practices such as outsourcing, the use of contract workers, the growing use of noncompete agreements, and executive compensation systems are taken as a given. The biggest success of the fantasy economy, then, is society's unyielding emphasis on the educational system as *the* vehicle for creating economic opportunity for the public.

But because of educational institutions' inherent inability to affect either wage rates or the labor market, a framing of economic opportunity rooted solely in education and training keeps both the K–12 and high-er education establishments in a permanently defensive political posture, enabling critics to continue to advance ill-advised reforms, many of which rely on data and research funded by vested interests and reformers them-selves. Here again, Grubb and Lazerson astutely observed these lopsided political dynamics and argued that the "individual benefits of formal schooling have also been exaggerated, leading to disappointment and a suspicion of formal schooling when its promises are not realized. . . . Higher levels of schooling cannot guarantee access to better employment and higher earnings; they may be necessary, but they are often not suf-ficient. Despite its popularity, the naïve version of human-capital theory has never been quite right" (2004, 155–156). Finally, the uncritical ac-ceptance of the fantasy economy's framing of economic opportunity has enabled austerity budgeting to become the default assumption in nearly all mainstream education policy discussion. For public education, doing "more with less" is not up for debate. Education is losing the larger po-litical debate about economic opportunity because the terms established by the fantasy economy have ensured that education cannot even mean-ingfully participate in this debate, let alone win.

The Great Recession, Higher Education Reform, and Conflicts of Interest in Research and Advocacy

For several decades, the education reform movement was focused on K–12 measures, including accountability, charter schools, and vouchers. But the Great Recession altered the larger debate about the economic prom-ise of higher education, as unemployment reached 10 percent and free market capitalism was subjected to increased scrutiny. The Republican Party seized on the public's economic anxiety to advance several auster-ity-driven priorities, including legislation inhibiting collective bargain-ing among public-sector workers, the expansion of market-based school reforms, and cuts to education funding. As Christopher Newfield has writ-ten, "economic downturns have always given states an excuse to cut col-leges. The financial crisis of 2008 gave states the mother of all excuses, and cut they did" (2016, 167). By 2016, levels of support for K–12 edu-cation in many states were still below where they had been several years earlier (Governing 2018). Public funding for higher education also con-tinued its long decline, and by 2018, states had reduced higher education funding to public colleges and universities by an average of over $2,300 per student, or "roughly one quarter," over 1987 levels (Webber 2018, 51). Public higher education had become largely tuition driven.

With the number of underemployed and highly indebted college graduates becoming too large to ignore, colleges and universities were increasingly blamed for the wage and labor outcomes of their graduates on the basis of the false assumption that higher education can control wage levels and jobs. Thus, anti-tenure campaigns were launched in several Republican-led states, including Iowa, North Carolina, Indiana, and Missouri. In early 2017, Missouri Republican state representative Rick Brattin introduced a bill eliminating tenure at the state's public colleges and universities and explicitly linked tenure to the poor employment outcomes of some university graduates. Brattin called tenure "un-American," saying: "This was brought to me by students and family members that have gotten degrees they were told was a great degree path and they got in the real world and can't find a job that it really applied to. They're working at a retail store for $12 an hour with $50,000 in debt. They feel like they were misled. That's a disservice, especially with a public university, and we need to ensure that what those public dollars are going to, and if these students are going to be making a good investment" (Zamudio-Suarez 2017).

The stories of underemployed, low-paid college graduates are all too real, and graduates' economic hardships are exacerbated by increasing levels of student debt. Yet such attacks on higher education resonate because of the overwhelming success of the fantasy economy narrative, which treats the roughly one-third of underemployed bachelor's degree holders—if it considers these millions of individuals at all—as a function of poor major or institution selection or a lack of individual skills as opposed to a reflection of structural labor market realities. Further, such attacks on higher education also fail to consider proximate causes of increasing student debt, including the long-term reduction in state aid to public higher education and decades of wage stagnation itself. As most people's wages have remained flat, their ability to save for their children's education has been substantially hampered. In 2013, only about 2.5 percent of all households reported using college savings plans, and just 0.3 percent of those below the fiftieth income percentile (Hannon et al. 2016). And with a long-term declining real minimum wage, most young people are unable to make significant contributions to their own college expenses and hence increasingly require student loans. Yet these attacks on higher education have had a significant impact, as recent polling has shown that a solid majority of Republicans and Republican leaning independents, 58 percent, believe that colleges and universities "have a negative effect on the country," as compared to just 19 percent of Democrats who feel similarly (Pew Research Center 2017). And as higher education became increasingly blamed for the poor labor market outcomes of their graduates, corporations and foundations launched a major higher education reform campaign.

The subject of conflicts of interest with respect to research funding sources has engulfed the sciences and medicine in recent years. This debate has led to major public policies, including the federal government's Open Payments database, in which consumers can search the financial relationships of their medical providers, as well as the increasingly common requirement in scholarly publishing of disclosing sources of research funding. But because of the lack of meaningful consideration of conflicts of interest in education and labor market research, corporate- and foundation-funded reports on the labor market and education system, often produced by university-based research institutes, are generally viewed as disinterested analyses. This has enabled the creation of one of the more influential tools of the fantasy economy, what I call alternative data. Alterative data is a type of data similar to that produced by public agencies but funded and produced by private sources and used as part of a political narrative to advance a policy agenda. Repeated interminably, alterative data often becomes *the* data.

The alternative data that lies at the heart of the fantasy economy campaign involves the educational requirements of the labor market. The U.S. Department of Labor's Bureau of Labor Statistics (BLS) has long produced data on the current and projected educational requirements of the labor market, and this data has consistently illustrated the realities of our economy, one still dominated by jobs typically requiring little formal education, most of which pay low wages. If private organizations produced their own data as an alternative to widely cited official data such as the unemployment rate or monthly jobs report, it would be quickly dismissed. But the relative obscurity of this data set has allowed the widespread dissemination and uncritical acceptance of alternative data on this crucial snapshot of our economy.

In 2008, according to the Bureau of Labor Statistics employment projections, approximately 31 percent of all jobs required postsecondary education or training for "most workers to become fully qualified," and this number was projected to increase very modestly over the next decade (Bureau of Labor Statistics 2009). The same year, the Center on Education and the Workforce (CEW) was founded at Georgetown University by Anthony Carnevale as a "unique collaboration between Lumina Foundation for Education, Ford Foundation and The Bill & Melinda Gates Foundation" (Center on Education and the Workforce 2009). The CEW argued that "the poor quality of the official projections cascades downward through state and local data systems into the hands of policy makers" (Carnevale, Smith, and Strohl 2010a, 1). Thus, the CEW began to produce its own, alternative data on current and future educational requirements of the labor market. And in 2010, the organization held that in 2007, 59 percent (91 million of 154 million) of jobs "required applicants with at least some college education" (Ibid., 14) and projected that by 2018, "about two-thirds of all employment will require some college education or better" (Ibid.). This data was far more encouraging for all those pursuing higher education. In 2011, the organization published a report entitled *The Undereducated American*, which affirmed: "The United States has been underproducing college-going workers since 1980. Supply has failed to keep pace with growing demand, and as a result, income inequality has grown precipitously" (Carnevale and Rose 2011).

Within short order, the CEW's alternative data had become, in effect, the only data in higher education circles. For example, in a 2020 article that did not mention either the CEW's funding sources or the Bureau of Labor Statistics' substantially different data on the educational requirements of the labor market, the *Chronicle of Higher Education* described the CEW's work as follows: "'By the year 2020, nearly two-thirds of all jobs will require postsecondary education and training.' Anyone who's been to a higher-ed conference or read a book on the topic in the past decade has no doubt heard some version of that prediction—some of us to the point of numbness" (Blumenstyk 2020). This assessment was clearly correct: the perception of a labor market dominated by jobs requiring post–high school education had become ever present in the higher education information ecosystem, and data from the Bureau of Labor Statistics showing a predominantly low-education labor market was much more difficult to find in mainstream discussion. As a political campaign, the fantasy economy is built on narratives, and the narrative of a labor market always requiring more highly educated workers had clearly become conventional wisdom. But I argue that considering the labor market illustrated in official data—in addition to public data illustrating consistently high underemployment rates of college graduates (Federal Reserve Bank of New York 2022a)—the uncritical acceptance of a high-education labor market has had debilitating political effects on higher education, thereby facilitating a continuous and largely unanswered call for a series of reformers' preferred policies, all of which are rooted in austerity budgeting.

In the perpetual, dual crises of the education system and labor force of the fantasy economy, there always seems to be some sort of looming demographic catastrophe. Demographic change was a major theme of the Reagan administration's 1987 report *Workforce 2000* (Johnston and Packer 1987), which maintained that such change could create a shortage of workers in the future. And in recent years, alternative data has also become a key component of another future demographic crisis linked to the labor force—the coming collapse in higher education enrollments, which has typically been referred to as the demographic cliff. Since 1964, the federal government has published detailed projections of education statistics, which have included future enrollments in both K–12 and higher education. In *Demographics and the Demand for Higher Education* (2018), economist Nathan Grawe created a model of future demand for higher education, and his work crystallized the narrative of the coming demographic cliff that had been building for decades.

Grawe embraces human capital theory, largely ignoring official labor market data when he affirms that "the economy's needs for greater educational attainment are substantially higher than we have achieved in recent years, it is possible to imagine plausible policy interventions that could hope to make significant progress on this front" (2018, 133). And his austerity-driven thesis argues that "beginning in 2026, the number of native-born children reaching college age will begin a rapid decline" (Ibid., 6). However, the U.S. Department of Education's projections published in the years before Grawe's book did not project a coming collapse in either future high school graduates or higher education enrollments as far as its data went into the future, roughly eight years (National Center for Education Statistics 2014, 8, 20; 2016a, 14, 24; 2016b, 14, 24; 2017a, 14, 24). Yet Grawe did not cite or discuss the federal projections in his model, which went through 2029, eleven years after the book's publication (Grawe 2018). The predicted crisis of future enrollments was reinforced by the higher education press (*Chronicle of Higher Education* 2019) and effectively became the only narrative in mainstream higher education debate.

Because public higher education has become largely tuition driven, even slight changes in enrollment can lead to significant changes in programs and staff. Higher education is therefore extremely vulnerable to any warnings of collapsing enrollments. And in the corporate-driven information ecosystem of higher education, the options available to address such a major enrollment crisis included the purchase of a growing number of products and services to maintain enrollments, the expansion of online education, curricular changes presumably better suited to the needs of the labor market, and even possible campus closures. Given higher education's structurally weak political standing and years of systematic defunding, increasing public funding through changes in taxation and spending was implicitly off the table. As with the adoption of a standardized testing regime in K–12 education resulting from No Child Left Behind, however, the likelihood of reversing such radical changes—no matter how unpopular, ineffective, or destructive to the very purposes of higher education—would be remote. Still, by the time of the COVID-19 pandemic in 2020, the narrative of a coming enrollment collapse had set the tone for all mainstream higher education discussion. Official enrollment projections that did not foresee such catastrophic trends were very difficult to find in mainstream discussion. The cliff was coming, and a significantly weakened higher education system was instructed to prepare in the present for substantially fewer students (and, implicitly, even less public funding) at some point in the distant future.

The Fantasy Economy Is Everywhere

As a political campaign, the fantasy economy has developed over a period of decades, its assumptions and messaging continually repeated in a wide variety of high-profile sources. Numerous influential reports have been part of this effort, the most well-known of which was *A Nation at Risk: The Imperative for Education Reform* (*ANAR*; National Commission on Excellence in Education 1983), published in 1983 by the Reagan administration's Department of Education and subject of countless analyses. Also in 1983, the Carnegie Foundation published the report *High School*, which argued that the nation's secondary education system was a "troubled institution" (Boyer 1983, 9). *Workforce 2000: Work and Workers for the 21st Century* (Johnston and Packer 1987), commissioned by President Reagan's Department of Labor and published by the Hudson Institute, was profoundly influential in creating the skills gap campaign, an essential component of the education reform movement. More recently, reports including the Bill Clinton administration's *Before It's Too Late* (National Commission on Mathematics and Science Teaching for the 21st Century 2000), the George W. Bush administration's *A Test of Leadership* (Secretary of Education's Commission on the Future of Higher Education 2006), and the National Academy of Sciences' *Rising above the Gathering Storm* (2007) reinforced previous arguments regarding supposedly inferior science and math education and, like *ANAR*, warned of inevitable American decline unless major actions were taken. The fantasy economy is, first and foremost, a political campaign, and, as we will see, privately created and funded organizations calling themselves "commissions" yet having no official status have also been a key part of these efforts.

Business interests have been the driving forces behind the fantasy economy campaign, both through their influence on politically appointed government commissions and through their own extensive political activities. Corporations and trade groups echo the fantasy economy's core claims about the many problems with the workforce and the need for significant education reforms. A growing number of educational consultants and technology firms repeat these claims while they profit from an austerity-based model positing an education system in constant crisis, failing students, employers, and the larger economy.

Foundations play an outsize role in the perpetuation of the fantasy economy. Major foundations fund a blizzard of research and initiatives promoting the assumption that the education system is the main institution responsible for providing economic opportunity. While foundations have long supported K–12 reform, they have also been active supporters of higher education reform, and these activities increased significantly in the aftermath of the Great Recession. Numerous organizations active in education policy and funded largely by foundations and corporations produce the data and research driving education reform and have also become extraordinarily influential. Despite relying on private funding—much of which comes from vested interests—and having clearly stated public policy agendas, such organizations are not typically seen as interest groups. Rather, they are seen as objective, data-producing organizations, giving them enormous influence on education debate and policy. And think tanks regularly produce research and reports echoing the fantasy economy's major assertions involving a purportedly high-education labor market and a failing education system.

In turn, the core assumptions of the fantasy economy are uncritically echoed in major media, including influential newspapers, cable news, and the business and education press. The tenets of the fantasy economy have also been elaborated in a seemingly endless line of popular books with titles such as *The World Is Flat: A Brief History of the 21st Century*; *Surpassing Shanghai: An Agenda for American Education*; *The New Education: How to Revolutionize the University to Prepare Students for a World in Flux*; *That Used to Be Us: How America Fell Behind in the World It Invented and How We Can Come Back*; *Creating Innovators: The Making of Young People Who Will Change the World*; *The Global Achievement Gap: Why Even Our Best Schools Don't Teach the New Survival Skills Our Children Need—and What We Can Do about It*; and *The Smartest Kids in the World: And How They Got That Way*. Thought leaders, many of whom are authors themselves, promote the fantasy economy paradigm in high-profile venues and elite conferences.

Finally, the fantasy economy's basic ideas have been given the imprimatur of higher education itself and of many scholars. With initial funding from the Reagan administration's National Institute of Education, the Institute on Education and the Economy (IEE), located within Columbia University's Teachers College, provided university-based research for the nascent skills gap campaign led by business interests at a time when news reports were dominated by the loss of industry and good jobs. And Georgetown University's CEW, funded by private interests, plays an outsize role in the data and research of the current higher education reform movement. Privately funded, university-based research institutes have also been central to K–12 education reform efforts, including the University of Washington's Center on Reinventing Public Education (CRPE), the University of Arkansas's Department of Education Reform, and the Center for Research on Education Outcomes (CREDO) at Stanford University's Hoover Institution.[1] I argue that as political entities, these organizations produce reports that—regardless of the findings—advocate the expansion of market-based education policies supported by their donors in a permanent campaign to keep the public discussion of economic opportunity focused squarely on education.

In addition, high-profile scholars also play an important role in shaping the fantasy economy narrative, despite the lack of any recent, comprehensive official labor market data in some of their most influential work (Bowen, Chingos, and McPherson 2009; Darling-Hammond 2010; Goldin and Katz 2008). In *The Flat World and Education: How America's Commitment to Equity Will Determine Our Future* (2010), Linda Darling-Hammond, the Charles E. Ducommun Professor of Education Emeritus at the Stanford Graduate School of Education and a noted progressive, acknowledges the support of several foundations, including Ford, Gates, Rockefeller, Wallace, and Spencer, among others (Ibid., xiii–xiv). Near the very beginning of the book, she states:

> In the last decades, mountains of reports have been written in countries around the world about the need for more powerful learning focused on the demands of life, work, and citizenship in the 21st century. The process of managing decisions and solving social and scientific problems in contemporary democracies is growing ever more complex. At least 70% of U.S. jobs now require specialized knowledge and skills, as compared to only 5% at the dawn of the last century, when our current system of schooling was established. . . . Furthermore, the nature of work will continue to change ever more rapidly. During much of the 20th century, most work-

ers held two or three jobs during their lifetimes. However, the U.S. Department of Labor estimates that many of today's workers will hold more than ten jobs before they reach age 40. The top 10 in-demand jobs projected for 2010 did not exist in 2004. Thus, the new mission of schools is to prepare students to work at jobs that do not yet exist, creating ideas and solutions for products and problems that have not yet been identified, using technologies that have not yet been invented. (Darling-Hammond 2010, 2)

It is not surprising that Darling-Hammond used this language. As any college faculty member or administrator could readily attest, these types of claims have become ubiquitous in the higher education information ecosystem in recent years. In the above passage, although a subsequent list of the six specific "new skills" necessary for the current labor market includes a citation to an essay by management consultant Peter F. Drucker and to Tony Wagner's *The Global Achievement Gap* (2008), the sentence claiming that "at least 70 percent of U.S. jobs now require specialized knowledge or skills"—an extraordinarily optimistic assessment of the educational requirements of the labor market—is not cited. One of Darling-Hammond's sources for this passage—the Department of Labor—is indeed reliable, but the source for the claim that the top ten in-demand jobs "projected for 2010 did not exist in 2004" is a book called *The Jobs Revolution: Changing How America Works*, published by Copywriters Incorporated, a division of the Greystone Group, a Washington-based consulting firm (Gunderson, Jones, and Scanland 2004).[2] Indeed, variations of this depiction of a labor market continuously inventing new, seemingly exciting jobs have become boilerplate in higher education, frequently directed at young people just beginning college and contemplating their employment futures in a world of increasing economic insecurity. In higher education, the fantasy economy is in the air we breathe.

Darling-Hammond subsequently coedited a 2015 book aimed at teachers entitled *Teaching in a Flat World: Lessons from High-Performing Systems* and became director, president, and CEO of the Learning Policy Institute (LPI), a California-based nonprofit research institute funded by many of the foundations most active in educational policy today. The LPI "conducts and communicates independent, high-quality research to improve education policy and practice" (Learning Policy Institute 2022). The organization further states: "In this new moment, there's very substantial ground on which Americans agree in terms of investing in the kind of education that moves our nation forward—one that guarantees that all children learn and graduate, find good jobs, and contribute to improving their communities" (Ibid.). Presumably, then, it is up to the education system to guarantee that graduates "find good jobs." Yet I argue that the LPI's funders, a list that includes many of the most influential foundations in education policy today (Ibid.), stand to benefit from a nearly exclusive emphasis on education's role in providing economic opportunity.

The tremendous success of the fantasy economy can be seen in the broad, bipartisan acceptance of its main ideas and education policy prescriptions among policy makers. While school vouchers remain largely partisan, charter schools have flourished under the leadership of both parties, and accountability policies, while often criticized, have generally been supported by majorities of elected Republicans and Democrats and most of the interest groups supporting both. Moreover, one hears little mainstream debate about the current higher education reform agenda, including curricular changes, accountability, or college completion, all of which depend on corporate-driven depictions of the needs of the labor market rather than on official data. Elites' acceptance of the assumption of a perpetually inadequate workforce in science and technology fields is best illustrated by the reflexive expansion of STEM education and the erosion of the liberal arts. STEM has become what political scientists call a valence issue: an issue in which there is universal agreement, such as support for a strong economy or opposition to crime. Anyone seeking elective office—from school board to the presidency—who questions the instinctive push for more STEM education does so at their own peril, as support for STEM approaches the political equivalent of support for our troops.[3] Close examination of U.S. student achievement in math and science or of the realities of the labor market are exercises generally left to a handful of researchers and only make an occasional appearance in mainstream discussion.

While the education establishment and public have also largely accepted the fantasy economy's depiction of the labor market, it is important to consider the larger context in which this sentiment has developed. Many individuals who accept and promote the major assertions of the fantasy economy are well meaning and sincerely concerned about education's role in shaping the future economic well-being of students, including that of their own children and grandchildren. They also know that economic opportunity has become much more elusive, and the claim that a computer science major necessarily creates better pathways to middle-class employment than a liberal arts major for any student seems quite plausible. And when the empirical claims of the fantasy economy are repeated enough times and receive no real scrutiny—as has happened within the educational establishment for decades—they are assumed to be self-evident. Therefore, many thoughtful people *believe* in the fantasy economy because there appears to be no alternative.

Yet the realities of the entirety of the labor market and education system are easily accessible. The U.S. Department of Labor and state-level agencies regularly publish comprehensive data on all aspects of the labor market, including the distribution of current and projected jobs, detailed information about wages, and education levels typically associated with specific jobs. And corporations and foundations, like anyone else, of course, have every right to represent their economic interests and fund whatever research they desire. Our political system is based largely on interest group advocacy. And because of the unique role of education in American political culture and history as well as the long-standing dominance of human capital theory, if any organization states that it is in favor of education—including *any* type of education reforms—then the data and research it produces tend to be seen as objective. But given the realities of the economy and labor market and the inherent inability of education to directly affect wage rates and the distribution of jobs, it is necessary to critically examine all data and research built on the assumption that reforming education alone can meaningfully address wage stagnation and growing inequality. Decades of ever-increasing educational attainment levels and substantially transformed K–12 and higher education systems within the context of growing inequality and stagnating wages for most workers should have made this abundantly clear long ago.

Moreover, widespread acceptance of the fantasy economy's overarching account of the labor market and higher education policy prescriptions should not be mistaken for public support for the major K–12 or higher education policies advocated by reformers. To the contrary, the education reform movement has been a continuous public relations effort to impose unpopular—and often ineffective—education policies on the public. Thus, reformers have constantly emphasized the theme of racial equity and cultivated the appearance of a racially and ideologically diverse coalition in their public appeals. Accountability, charter schools, and vouchers, along with more recent efforts regarding STEM education, K–12 school funding, college completion, and online education, have all been promoted in terms of increasing racial equity. For example, EdBuild, funded by the Gates, Walton Family, and Broad Foundations as well as the Center for American Progress, among others (EdBuild 2019a), "focused on bringing common sense and fairness to the way states fund public schools" (EdBuild 2019b). With a photograph of a young African American male in an urban setting in the backdrop, EdBuild's website correctly labeled our current school funding systems "outdated, arbitrary, and segregating" (Ibid.). Citing an "urgent and growing need for talent," the Lumina Foundation emphasized the impact of the country's "centuries-long history of slavery, segregation, and discrimination" on educational outcomes, and the foundation's stated goal is that 60 percent of all Americans will have a "college degree, certificate, industry certification, or other credential of value by 2025" (Lumina Foundation 2022a). The Gates Foundation's Every Learner Everywhere grant "advocates for equitable outcomes in U.S. higher education through advances in digital learning" (Every Learner Everywhere 2022).

Yet EdBuild was only a "limited-term, catalytic organization," and "as planned, it closed its doors in June 2020" (EdBuild 2022). And the goal of expanding post–high school education among the disadvantaged—whether through online or face-to-face education—implicitly depends on alternative labor market data funded, in part, by the Lumina and Gates Foundations. Such efforts are embraced by higher education because they have the potential to keep tuition dollars flowing at a time when state support has been significantly scaled back and because the fantasy economy campaign itself has seen incredible success. I suggest that reformers' advocacy of college completion and post–high school education generally is also politically astute, as it softens potential opposition to reformers' less popular priorities, including online education and accountability. But maintaining an emphasis on equity has been an indispensable component of the modern education reform movement, which frames its overriding purpose as concern for the disadvantaged even as it rarely discusses the decidedly unpopular tenets of a neoliberal economic order that has left most workers—particularly the disadvantaged—behind.

The Building Blocks of the Fantasy: Technology, Free Markets, and Data

In *The Education Gospel*, Grubb and Lazerson (2004, 251) insightfully point out the "strong tendency to simplicity and sloganeering" inherent in the education gospel narrative. Because the fantasy economy is a comprehensive portrayal of the economy and education system, however, mere sloganeering is insufficient. And three overarching themes underlie this campaign—technology, free markets, and data.

The tech-centric, futuristic fantasy economy assumes that convenience is the ultimate motivation, and therefore the notion that digital reality is perpetually on the cusp of taking over face-to-face life is rarely questioned. Society and the workplace are understood substantially through the lens of technology, and as a result, tech supremacy has been a central feature of the modern education reform movement since its inception. In 1983, *ANAR* declared that "computers and computer-controlled equipment are penetrating every aspect of our lives—homes, factories, and offices. . . . Technology is radically transforming a host of other occupations. They include health care, medical science, energy production, food processing, construction, and the building, repair, and maintenance of sophisticated scientific, educational, military, and industrial equipment" (National Commission on Excellence in Education 1983, 10). The same year, the Carnegie Foundation's Ernest Boyer argued that the "prospects for a technology revolution in education go far beyond computers" (Boyer 1983, 197). But he lamented the fact that low-income children, because of a lack of access to the latest technology in schooling, "will fall further behind in the struggle for equal opportunity" (Ibid., 189) and chided school districts for not taking advantage of local channels set aside by cable television companies specifically for schools (Ibid., 197). Technology was also one of the nine items identified by the Business Roundtable in 1989's *Essential Components of a Successful Education*, which argued that "technology is a critical part of a program of systemic change, for it provides the means to improve productivity and access to learning" (Business Roundtable 1989, 8). In 1991, Carnegie reiterated its support for the power of television as a teaching tool, making an argument that would be repeated years later regarding the potential educational power of the internet: "Television sparks curiosity and opens up distant worlds to children. Through its magic, youngsters can travel to the moon or the bottom of the sea. They can visit medieval castles, take river trips, or explore imaginary lands" (Boyer 1991, 79–80).

Technology took on an even greater role in both K–12 and higher education reform with the introduction of the internet. By the late 1990s, the American Association for Higher Education (AAHE) was heavily involved in advancing technology in higher education by "building better bridges between *academic leaders*—including faculty and others committed to improving teaching and learning—and *campus professionals and vendors* who have expertise in information technology and information resources" (American Association for Higher Education 1997, emphasis in original). The AAHE promoted technology's ability to create "significant educational (and societal) change" (Ibid.). More recently, the American Legislative Exchange Council has argued that technology was "part of the larger opening up of the system to choice" (Abamu 2017).

Tech supremacy in education is justified through a depiction of the workplace as dominated by technology. Phrases like "twenty-first Century jobs," "knowledge worker," "knowledge economy," and "future-focused" programs of study are continually invoked but rarely concretely defined. This vacuous terminology emphasizes the increasing complexity of today's jobs while positing an unimaginable future because of the "accelerating rate of change." In her 2017 book, Cathy Davidson, the founding director of the Futures Initiative of the City University of New York, references the "jobs of the future" and argues that "technophobia" limits students "instead of arming them to deal with the complexities of a world, a workplace, and a future that most of us cannot begin to grasp or predict" (Davidson 2017, 132, 100). Davidson's book is called *The New Education: How to Revolutionize the University to Prepare for a World in Flux* for a reason—she implicitly takes economic insecurity and wage stagnation as inevitable, and her project is to change the education system, not formulate public policies or transform business culture in a manner that could lead to increased wages and greater economic opportunity for the citizenry.

The emphasis on technology is perhaps best illustrated by one of the fantasy economy's key concepts, STEM, which as a work of public relations is difficult to beat. The noun "stem" refers to the "main body or stalk of a plant," while the verb "to stem" means, among other things, "to originate from or be caused by." STEM is seen as the foundation of national prosperity, and advocating for increasing STEM education on the basis of a supposedly boundless supply of high-paying jobs in these fields has become an article of faith for a wide variety of powerful institutions. STEM has penetrated every level of education, from elementary school, where STEM has often been added alongside traditional science instruction, through higher education, where universities increasingly emphasize the expansion of STEM programs during a time of austerity. STEM encapsulates technology and complexity in one concise, extraordinarily marketable term.

While elites have continually painted a picture of a tech-dominated workplace and reflexively promoted the expansion of technology in education, the public has been less enthusiastic about technology's role in either employment or schooling. Generations of Americans grew up in a culture in which conventional wisdom assumed that too much television would rot your brain, and today parents continually monitor children's screen time while worrying about technology replacing their jobs. And as the nationwide experiment of remote learning during the COVID-19 pandemic made abundantly clear, the public appreciates the human interaction at the heart of the educational process. As a result, television never replaced teachers, and the demand for online education has long been overhyped.

Tech-centric predictions are also replete with doomsday scenarios adding a healthy dose of fear to the fantasy economy. Popular media continually reminded us to prepare for the technology-related devastation that would accompany Y2K (the year 2000), which turned out to be a nonevent. From the perspective of workers and students, the most frightening current prediction involves automation taking over large segments of the labor market, a thesis regularly advanced by education reformers despite the lack of any systematic empirical evidence to support it. Notwithstanding its tenuous connection to reality, the automation-induced panic further focuses public and elite attention on education and training as the antidote to the inevitable robot-driven plague. The excessive focus on technology has led to many other erroneous predictions, including the failure of e-books to replace physical books and the rather limited uses for 3D printers in our everyday lives. Still, the prospect of self-driving cars clogging our highways in the immediate future is repeated uncritically, as if the boy has never cried wolf before. And because of the multitude of corporate interests driving education reform, tech supremacy continues unabated, albeit in messaging that often minimizes explicit references to technology itself.

As a justification for neoliberalism, free markets are foundational to the fantasy economy. School choice and accountability policies are built on free market assumptions, while higher education programs are evaluated in terms of their purported labor market value, as if faculty members determine the wages employers pay to graduates. But because the public is also skittish about the promotion of free market policies in education, the K–12 education reform movement has long downplayed market language, as evidenced by the adoption of terms such as "public charter schools" and steadfast avoidance of the word "voucher" in the promotion of school voucher programs. And within higher education, the discussion of the labor market is dominated by euphemistic language downplaying the many negative effects of unregulated free markets on workers. Economic insecurity is romanticized with terms such as "gig economy," and students are told they will have to be nimble or agile, likely even needing second jobs, which are playfully called a side hustle. Despite the low wages and underemployment of millions with bachelor's and graduate degrees, students, employees, and educators are reminded of a perpetual skills gap, a concept created by business interests at the height of deindustrialization. Yet educational consultants rely on structural underemployment to sell a growing list of products and services to higher education that ostensibly create better "pathways" to gainful employment for graduates. Such terminology incorrectly assumes that every college degree program is associated with a finite list of specific occupations while ignoring the long-term wage stagnation experienced by many working in jobs requiring bachelor's and advanced degrees, yet it shrewdly shifts the discussion back to the shortcomings of education.

In recent years, because of the lack of popular appeal of the themes of technology and free markets in education policy, however, reformers have frequently subsumed these concepts under a broader rubric of innovation. Innovation has come to represent nearly all K–12 and higher education reforms promoted by economic elites, including school choice, online instruction, STEM programs, or seemingly any new educational product or service. Paying educators more, addressing the contingent teaching workforce in higher education, reversing decades of defunding both public K–12 and higher education, decreasing class sizes at any level of schooling, or treating students with compassion are not considered innovations. Innovation is necessarily positive, and those who question innovation are labeled as agents of the status quo, responsible for facilitating the reproduction of inequality.

Finally, the most important element of the fantasy economy campaign is the concept of data. Virtually all activity is thought to be measurable with quantitative metrics, and major claims are typically backed by the requisite data. The use of standardized tests, value-added models in teacher evaluations, and assessment in higher education illustrate the triumph of quantitative data in education policy. Universities add majors in data science at the expense of liberal arts programs because Big Data is believed to be central to our collective economic future. The *Chronicle of Higher Education*'s report *Preparing for Tough Conversations* advises higher education administrators to "use data to establish and define the problem. Empirical evidence is the best counter to suspicions of administrative overreach" (Gardner 2019, 15). In sum, quantitative data has been instrumental to the fantasy economy's overarching education policy agenda.

But data has come to mean much more than simple quantitative information. The metric fixation identified by Jerry Z. Muller (2018) can be traced to management consultants and the business schools that trained them to present the illusion of total objectivity in decision-making. And in the education reform movement, what was once called "statistics" or casually referred to as "figures" or even "numbers" became "data," giving the concept a much greater aura of authority. As a result, merely invoking the *word* "data" and presenting *any* quantitative metrics implies complete objectivity, and as Theodore Porter has argued, "Objectivity means the rule of law, not of men" (1995, 74). Thus, the word "data" has taken on an almost religious connotation in education—something that cannot, and should not, ever be questioned. If you have numbers in support of your position and label those numbers as data, you are necessarily in a position of power and can much more easily impose your preferences.

But while scholars in nearly every other field have been compelled to grapple with the uncomfortable yet necessary questions of how funding sources influence research agendas, results, and interpretation, the education policy ecosystem has yet to adequately consider these critical issues. Thus, in education policy, data simply exists, and the researcher's job is to locate and explain it. The press releases and public statements of education reformers talk incessantly about being data driven and going where the data leads, as if data requires no human choice at all. Under these assumptions, whatever quantitative metrics are presented are assumed to be the one, objective account of the phenomenon in question and therefore not open to multiple explanations or interpretations. In education policy, data just is, and the policy preferences and economic interests of research funders are not acceptable lines of inquiry.

Moreover, despite its overwhelming importance in contemporary education policy and practice, our everyday experiences with schooling immediately call into question basic assumptions surrounding quantitative measurement. For example, if one asks a professional educator at any level the qualities of a good instructor, one will inevitably hear about the importance of traits that are difficult to measure quantitatively, such as inspiring, enthusiastic, articulate, patient, kind, interesting, humorous, self-deprecating, inquisitive, compassionate, curious, empathetic, honest, hardworking, and joyful. And when educators talk about their students, they also discuss the many personal qualities affecting their ability to learn that defy easy measurement and are also constantly subject to change. Further, employers value a variety of skills in current and prospective employees, many of which are, by definition, difficult to capture with any quantitative metrics.

In addition, in other critical areas of life, such as health care, the use of qualitative data based on judgment is a necessity. Because numerous physical and psychiatric conditions are not subject to laboratory tests or imaging, medical providers routinely utilize clinical diagnoses to treat a wide variety of ailments. Medical treatments are offered and drugs prescribed entirely on the basis of "soft" data—observation, history, context, and the patient's self-reporting. Yet education reformers—few of whom have ever been teachers—dismiss this approach, hence the constant quest for more quantitative data as the professional judgment and discretion of teachers and educational professionals is deliberately diminished. As a result, popular policies fall back on what is most easily measured, minimizing the complexities of the interpersonal interaction and contextual variables that are at the heart of the teaching and learning process. In education, we are ruled by what Muller's volume is aptly called: *The Tyranny of Metrics* (2018).

While the messaging of the fantasy economy tends to convey a consistent picture, like other large-scale political projects, it is sometimes confusing or contradictory. School-age students participating in corporate-sponsored robotics teams will eventually be told they need to develop robot-proof skills for the workplace. And the anti-science Trump administration, without a hint of irony, argued that it sought to "ensure that all Americans have access to quality STEM education and safeguard America's place as the global leader in STEM innovation and employment" (Office of Science and Technology 2018). More fundamentally, the obvious question of whether technological advances make everyday life easier or increasingly complex is rarely directly confronted as such a discussion would undermine the prescription of more education and training as the only solution to economic insecurity. Ultimately, however, the ubiquity of the themes of the fantasy economy overwhelms these periodic inconsistencies, leaving elites' campaign to frame economic inequality as solely a problem of inadequate education and training with little sustained opposition.

Conclusion

At the outset, I want to make clear my underlying beliefs. As a college professor for over twenty years, I place an extraordinarily high value on education. And as a political scientist, I am deeply troubled by the historical moment in which we find ourselves, and view education as fundamental to maintaining democracy. I have also spent a career researching many of the causes and effects of racial and economic inequalities in the urban and metropolitan context, including education (Kraus 2000, 2008, 2013). I take it as a given that policies should be adopted to address the extreme inequalities in K–12 schooling and that higher education should be made easily accessible and affordable to all.

But no education policies can change the fact that the economy is dominated by low-wage jobs typically requiring little formal education or the fact that the combined number of bachelor's and advanced degree holders substantially outnumber jobs typically requiring these higher levels of education. Further, no education reform policies can alter the wage stagnation suffered by millions of highly educated Americans working in jobs commensurate with their educational attainment. Nor can channeling students into STEM fields change the number of engineering or technology-related positions in the labor market. Yet low wages for teachers, civil servants, and workers in the nonprofit sector almost certainly decrease interest in these fields among many students. If we were to wave a magic wand and give the roughly 15 percent of Americans who have completed some college but have no degree either associate's or bachelor's degrees, what jobs would be available for them? What would these jobs pay? What if every high-poverty school had the college attendance rates of the best charter, wealthy suburban, or private schools? Would that allow every young person to have access to a job with a livable wage one day? These are questions that the fantasy economy campaign does not even want to ask, let alone try to answer, yet they are a prerequisite for a serious discussion of economic opportunity in the United States today. I wrote this book because I discovered the extraordinary gulf between what I call the fantasy economy and the real economy, the one in which my students and their families and all of us live, and I argue that placing a high value on equitable educational opportunities and outcomes must not limit discussion of the causes of and prescriptions for wage stagnation and inequality, as powerful interests very conspicuously seek to do.

The following chapters describe and evaluate the claims of the fantasy economy and how it has shaped the education reform movement. Chapter 1 lays out fantasy economy's historical influences, major claims, and evolution over the past several decades. Chapter 2 uses a combination of data and research from government agencies and scholars to illustrate the substantial empirical flaws of claims of an inferior education system and inadequate workforce. Chapter 3 situates the fantasy economy's use of data and research within the larger discussion of conflicts of interest and documents reformers' widespread use of misleading data techniques, including the creation of alternative data. Chapters 4 and 5 provide a history of the political campaigns behind accountability and school choice. The Conclusion briefly documents the growth of inequality in recent decades, summarizes the book's main findings, and offers several suggestions for getting beyond the fantasy economy. The epilogue surveys recent events involving education politics and policy and economic opportunity.

Throughout the chapters, I rely primarily on two main types of sources—literature, data, and research on the labor market and education system funded and produced by private organizations in juxtaposition with data and research produced by government agencies and scholars. I maintain, therefore, that official statistics are the most objective data available. And considering society's widespread reliance on official data, the objectivity of official data is a widely held belief in our political culture. The federal economic and education data and research utilized is produced primarily by five agencies: the Bureau of Labor Statistics/Department of Labor; Department of Education; Census Bureau; Federal Reserve; and Government Accountability Office. I also examine the funding sources, tax documents, and articles of incorporation of private organizations and draw on the extensive body of scholarly work on education and economic inequality.

Ultimately, I argue that the larger debate about economic opportunity must be grounded in the real economy and explicitly acknowledge that wage stagnation and inequality have resulted from decades of neoliberal decision-making. Once we see that the fantasy economy is an illusion, we can meaningfully discuss prescriptions for inequality and restore education's multifaceted role as an institution designed to cultivate informed democratic citizenship and help students find meaning and purpose in life.

1

The Creation of a Fantasy

Nevermind. In the sweeping public verdict of 1981, the
schools are failing.
—NEWSWEEK, "Why Public Schools Are Flunking"

The jobs that will be created between 1987 and 2000 will
be substantially different from those that exist today. A
number of jobs in the least-skilled job classes will disappear,
while high-skilled professions will grow rapidly. Overall,
the skill mix of the economy will be moving rapidly upscale,
with most new jobs demanding more education and higher
levels of language, math, and reasoning skills.
—WILLIAM B. JOHNSTON AND ARNOLD H. PACKER,
    Workforce 2000: Work and Workers for the
    21st Century

Introduction

Chapter 1 documents the historical development of human capital theory
beginning in the 1950s. In the aftermath of the Great Depression during
the mixed economy of the New Deal, the Keynesian paradigm, which
advocated an activist state and a balancing of interests between capital
and labor, became dominant. But human capital theory challenged the
assumptions of Keynesianism and eventually became an essential component of the larger framework of neoliberalism, which was built on free
markets, a limited state, and the supremacy of shareholder interests. But
neoliberalism, which advocated deregulation, tax cuts for corporations
and the wealthy, erosion of the social welfare state, and free trade, along
with the new business culture focused exclusively on maximizing returns
on capital at the expense of labor, did not engender widespread support.
The loss of manufacturing employment in the United States was especially unpopular, as good jobs for those without a college degree, many
of which were unionized, were replaced largely by low-education, service-sector jobs that were largely nonunionized.

Thus, I argue that elites needed a strategy to advance the major tenets of neoliberalism, which led to a permanent political campaign positing the chronic deficiencies of the education system and labor force within a purportedly high-education, high-skill economy. By the early 1980s, major media had adopted the framing of a failing K–12 school system as the primary culprit behind poverty and declining economic opportunity, and this campaign was furthered by two reports of the Reagan administration, *A Nation at Risk* and *Workforce 2000*. And the Reagan administration's politicization of the National Institute of Education led to the creation of Columbia University's Institute on Education and the Economy, as claims of an inferior education system and insufficiently skilled workforce became omnipresent.

Human Capital Theory and the Focus on Education and Training

In the years after World War II, with the devastation of the Great Depression still in recent memory, what Jacob S. Hacker and Paul Pierson (2016) have labeled the mixed economy became the guiding framework for policy making in the United States. Fiscal and monetary policies based on the work of economist John Maynard Keynes "were widely deployed to dampen business cycles and to ensure reasonably full employment" and a "'class compromise' between capital and labour was generally advocated as they key guarantor of domestic peace and tranquility" (Harvey 2005, 10). During this period, most workers did not finish high school, and very few attended higher education. But labor unions were growing, and manufacturing employment was plentiful. To be sure, racism was embedded in the social and political order, causing acute economic hardship for persons of color. Yet because of the strong state of the New Deal, one's economic standing was certainly not solely a function of one's education and formal training. The post–World War II period of economic growth and expansion in which income and wealth gains were more widely shared constituted a "high point of the business community's acceptance of a consensus politics that included organized labor and government officials" (J. Hacker and Pierson 2016, 134).

But corporate opposition to the New Deal and support for libertarian, free market principles remained a major factor in American politics. And these sentiments found a natural ally in an emerging line of thinking advanced by economists in the 1950s called human capital theory. Human capital theory relied on a reinterpretation of some of Adam Smith's limited work on education and developed "an increasingly technical understanding of education's monetary value as human capital" (Kamola 2019, 127). By the late 1950s and early 1960s, human capital theory had crystallized, and it maintained that incomes are directly correlated with the amount of education and training individuals receive. In 1958, economist Jacob Mincer used the concept of human capital to explain income inequality (Ibid., 128), laying the groundwork for the future emphasis of corporate reformers on the education system as the root cause of economic dislocations decades later. Gary Becker's highly influential work *Human Capital: A Theoretical and Empirical Analysis, with Special Reference to Education* was first published in 1964. Human capital theory placed substantial emphasis on the impact of formal education and training on income and fit squarely within the neoclassical economics tradition.

This overarching approach suggested that society's increasing investment in education would lead to higher overall levels of attainment, which would, in turn, lead to increased economic growth and productivity and, presumably, ultimately to higher wages for all. Human capital theory's "close cousin" (Brown, Lauder, and Cheung 2020, 37), skill-biased technological change, assumed that advancing technologies would create an increasing number of jobs for the highly educated, thus providing ostensive support for the human capital approach. This thinking was advanced further in Daniel Bell's *The Coming of Post-industrial Society*, published in 1973. Relying on a picture of the labor market based on limited data, Bell argued that a "new intelligentsia—in the universities, research organizations, professions, and government" would be "decisive for post-industrial society" (Bell 1973, 15). While Richard B. Freeman's (1976) pioneering work empirically questioned human capital theory's assumptions about the necessary economic benefits of education, by this time, human capital theory had become entrenched in mainstream education policy discussion and scholarly research.

A fundamental reason for human capital theory's enduring popularity is its implicit acceptance of long-standing aspects of American political culture involving economic opportunity, individualism, and belief in limited government. Further, many commonly cited statistics appear to affirm the merits of human capital theory. Statistical averages or medians seem to indicate that the economic fate of those with bachelor's and advanced degrees is indeed much better than for those with less formal education. Yet however intuitively convincing these aggregate average wage statistics appear, they obfuscate several underlying characteristics of the contemporary labor market, including widespread underemployment at every level of formal education beyond high school as well as wage stagnation among those employed in jobs at all educational attainment levels. Moreover, favorably comparing the wages of those in many jobs requiring bachelor's degrees (e.g., teachers, civil servants, social workers) to the wages of individuals in jobs requiring high school degrees or less (e.g., retail and food-service workers) ignores the realities of wage stagnation all together. For example, a schoolteacher earning a wage of $40,000 does in fact make 60 percent more than a food-service worker being paid $25,000. But both these wages paid in 2022 are quite low. However, the uncritical comparisons of average or median wage data among individuals with different formal education levels is powerful evidence of the enduring popularity of human capital theory and elites' success in framing public discussion of economic opportunity on formal education.

The Transformation of Business, Policy, and Politics: The Triumph of Neoliberalism

By the late 1970s, the underpinnings of the mixed economy began to crumble, and, with the election of Ronald Reagan in 1980, neoliberalism began to firmly take hold. The new political economy resulted from a significant shift in business culture that depended on a form of amnesia regarding the critical role that government played in creating the economic prosperity of the twentieth century (J. Hacker and Pierson 2016). Corporations began to focus much more explicitly on shareholder interests over all others. Business opposition to regulation and support for tax cuts—particularly for the wealthy, corporations, and capital income—were fueled by an overarching hostility toward government, as business interests increasingly blamed government for their perceived problems. Pressures to integrate into the global economy resulted in a constant fixation on stock returns, and escalating executive pay was increasingly tied to stock price. Major business interest groups such as the Business Roundtable and Chamber of Commerce espoused these new sentiments: "Like the Roundtable's descent into a C.E.O. lobbying shop, the Chamber's metamorphosis from a consensus-based organization into a hard-right influence machine illuminates a larger story. It is a story of growing business clout, mounting hostility to the mixed economy, and an increasing focus on the promotion of narrow interests" (J. Hacker and Pierson 2016, 213).

A critical aspect of neoliberal thought was a nonstop attack on public institutions, including the very notion of the "public" itself, a pattern that has been evident in many democratic societies (Suleiman 2003). Neo-liberal critics, consisting initially of ideological conservatives, argued that public services are inherently inferior to what the private market could deliver, and K–12 education policy became a central exhibit in this discussion with the publication of *A Nation at Risk* (National Commission on Excellence in Education 1983) in 1983. President Reagan's assertion in his 1981 inaugural address that "government is not the solution to our problem, government is the problem" reflected neoliberalism's growing influence, and the administration's 1984 *Grace Commission* report about waste and inefficiency in the federal government provided additional fodder for critics of public institutions, including public education.

During his second term, President Reagan's attack on government continued, and I argue that his administration's 1987 report, *Workforce 2000* (Johnston and Packer 1987), produced by the Hudson Institute, was critical in the creation of the fantasy economy campaign as well as the larger neoliberal project. In the preface, Assistant Secretary of Labor Roger D. Semerad implicitly linked the report's account of the future labor market to the goal of dismantling the social welfare state: "Most of the policies that guide today's economy and labor markets were originally devised during the 1930s or 1960s in response to the conditions and problems of those decades. Social Security, welfare, unemployment insurance, trade adjustment assistance, training programs, and many other federal programs trace their roots either to the New Deal or to the Great Society. As times have changed, the relevance of these programs from earlier eras must increasingly be called into question. As change continues to unfold between now and the year 2000, many of the policies from past decades are likely to become irrelevant to the needs of the 1990s and beyond" (Johnston and Packer 1987, viii). Semerad, executive director of the 1980 Republican Platform Committee and executive vice president at the Brookings Institution from 1981 to 1985 (*Washington Post* 2012), also coauthored the popular business book *Reinventing Education: Entrepreneurship in America's Public Schools*, with the CEO of IBM, Louis V. Gerstner Jr.; Denis Philip Doyle; and William B. Johnston (one of the two main authors of *Workforce 2000*; Gerstner 1994). While most of this agenda was—and remains—politically untenable, *Workforce 2000* made clear the administration's domestic policy agenda, and the longer-term demonization of public services, including public schools, was firmly established.

Arguments opposing government and long-standing social welfare programs were most forcefully championed by Republicans, yet many leading Democrats accepted the new terms of the debate, and defense of public institutions and government generally became increasingly rare. The supremacy of free markets to government became conventional wisdom, and neoliberalism became understood as "not a particular ideology nor even an ideology at all. It is simply the way things are, the set of 'realistic' policies that 'work'" (Kotsko 2018, 11). Human capital theory squared well with neoliberalism's free market supremacy, and economic opportunity was increasingly framed as a function solely of education and training. As opposition to government and taxation increased, the Democratic Party moved toward the center, a trend best exemplified by the 1992 election and administration of President Bill Clinton, who labeled himself a New Democrat. These trends were expedited by the fall of the Soviet Union and the lack of any major countervailing ideology to free market capitalism.

Some of the Clinton administration's highest-profile policy accomplishments illustrated this policy orientation. Welfare reform, passed in 1996, repealed Aid to Families with Dependent Children (AFDC) and created Temporary Assistance to Needy Families (TANF). This specific policy change was also suggested in *Workforce 2000*, which affirmed: "Now that a majority of nonwelfare women with young children work, it no longer seems cruel to require welfare mothers to do so. The current system should be replaced with one that mandates work for all able-bodied mothers (excluding those with infants), while providing training, day care, and job counseling" (Johnston and Packer 1987, 113–114). Subsequently, the Hudson Institute was a central force in shaping the nation's welfare reform law passed in 1996 (*Washington Examiner* 2011). Clinton also presided over the passage of the North American Free Trade Agreement (NAFTA), the repeal of the New Deal–era banking regulation known as Glass Steagall, and the Telecommunications Act of 1996, which deregulated media ownership.

As part of this larger trend within the Democratic Party, Clinton also continued the critique of government established by the Grace Commission, albeit in a softer form. He created the National Partnership for Reinventing Government, led by Vice President Al Gore, the purpose of which was to improve the functioning of the federal government primarily by streamlining processes and procedures across multiple agencies. Within this paradigm, citizens are viewed more as consumers or clients, a model that fits well with market-based education reform such as charter schools or vouchers. The Clinton administration exemplified the consensus emerging among elites in both parties that economic inequality was primarily a function of education. As Tom Frank has argued: "To the liberal class, every big economic problem is really an education problem, a failure by the losers to learn the right skills and get the credentials everyone knows you'll need in the society of the future" (2016, 34). This approach led Democrats away from advocating for the needs of their traditional constituencies, including the working class, poor, and organized labor, as they courted highly educated, upper-middle-class voters. Thus, during the Clinton years, many leading Democrats embraced market-based education policies, including accountability and charter schools.

The new terms of political debate were evident in the 2000 presidential election. The Democratic candidate, Clinton's vice president Al Gore, stressed the Clinton administration's fiscal discipline and job creation and pledged to continue these policies, which he linked with prosperity. Yet Gore rarely discussed the types of jobs created and wages paid, a fact emphasized by the Green Party candidate and longtime consumer activist Ralph Nader. Rather than meaningfully address the continued proliferation of low-wage jobs amid rising educational attainment levels, candidates Gore and Republican George W. Bush spent considerable time discussing various education policies based on the unquestioned assumptions of human capital theory and free market supremacy. After eight years of Democratic rule, Bush labeled himself a "compassionate conservative" and advanced the emerging elite framing that economic opportunity was solely a function of education. He vigorously cultivated the support of minority communities in his quest for K–12 education accountability. Substantially assisted by the monumental distraction of 9/11, No Child Left Behind became law in 2002.

Elected during the financial crisis of 2008, President Barack Obama's public policy priorities were largely a continuation of those of the Clinton administration. Obama implicitly accepted the neoliberal consensus and the assumptions of human capital theory. Passed in 2009, the Obama administration's $4.3 billion Race to the Top initiative incentivized states to adopt market-based education policies within the larger framing of education as an antipoverty program. Writing two years later, Gary Becker (2011) conceded that economic inequality had increased but argued that such increases were "due in large measure to globalization and technological progress that raised the productivity of more educated and more skilled individuals." President Obama's policies largely reflected similar assumptions, and apart from school vouchers, a commitment to market-based education reforms based on a purportedly high-education, high-skill labor market had become accepted by elites in both parties.

Republican attacks on public institutions, including schools, boiled over with President Donald Trump. In his inaugural speech, Trump took direct aim at urban public schools' alleged greed and inability to educate their students: "Mothers and children trapped in poverty in our inner cities; rusted-out factories scattered like tombstones across the landscape of our nation; an education system, flush with cash, but which leaves our young and beautiful students deprived of all knowledge; and the crime and gangs and drugs that have stolen too many lives and robbed our country of so much unrealized potential" (Trump 2017). Trump's singling out the public schools for such harsh criticism was illustrative of criticisms espoused within the conservative coalition for many years.

The effects of neoliberalism have been profound and have substantially contributed to the public's growing loss of trust in government. And as government has become increasingly demonized, defense of the public sector has become almost nonexistent, as "even defenders of government often reluctantly join the spiral of silence, concluding that the best defense of our government's diminishing capacity is not to talk about government at all" (J. Hacker and Pierson 2016, 340). Yet neoliberalism required a political campaign to bring its free market–based paradigm and prioritization of shareholder interests to fruition, and by the early 1980s, this campaign had begun in earnest and was built on two major claims—the schools and the workforce were woefully inadequate.

America's Failing Schools: A Mantra Is Born

By the late 1970s and early 1980s, the U.S. economy was in recession, with unemployment rates increasing and inflation and interest rates skyrocketing. As part of the new business culture's emphasis on minimizing the cost of labor, domestic manufacturing facilities were being shuttered across much of the nation. Armed with the growing support for human capital theory and neoliberalism's antigovernment message, elites used the moment to define the primary problem in the United States as the education system in the larger campaign for free market supremacy. Americans were increasingly told that the public schools were the primary cause of increasing economic insecurity and the loss of good jobs. This reasoning had roots in the business-driven standards movement, which saw public schools as unduly influenced by education trends at the expense of academic content.

Many years before the 1983 publication of A Nation at Risk (ANAR), popular media gave substantial attention to the ostensibly failing school system. These accounts, based largely on anecdotes, speculation, and decontextualized data, used sensational language to connect various social ills to the K–12 school system. For example, a cover story from *Time* magazine from June 1980 entitled "Help! Teacher Can't Teach!" stated: "Like some vast jury gradually and reluctantly arriving at a verdict, politicians, educators and especially millions of parents have come to believe that the U.S. public schools are in parlous trouble. Violence keeps making headlines. Test scores keep dropping. Debate rages over whether or not one-fifth or more adult Americans are functionally illiterate" (*Time* 1980, 54). *Newsweek* ran a special report the next year entitled "Why the Public Schools Are Flunking" (*Newsweek* 1981). After a brief discussion of the recent history of educational policy debates, the report concluded: "Nevermind. In the sweeping public verdict of 1981, the schools are failing" (Ibid., 62). Significantly, the *Newsweek* series focused as much on public opinion polls showing that Americans had become much more critical of the public schools as on the actual policies, practices, and results of the education system. Similar stories appeared in other mainstream news and opinion publications and helped set the tone for the influential policy debates that followed.

Then, in 1983, with the publication of the *ANAR*, the overarching conventional wisdom about the U.S. school system that had been percolating for several years was made official. In dramatic language, the report advanced the argument that American schools and students were underperforming those of many other nations and that this threatened the future of the United States itself: "Our Nation is at risk. Our once unchallenged preeminence in commerce, industry, science, and technological innovation is being overtaken by competitors throughout the world. . . . What was unimaginable a generation ago has begun to occur—others are matching and surpassing our educational attainments" (National Commission on Excellence in Education 1983, 5). At the same time, the authors qualified the exclusive linkage of the education system to economic changes by affirming that *ANAR* was "concerned with only one of the many causes and dimensions of the problem, but it is the one that undergirds American prosperity, security, and civility" (Ibid.). In 1983, the skills gap campaign was not yet fully developed, and wage stagnation and growing economic inequality would not be linked exclusively to schooling until several years later. Still, despite reliance on limited data consisting mainly of average test scores as well as commissioned research, *ANAR* solidified two key assumptions of the fantasy economy: (1) The achievement of American students had declined over time; and (2) American students were significantly inferior to those of many other nations. In the intervening years, these two claims became conventional wisdom, echoed in seemingly countless works on the education system.

The report offered numerous recommendations on a variety of subjects, including educational content, expectations of teachers and schools, time spent on the educational process, and the teaching profession. But as education scholar Diane Ravitch has pointed out, the overarching narrative that *ANAR* created was the "unfounded belief that America's public schools were locked into an arc of decline" (2013, 39). This belief was buttressed by an "explosion of independently generated books and commission reports about American education" with titles such as *America's Competitive Challenge: The Need for a National Response*; *Horace's Compromise: The Dilemma of the American High School*; and *Action for Excellence: A Comprehensive Plan to Improve Our Nation's Schools*, among many others (Berliner and Biddle 1995, 140). By the middle 1980s, the stage was set for the major education reform policies of the coming decades.

While *ANAR* did not emphasize market-based solutions to the educational system's professed ills, the Reagan administration used the report's publication to launch a campaign for market-based school policies. As pointed out by Deborah Duncan Owens, in celebrating the report's release, after discussing the general finding of failing public schools, President Reagan pivoted to push his administration's education priorities, which bore little resemblance to the report's recommendations: "So, we'll continue to work in the months ahead for passage of tuition tax credits, vouchers, educational savings accounts, voluntary school prayer, and abolishing the Department of Education. Our agenda is to restore quality to education by increasing competition and by strengthening parental choice and local control" (Owens 2015, 27).

In the years after its publication, the Reagan administration took several important steps to justify the fantasy economy's exclusive emphasis on education's role in shaping economic opportunity, including the Labor Department's funding of *Workforce 2000*, produced by the Hudson Institute, which argued in favor of far-reaching, market-based education policies: "In school districts with the most serious problems, not only vouchers but complete privatization of the schools should be considered. Performance standards should be applied, not only to teachers but to students, administrators, and schools themselves. In practice, this might mean not only support for magnet schools that can be islands of excellence, but a willingness to close the worst schools, fire incompetent teachers, and expel disruptive students" (Johnston and Packer 1987, 115). The report was steeped in the culture-of-poverty approach, which sought to blame poverty on the values of those in poverty: "The choices are not simply between on-the-job training and basic skills remediation programs for teenagers, but among investments in child care, pregnancy prevention, welfare reform, big brother programs, and other possible interventions. Before minority unemployment can be significantly reduced, there must be change in the cultural values that make it seem more attractive to sell drugs or get pregnant than to do well in school and work at McDonald's" (Ibid.). While political necessity would require that elites drop explicit cultural analysis rooted in racist stereotypes as well as such straightforward discussion of the labor market, *Workforce 2000* extended the narrative about failing schools established by *ANAR* and provided a more fully articulated justification for major education reform—the presumed high-education, high-skill labor market of the near future.

During the 1980s, educational attainment levels were much lower than today, and underemployment of college graduates had not yet become a major issue of public discussion. Thus K–12 schooling remained the focus of education reform. But higher education was not spared from education policy discussion during the Reagan administration. In 1984, the Department of Education's National Institute of Education (NIE) published *Involvement in Learning: Realizing the Potential in American Higher Education*. Like *ANAR*, many of the NIE report's findings and recommendations have largely been forgotten. For example, the authors expressed dismay with the increasing use of part-time faculty and declining enrollments in the arts, humanities, and sciences at the expense of vocational and professional fields, and they advocated strongly for increasing student involvement in higher education. The report also questioned a tuition-driven funding system: "Indeed, a funding system based principally on enrollments sends a clear message to colleges that quantity is valued over quality" (National Institute of Education 1984, 12). The report's main legacy, however, is its advocacy for assessment (Cumming and Ewel 2017), which, I argue, is also a by-product of the success of the skills gap campaign. If the economic value of a college degree in the labor market were self-evident—as it may have been decades ago when educational attainment rates were much lower—there would be no political pressure on higher education to prove its educational value as defined by labor market outcomes by assessing student learning.

Not Just Any Curriculum:
The Emergence of STEM

While the reports of the 1980s discussed the decline of education generally, many were also part of long-standing campaigns emphasizing the qualifications of workers in math and science fields. Since at least the middle twentieth century, elites have argued that shortcomings in math and science education would lead to a shortage of qualified scientists and engineers, which would imperil the nation's economy and national security (Teitelbaum 2014a). In turn, federal policy makers increasingly viewed "engineers (and scientists) as essential to the military and economic strength of the nation" (Kuehn and Salzman 2018, 20–21). The political push for increasing math and science education was given a tremendous boost with the creation of the acronym STEM, which stands for "science, technology, engineering, and math." Originally referred to as SMET, the term was changed in 2001 by Judith Ramaley, a member of the National Science Foundation. When asked in 2011 about changing the name, Ramaley said she "didn't like the sound" of SMET and thought STEM had a "much better ring to it" (Christenson 2011). The term gained widespread usage, despite inconsistent definitions of the fields included in this category.

The emphasis on STEM education increased significantly in the early years of the twenty-first century. Reports such as *Before It's Too Late* (National Commission on Mathematics and Science Teaching for the 21st Century 2000), *Innovate America* (Council on Competitiveness 2005), *Tapping America's Potential* (Education for Innovation Initiative 2005), *Rising above the Gathering Storm* (National Academy of Sciences et al. 2007), and *Tough Choices or Tough Times* (National Center on Education and the Economy 2008) stressed increasing STEM education at all levels and thereby increasing the supply of STEM workers. This literature utilized international assessments in math and science showing American students behind many other nations in average test scores. The foreword of *Before It's Too Late*, by Commission Chair John Glenn, linked the future of the nation itself to math and science education and sounded strikingly similar to *ANAR*: "First, at the daybreak of this new century and millennium, the Commission is convinced that the future well-being of our nation and people depends not just on how well we educate our children generally, but on how well we educate them in mathematics and science specifically" (National Commission on Mathematics and Science Teaching for the 21st Century 2000, 4). *Tapping America's Potential* was backed by a coalition of many of the nation's biggest business-interest groups, including the Business Roundtable, the U.S. Chamber of Commerce, and the Council on Competitiveness, and sought to double the number of STEM bachelor's degree recipients by 2015 (Education for Innovation Initiative 2005). And the lengthy report by the National Academy of Sciences, National Academy of Engineering, and Institute of Medicine, *Rising above the Gathering Storm: Energizing and Employing*

America for a Brighter Economic Future, lent an aura of scientific expertise to the push from the nation's biggest business interests for increased and improved STEM education.

Rather than providing scholarly cover, however, the background and contents of the *Gathering Storm* report further illustrate the magnitude of the political push for STEM education that was enveloping Washington. The report resulted from a request from four members of Congress asking the National Academies/National Research Council for specific suggestions as to how federal policy makers could "enhance the science and technology enterprise so that the United States can successfully compete, prosper, and be secure in the global community of the twenty-first century" (Teitelbaum 2014a, 13). The committee appointed to write *Gathering Storm* was "dominated by current or former C.E.O.s of large corporations and leading research universities" (Ibid.). The report was over five hundred pages, but time constraints "limited the ability of the committee to conduct an exhaustive analysis" (National Academy of Sciences et al. 2007, 2). For these reasons, *Gathering Storm* merely reiterated the major themes of numerous other reports: U.S. students lagged their international counterparts in science and math, and future economic prosperity and national security depended on increased investments in science and math education at every level of the education system.

Yet in short order, the report became extraordinarily influential on educational policy debate and "can fairly be described as one of the most politically influential reports ever produced by a National Research Council committee" (Teitelbaum 2014a, 18–19). Many of its suggestions became legislative proposals, some of which were adopted as part of the America COMPETES Act of 2007. Although the budget impasse of 2008 and the subsequent Great Recession prevented much of this original act from receiving funding, some proposals originating in the *Gathering Storm* report did become law as part of the economic stimulus legislation of 2009. Scholars have also stressed the need to invest heavily in STEM education and increase the number of STEM graduates. In *The New Education*, although stipulating that "S.T.E.M. is not the problem. Nor is S.T.E.M. the solution," Cathy Davidson concludes that it is "indisputable that we need more people trained in S.T.E.M. fields, and that the United States is poor at training the next generation of S.T.E.M. experts" (2017, 137). Economists Laura Tyson and Michael Spence affirm that "few question the need for more education in S.T.E.M. fields (science, technology, education, and mathematics). Digital technologies will continue to complement the demand for workers in these fields, and increasing their supply will moderate the skill premium and reduce inequality" (Tyson and Spence 2017, 205).

Because it is a valence issue, policy makers have endorsed STEM expansion automatically. The anti-science Trump administration offered a full-throated defense of STEM, even linking it to improving the economic prospects for children in poverty, when it declared it would "do everything possible to provide our children, especially kids in underserved areas, with access to high-quality education in science, technology, engineering, and math" (Office of Science and Technology 2018). Promoted endlessly by elites, STEM education has become an essential component of the fantasy economy.

The Permanently Deficient Workforce: Growing Inequality and Education Reform

A political campaign that focuses on failing schools and the qualifications and supply of STEM workers is inherently limited. Depending on the educational and skill levels required by the labor market, the larger significance of an education system thought to be underperforming is not necessarily straightforward. And notwithstanding the constant lobbying of business interests, objective data on STEM job markets is easily accessible through the U.S. Department of Labor. I argue, then, that to justify emerging patterns of wage stagnation and growing inequality, the narrative of failing schools had to be explicitly linked to a much more comprehensive account of a chronically deficient workforce. This framing deflects all attention away from public policies and business practices that directly and indirectly affect wage rates and jobs. While business interests had historically advanced claims of worker shortages, in the 1980s, the rhetoric of workforce inadequacies transformed and expanded. And because of increasing educational attainment levels vis-à-vis the relatively low educational requirements of the labor market revealed in official data, I argue that the fantasy economy's focus on education and training mandated a rhetorical emphasis on skills—rather than education per se—hence the "skills gap" between the abilities of the workforce and requirements of the labor market. As Ellen Ruppel Shell has argued, the skills gap has been so widely cited in recent years it has become a sort of "cultural meme" (Ruppel Shell 2018, 163). Still, the concept of a skills gap remains central to the language of both K–12 and higher education reform today, decades after its introduction.

Arguments positing worker shortages and skills gaps rest on a depiction of the labor market in which demand for greater levels of education and training is strong and constantly growing. This campaign has had two major dimensions: (1) Jobs that have historically required little formal education (manufacturing, retail, etc.) are becoming increasingly complex and therefore now require more formal education and training; and (2) Jobs historically requiring greater formal education and training (STEM fields, management, professional services, etc.) are increasing as a share of the total labor market. The skills gap campaign has included a focus on increasing the number of college graduates and increasing the number of workers qualified in STEM and technical fields, as well as a generic emphasis on increasing workforce education and skills as evidenced in the frequent use of terms such as "upskilling" and "reskilling." Uniting all this messaging are the assumptions of a workplace that is increasingly complex and a labor market dominated by jobs requiring highly educated and trained workers. Because without the assumption of a permanently inferior workforce grounded in a high-education labor market, there is little ammunition left for the education reform movement.

The emphasis on the labor market's need for workers with more formal education and greater skills was articulated in *A Nation at Risk*, which asserted that "knowledge, learning, information, and skilled intelligence are the new raw materials of international commerce" (National Commission on Excellence in Education 1983, 7), and subsequent literature expounded on the prediction of an increasingly complex labor market requiring more education and training. In 1987, *Workforce 2000* was published, and it is widely credited as being the single most important influence on the emerging skills gap narrative. The report declared that the *"new jobs in service industries will demand much higher skill levels than the jobs of today"* (Johnston and Packer 1987, xiii, emphasis in original). Although funded by the Department of Labor, the report provided an account of the educational requirements of the labor market seemingly at odds with official data: "The jobs that will be created between 1987 and 2000 will be substantially different from those in existence today. A number of jobs in the least-skilled job classes will disappear, while high-skilled professions will grow rapidly. Overall, the skill mix of the economy will be moving rapidly upscale, with most new jobs demanding more education and higher levels of language, math, and reasoning skills" (Ibid., 96). The report went on to claim that "of all the new jobs that will be created over the 1984–2000 period, more than half will require some education beyond high school, and almost a third will be filled by college graduates" (Ibid., 97).

Another major theme of *Workforce 2000* was the demographic crisis that was presumably facing the nation's economy. According to the report, the future workforce would *"grow slowly, becoming older, more female, and more disadvantaged"* (Johnston and Packer 1987, xiii; emphasis in original). These trends, in conjunction with the coming high-skill labor market, would create shortages of sufficiently skilled labor, thereby inhibiting economic growth. The "shrinking numbers of young people, the rapid pace of industrial change, and the ever-rising skill requirements of the emerging economy make the task of fully utilizing minority workers particularly urgent between now and 2000. Both cultural changes and education and training investments will be needed to create real equal employment opportunity" (Ibid., xiv). Women entering the workforce in larger numbers were also implicitly linked to the larger neoliberal public policy and corporate agenda, as the authors stated that "most current policies and institutions covering pay, fringe benefits, time away from work, pensions, welfare, and other issues were designed for a society in which men worked and women stayed home" (Ibid., xiv).

Despite the impact of the report, it took several years for elites to unify around a consistent message of the high-education, high-skill labor market and permanently deficient workforce. Even *Workforce 2000* seemed to undermine its central prediction of a high-education, high-skill labor market when it affirmed that "very few new jobs will be created for those who cannot read, follow directions, and use mathematics" (Johnston and Packer 1987, xiii), a characterization of the skills of a typical high school graduate. Such language would gradually fade from subsequent literature, which emphasized the critical need for citizens to obtain formal education and skill levels well beyond high school to achieve any measure of economic security. But the significance of *Workforce 2000* on shaping the skills gap campaign and larger fantasy economy narrative cannot be overstated.

The continuing loss of industry was also a major theme of *Workforce 2000*, which declared that *"U.S. manufacturing will be a much smaller share of the economy in the year 2000"* and that "service industries will create all of the new jobs, and most of the new wealth, over the next 13 years" (Johnston and Packer 1987, xiii, emphasis in original). At the time, deindustrialization was a major political issue and led to the passage of the federal Worker Adjustment and Retraining Notification Act of 1988. The largely symbolic act required most employers with one hundred or more workers to provide sixty-day advance notification of any plant closings and mass layoffs. Yet President Reagan compared the proposal to "European labor policy," called it "political shenanigans," and allowed its passage without his signature (Ronald Reagan Presidential Library and Museum 1988). These events led business elites to begin presenting a more unified public campaign declaring that the skills gap was the cause of manufacturing-job loss. Within this context, Reagan's vice president, George H. W. Bush, was elected in 1988 and declared that he would be the Education President. And in the fall of 1989, coinciding with President Bush's Education Summit for the country's governors at the University of Virginia, business interests began an intense political campaign that continues to the present day, arguing that the real problem the nation faced was a poorly educated, insufficiently skilled workforce.

The new skills gap campaign began from the assumption that the nation had entered a "knowledge" or "information" economy, implicitly accepting human capital's overarching emphasis on education. In September 1989, John Sculley, the CEO of Apple Computer, articulated the idea of a postindustrial economy, telling the *New York Times* that "in the days when resources came out of the ground, we were a resource-rich country. . . . Now resources are what come out of people's heads, and we're no longer resource rich" (Fiske 1989a). Shortly thereafter, the *Times* ran an article on the top of page 1 that outlined a comprehensive corporate response to the steady drumbeat of bad economic news. "Impending U.S. 'Disaster': Work Force Unqualified to Work," which was over 1,600 words, painted a detailed picture of an increasingly complex labor market and adopted a much more cohesive and urgent tone about workforce deficiencies (Fiske 1989b). The piece included quotations from several CEOs describing the difficulties they experienced in finding qualified workers and pointing at the schools as the main cause of this problem and concluded that, according to "leaders in government, business, and education . . . America is developing into a nation of educational haves and have nots, who are fast becoming employment haves and have-nots; that this polarization follows racial lines, and that the effect on the economy and the country could be devastating" (Ibid.). The *Times* article stated that both prongs of the skills gap were "documented by the Hudson Institute, a research organization, in a Labor Department study titled 'Workforce 2000: Work and Workers for the 21st Century'" (Ibid.). In the article, one of the report's authors, Arnold H. Packer, maintained that because of the difficulty of finding qualified workers, industry had few options, including sending skilled jobs abroad, "[automating] to accommodate a low-skilled domestic labor force," or choosing not to upgrade operations and the "concomitant skill levels of employees" (Ibid.). Packer concluded: "Jobs will get filled . . . but you're talking about lower productivity and thus a lower standard of living for everyone" (Ibid.).

Two individuals affiliated with Columbia University's newly established Institute on Education and the Economy, which was part of the university's prestigious Teachers College, were also quoted in the piece: Senior Research Associate Thomas Bailey and Director Sue E. Berryman. Berryman linked an individual's future economic prospects solely to their education: "The well educated face a future of expanding job opportunities and rising wages . . . while those not well educated face a future of contracting opportunities and poverty" (Fiske 1989b). Bailey argued that the labor market was "upskilling" and claimed that "new opportunities for workers with no more than a high school degree are falling sharply" (Ibid.). The *Times* piece brought the central narrative of *Workforce 2000* to a much larger audience and was a critical piece in framing the problem of wage stagnation and inequality: the inadequate skills of the workforce were at the root of the problem, and the school system was ultimately responsible.

Yet contemporaneous assessments of this period undermined the notion that the labor force lacked workers with sufficient skills and education. A 1984 report by the National Academy of Sciences entitled *High Schools and the Changing Workplace: The Employers View* concluded that those with only a high school degree "represent the largest segment of the American workforce and play a central and critical role in the nation's economy" (National Academy of Sciences 1984, viii). Early work produced by the National Center on Education and the Economy (NCEE) relied on Bureau of Labor Statistics (BLS) data on the educational requirements of the labor market and acknowledged the relatively low level of formal education required by most jobs. The NCEE originated with the Carnegie Corporation of New York's 1985 Forum on Education and the Economy and was formally established in 1988 in Rochester, New York. The NCEE created the Commission on the Skills of the American Workforce to assess the educational and skill requirements of the labor market. In 1990, the commission published *America's Choice: High Skills or Low Wages!* which cited BLS data on the educational requirements of the labor market, concluding that "more than 70 percent of the jobs in America will not require a college education by the year 2000. These jobs are the backbone of our economy, and the productivity of workers in these jobs will make or break our economic future" (National Center on Education and the Economy 1990, 3, 26). Based on an extensive survey of employers, *America's Choice* concluded that "only five percent of employers were concerned about a skills shortage," while more than 80 percent were concerned about "finding workers with a good work ethic and appropriate social behavior: 'reliable,' 'a good attitude,' 'a pleasant appearance,' 'a good personality'" (Ibid., 3). There was no skills gap: "With some exceptions, the education and skill levels of American workers roughly match the demands of their jobs" (Ibid.). The rationale for education reform, then, was to increase worker productivity in a predominantly lower-education labor market on the assumption that increased productivity would lead to increased wages. *America's Choice* acknowledged only six funders: the Carnegie Corporation of New York, the State of New York, Towers Perrin, Cresap/Telesis, SJS, and the German Marshall Fund (Ibid., 129).

Despite this inconsistency in elite messaging, the skills gap campaign had substantial momentum. After the publication of the *Times* cover story in 1989, the foundation- and corporate-funded Institute on Education and the Economy at Columbia lent academic credibility to the skills gap narrative through the publication of numerous reports on the educational and skill needs of the labor market. In 1992, the institute published *The Double Helix of Education and the Economy*, by Berryman and Bailey (1992b), which argued that economic changes led to several major developments in the workplace, including the reduction in lower-skill jobs and the necessity of workers to acquire higher-level skills. Like the *Times* piece and *Workforce 2000*, the executive summary for *The Double Helix* focused on new jobs—as opposed to all jobs—and argued that "thirty percent of all *new* jobs expected to be created between 1990 and the year 2005 will go to college graduates" (Berryman and Bailey 1992a, 3, emphasis in original). Berryman and Bailey implicitly relied on official data in their analysis but minimized aggregate labor market data that showed the dominance of low-wage, lower-education jobs: "Although tales of the proliferation of fast-food workers and janitors have had a strong influence on public opinion, looking at absolute growth in particular occupations can be misleading" (Berryman and Bailey 1992b, 31).

Berryman and Bailey's comments directed at the education establishment were hard hitting: "Our schools routinely and profoundly violate what we know about how people learn most effectively and the conditions under which they apply their knowledge appropriately to new situations" (Berryman and Bailey 1992a, 3). And *The Double Helix* crystallized the fantasy economy's emerging political framing of inequality by affirming that policy makers should *"change the mission of K–12 schools to take educational responsibility for the economic futures of all students"* (Ibid., 7, emphasis in original). I suggest that with the creation of the Institute on Education and the Economy at an Ivy League university, the fantasy economy had acquired academic legitimacy, and throughout the 1990s, business interests repeatedly declared that the real problem at the heart of declining economic opportunity was an unskilled workforce rooted in a poorly performing education system.

By the turn of the millennium, arguments advancing the skills gap thesis were increasingly given official status, and analyses of the workplace virtually always included the language of technology. In 2000, the Clinton administration's *Before It's Too Late* argued that "'knowledge work' is replacing low end, low wage jobs" (National Commission on Mathematics and Science Teaching for the 21st Century 2000, 13). After its first report in 1990, the National Center on Education and the Economy relocated from Rochester, New York, to Washington, DC; began to receive significant funding from corporations and foundations; and became a major actor in the education reform movement. Founding CEO Marc Tucker authored or edited several popular education reform books, including *Surpassing Shanghai: An Agenda for America's Education Built on the World's Leading Systems* (Tucker 2011).

The second NCEE report, based on the New Commission on the Skills of the American Workforce, was entitled *Tough Choices or Tough Times*. Published in 2006, the report adopted a very different argument about the educational requirements of the labor market. The NCEE declared that a "very high level of preparation in reading, writing, speaking, mathematics, science, literature, history, and the arts will be an indispensable foundation for everything that comes after for most members of the workforce" (National Center on Education and the Economy 2008, xxiv). The report also expanded on an increasingly popular assertion of reformers (and one articulated in the 1989 *New York Times* cover story) that the country was "developing into a nation of educational haves and have nots" by arguing that "America Has Been Divided into College Haves and Have-Nots" (Ibid., 2). Despite increasing levels of educational attainment since the publication of the NCEE's 1990 report, *Tough Choices or Tough Times* attributed over two decades of increasing inequality and wage stagnation to the inferior educational qualifications of the American workforce, and the report did not rely on BLS data on the educational requirements of the current and future labor market. The report observed: "Today, Indian engineers make $7,500 a year against $45,000 for an American engineer with the same qualifications. If we succeed in matching the very high levels of mastery of mathematics and science of these Indian engineers—an enormous challenge for this country—why would the world's employers pay us more than they have to pay the Indians to do their work? They would be willing to do that only if we could offer something that the Chinese and Indians, and others, cannot" (National Center on Education and the Economy 2008, xxiii).

The solution to wage stagnation and growing inequality, then, was to increase both the educational attainment and achievement of the American workforce. The New Commission acknowledged the Annie E. Casey, Bill and Melinda Gates, Lumina, and William and Flora Hewlett Foundations for financial support and identified Anthony Carnevale as the director of labor market and economic study (New Commission on the Skills of the American Workforce 2011a, 2011b). And by 2020, the NCEE listed numerous corporations, foundations, and individuals that supported its work "over the years," including Apple, Ford, Target, Boeing, Union Carbide, Jewel-Osco, Xerox, the Annie E. Casey Foundation, John D. and Catherine T. MacArthur Foundation, Lumina Foundation for Education, the Bill and Melinda Gates Foundation, and Pew Charitable Trusts, among many other corporations and foundations (National Center on Education and the Economy 2020).

Yet by the first decade of the twenty-first century, a labor market requiring high levels of education was not materializing. In 2010, BLS data still showed that nearly 70 percent of all jobs typically required only a high school degree or less (Bureau of Labor Statistics 2012, 14), making the skills gap argument much more challenging. While the emphasis on education reform had been on K–12 schools, by this time, elites turned more of their attention to higher education. In 2006, Columbia's Institute on Education and the Economy was absorbed into the university's newly formed Community College Research Center (CCRC), under the leadership of Thomas Bailey. And then the Great Recession exacerbated the decades-long increase in inequality and brought increased attention to unemployment and underemployment among the highly educated. Within the context of the larger discussion in which the value of a college degree was increasingly questioned, elites reaffirmed their focus on higher education reform.

But the educational attainment levels illustrated in official data, as well as the millions of low-wage, low-skill jobs that the economy regularly produced, undermined an emphasis on the unambiguous benefits of higher education. I argue that placing political pressure on higher education would be extremely difficult if one relied only on official education and labor market data. And in 2008, as a "unique collaboration between Lumina Foundation for Education, Ford Foundation and The Bill & Melinda Gates Foundation" (Center on Education and the Workforce 2009), the Center for Education and the Workforce (CEW) was founded by Anthony Carnevale at Georgetown University. The CEW began to produce alternative data showing a very different labor market than the one illustrated in official data. Specifically, the CEW's data showed a job market dominated by occupations requiring post–high school education and training. The press release for the CEW 2010 employment projections summarized its research and higher education agenda, including what it saw as the costs of not substantially increasing higher education attainment levels: "'America needs more workers with college degrees, certificates and industry certifications,' said Anthony P. Carnevale, the Center's director. 'If we don't address this need now, millions of jobs could go offshore'" (Center on Education and the Workforce 2010, 1, emphasis in original). One of the early CEW reports explicitly articulated elites' preferred solution to growing inequality: "If we were to add 20 million postsecondary-educated workers to the workforce, income inequality would decline" (Carnevale and Rose 2011). The CEW's alternative data on the educational requirements of the labor market was embraced by the higher education establishment, and, for all intents and purposes, it supplanted BLS data on the labor market's demand for post–high school education.

The Great Recession also required a ratcheting up of arguments suggesting shortages of workers with less formal education, specifically manufacturing workers. As Andrew Hacker has pointed out, claims of shortages of lower-skilled workers have been made by business interests for decades: "For at least a half century, America's agricultural industries have contended that they cannot find enough homegrown citizens to pick and pack crops" (A. Hacker 2016, 37). And the high unemployment rates of the Great Recession led business interests to engage in an extensive public relations effort regarding a persistent skills gap in the manufacturing sector. For example, in 2011, with the unemployment rate hovering around 9 percent, Deloitte published a report for the Manufacturing Institute (affiliated with the National Association of Manufacturers) entitled *Boiling Point? The Skills Gap in U.S. Manufacturing* (Deloitte 2011). Based on a survey of 1,123 executives in manufacturing fields, the report took the skills gap and worker shortage as givens: "As many U.S. manufacturers look to regain momentum, they will likely face some well-documented challenges. Not least among these is the issue of talent. This is not new—for years, manufacturers have reported a significant gap between the talent they need to keep growing their businesses and what they can actually find" (Ibid., 1).

Accordingly, Deloitte and the Manufacturing Institute created a series of reports on the skills gap and released a report in 2018 that posed the question "The jobs are here, but where are the people?" (Deloitte 2018). Other major business interests asserted similar claims. In 2019, the Business Roundtable sounded the alarm: "American businesses are facing an unprecedented challenge: the labor force simply doesn't have enough qualified workers. In fact, the labor force doesn't have enough workers—*period"* (Business Roundtable, n.d., emphasis in original). And in January 2020, Tom Donohue, the CEO of the U.S. Chamber of Commerce, called both the skills gap and worker shortages an "urgent priority" (U.S. Chamber of Commerce 2020).

Within the context of a declining manufacturing sector and the proliferation of low-wage service-sector jobs in the United States, the skills gap has also been used to justify domestic firms' decisions to locate manufacturing facilities abroad. In 2015, the CBS show *60 Minutes* interviewed Apple's CEO Tim Cook. Like so many other manufacturers, Apple has a large presence in China, where, according to CBS, "Apple products are manufactured by one million Chinese workers in the factories of Apple contractors, including its largest: Foxconn" (C. Rose 2015). Cook was asked why Apple employs so many workers in China, and, according to CBS, he "insists that China's vast and cheap labor force is not the primary reason for manufacturing there" (Ibid.). Rather, according to Cook, it was the skills of the Chinese workers instilled by the country's educational system:

> COOK: Yeah, let me—let me—let me clear, China put an enormous focus on manufacturing. In what we would call, you and I would call vocational kind of skills. The U.S., over time, began to stop having as many vocational kind of skills. I mean, you can take every tool and die maker in the United States and probably put them in a room that we're currently sitting in. In China, you would have to have multiple football fields.
> INTERVIEWER: Because they've taught those skills in their schools?
> COOK: It's because it was a focus of them—it's a focus of their educational system. And so that is the reality. (C. Rose 2015)

Once again, the implication was clear: the skills gap was a given, and the education system was to blame for the jobs and wage levels available to U.S. workers.

Warnings of shortages of manufacturing workers are typically taken at face value by the business press. A headline from the business pages of the Minneapolis *Star Tribune* from early 2019 is representative: "Manufacturing Advocates Warn of Looming Labor Crisis at Twin Cities Event" (DePass 2019). The article, relying largely on data and quotations provided by business interests, describes a doomsday scenario of a lack of skilled workers looming in the coming years: "The number of unfilled

U.S. manufacturing jobs will swell to 2.4 million in a decade unless aggressive recruiting and training begin now" (Ibid.). The piece neglected to mention that at any one point in time, because of worker mobility, retirements, and deaths, there are large numbers of job openings in the national labor market.

Immigration policy has also been advanced by business interests as a method of addressing alleged worker shortages and skills gaps, and the H-1B visa program is the most visible manifestation of the political power of these arguments. The H-1B program allows skilled workers into the United States under certain conditions and was created as part of the 1990 Immigration Act "after strong lobbying from industry and employer groups" (Teitelbaum 2014a, 57). The work visas are valid for a three-year period, can be easily renewed for another three years, and may be "extended permanently beyond the six-year period if a petition for permanent resident visa is pending" (Ibid.). Although popular discussions describe the jobs filled as "highly skilled," the "actual qualifications are quite modest" (Ibid.). The job "must require a bachelor's or higher degree or its equivalent, and the visa recipient must have completed such a bachelor's or higher degree at an accredited U.S. college or university, hold an equivalent degree from a foreign institution, or have gained experience in the specialty that is equivalent to the completion of such a degree" (Ibid.). Because it is a guest worker program, the terms of the visa are controlled entirely by the employer. Support for the H-1B has become a formidable political force, uniting business interests and many left-leaning immigrants' rights groups.

Technology interests have engaged in a continuous, high-profile lobbying campaign in support of the H-1B program. Because wage stagnation and underemployment among bachelor's and advanced degree holders have become politically inescapable, corporate interests have couched their support for the H-1B as a method of improving the economic situation of all workers. In 2008, Bill Gates testified before the U.S. House of Representatives Committee on Science and Technology about immigration and education. Gates introduced himself as chairman of Microsoft and, with his wife, Melinda, "founder of the Bill & Melinda Gates Foundation" (Gates 2008). Gates maintained that the nation's status as the "world's center for innovation" was "at risk." One of the two main reasons for this risk was that "U.S. companies face a severe shortfall of scientists and engineers with expertise to develop the next generation of breakthroughs" (Ibid.). For Gates, the United States was also underinvesting in "the basic research needed to drive long-term innovation" (Ibid.). Unless these trends were reversed, he argued, "our competitive advantage will erode. Our ability to create new high-paying jobs will suffer" (Ibid.). He went on to discuss the recent efforts of both Microsoft and the Gates Foundation to address these issues and went on to say that "as a recent study shows for every H-1B holder that technology companies hire, five additional jobs are created around that person" (Ibid.). Gates then provided a list of specific policy requests, including "extending the period that foreign students can work here after graduation, increasing the current cap on H-1B visas, clearing a path to permanent residency for high-skilled foreign-born employees, eliminating per-country green card limits, and significantly increasing the annual number of green cards" (Ibid.).

In 2012, Microsoft elaborated on these priorities in *A National Talent Strategy: Ideas for Securing U.S. Competitiveness and Economic Growth*, which restated long-standing claims regarding the comparatively inferior quality of American achievement in math and science as well as the insufficient quantity of STEM workers. Microsoft affirmed that there was an "urgent demand for workers trained in the STEM fields" but that there were "not enough people with the necessary skills to meet that demand and help drive innovation" (Microsoft 2012, 3). The corporation also promoted its own philanthropy, stating that "we have decided to help" and that it was "reorienting a large portion of corporate philanthropy to focus on these challenges, investing $500 million in a wide range of company resources over the next three years to expand opportunities for education, employment and entrepreneurship for over 50 million young people in the United States and 300 million youth worldwide" (Ibid., 4). The corporation argued in favor of a "two-pronged approach that will couple long-term improvements in STEM education in the United States with targeted, short-term, high-skilled immigration reforms" (Ibid.). Microsoft requested that national policy makers strengthen STEM education in K–12, "broaden access to computer science in high school," and address "our national crisis in college completion by helping students who start college to finish it faster and expand higher education capacity to produce more STEM degrees, with a particular focus on computer science" (Ibid., 4–5). The corporation also requested that a "new allocation of 20,000 H-1B visas for foreign nationals with a U.S. bachelor's degree or equivalent foreign degree in a STEM discipline should be established" (Ibid., 24).

Today, the rhetoric of "skills" is central to the marketing efforts of higher education consulting firms. In July 2017, Bill Hansen, a former George W. Bush administration official in the Department of Education and CEO of the newly created Strada Educational Network, a nonprofit holding company, argued that the college-educated workforce was still inadequate: "Our universities are not producing graduates with the skill sets our businesses and companies are looking for" (Columbo 2017). According to 2019 tax filings, the CEO earned over $1.6 million in reportable compensation plus over $64,000 in other compensation, while the nonprofit also paid fifteen individuals between roughly $57,000 and $98,000 solely for their board service (Strada Education Network 2019). In 2020, Emsi, one of Strada's holdings (Strada Education Network 2018), promoted products intended to help higher education institutions "skillify their curriculum, translating it into the same skill-based language used by employers and job seekers" (Verougstraete 2020), including the identification of regional "skill clusters" as part of a "New Geography of Skills" (Repp 2020). In recent promotional materials, the assessment firm ACT maintained: "Individuals are entering the workforce without the skills employers need. ACT WorkKeys assessments is a first step toward closing skills gaps and improving workforce quality" (ACT 2022).

From Threat to Permanent Prediction: The Robots Are Always Coming

The skills gap's rhetorical emphasis on technology and workplace complexity has included a growing emphasis on automation and robots, which, in turn, have also become a recurring theme among education reformers. Specifically, predictions that large segments of the workforce are poised to become automated have become commonplace, and these predictions are typically accompanied by the recommendation that the public pursue additional education and training. Automation predictions have been advanced since early in the twentieth century and, tellingly, nearly always presented in language that implicitly acknowledges the lack of any empirical basis for such claims. In the 1980s, elites warned that "routine" jobs were "at risk," while in more recent years, the public has been cautioned that a much larger variety of middle-class jobs requiring more formal education are "vulnerable" or "susceptible" to automation. Many discussions of workplace automation often conflate job loss resulting from real trends such as offshoring or the use of contingent employment with automation itself, which implies that automation replacing employees is as likely as these other real developments.

Public discussion of automation during the Reagan administration was intertwined with the president's anti-labor policies. In 1982 the Reagan administration's National Commission on Employment Policy warned that workers should be ready to accept lower wages and potentially even job loss resulting from automation: "Workers may be threatened in the short term by loss of their jobs due to rapid automation of manufacturing plants and in the long term by possible crippling of whole industries if manufacturers fail to automate rapidly enough or otherwise change their production techniques or wage costs to meet foreign competition" (Sherman 1983, 9). In 1987, *Workforce 2000* predicted waves of automation touching on numerous types of jobs: "Silicon secretaries that can take dictation and edit letters, reservation clerks that understand speech in any language, or robots that can load a truck or pick strawberries are easily within the reach of technologies being developed now" (Johnston and Packer 1987, 34). In the 1989 *New York Times* cover story on the skills gap, *Workforce 2000* coauthor Arnold Packer stated that if schools were not improved, employers would have few alternatives, one of which was to automate employment to "accommodate a low-skilled domestic labor force" (Fiske 1989b). A few decades later, the NCEE's *Tough Choices or Tough Times* emphasized the loss of "routine" work but also claimed, with scant evidence, that such work was not confined to low-wage jobs: "Many good well-paying, middle-class jobs involve routine work of this kind and are rapidly being automated" (National Center on Education and the Economy 2008, xxiii).

The current discussion of workplace automation has been driven by the 2017 work of Carl Benedict Frey and Michael A. Osborne, which stunningly claimed that "around 47% of total U.S. employment is in the high risk category" of being automated "relatively soon, perhaps over the next decade or two" (Frey and Osborne 2017, 268). As of June 2022, according to Google Scholar, Frey and Osborne's article had been cited over ten thousand times. Their predictions are based on a statistical model that quantifies several different tasks involved in specific jobs and fails to consider any historical data on automation. Also published in 2017 was the *Chronicle of Higher Education*'s report *The Future of Work*, by Scott Carlson, aimed at higher education administrators. *The Future of Work* grouped automation with existing trends that had created workplace instability for millions of workers, including part-time employment and independent contracting, and suggested that in the future "employment may become more tenuous, as computers and robots reinvent and even eliminate some kinds of jobs, while other jobs become freelance and part-time 'gigs'" (Carlson 2017, 9–10). The report also affirmed: "Many experts in artificial intelligence see a future where any routine task—and perhaps some non-routine ones—are candidates for automation: accountants, clerks, telemarketers, movie projectionists, receptionists, and even pharmacists, archivists, and janitors" (Ibid., 18). This ominous picture of a future workplace dominated by automation and robots was also vividly captured in Davidson's *The New Education*, in which the automation threat is again commingled with an existing trend, offshoring: "As we are seeing, many S.T.E.M. positions and whole occupations are susceptible to automation and offshoring" (Davidson 2017, 139). Davidson's depiction of the future for workers can fairly be labeled cataclysmic: "With artificial intelligence powering robots to do everything from drive our cars to fill out tax forms, it is not clear what new jobs will be created to offset the massive layoffs portended ahead" (Ibid.).

Two 2019 reports on the future of employment published by the Brookings Institution and McKinsey also embrace Frey and Osborn's work and predict a future workplace with extensive automation and robots. The McKinsey report, which elaborated on the firm's previous work, warned that the "next wave of automation will affect occupations across the country, displacing many office support, food service, transportation and logistics, and customer service roles" (McKinsey Global Institute 2019, vi). McKinsey stressed that individuals with less formal education would bear the brunt of this trend, arguing that those with a high school degree or less were four times more likely to hold "highly automatable roles" than those with bachelor's degrees (Ibid.). Because of existing racial disparities in employment patterns, McKinsey argued that Hispanics and African Americans "may be hardest hit, with 12 million displaced" (Ibid.). However, the report also argued that the livelihoods of workers over fifty were in danger as this group holds 11.5 million "at-risk" jobs (Ibid.). Yet more educated workers were also at serious risk because automation and artificial intelligence "could replace millions of workers in middle- to high-wage accounting, finance, business, legal, and support functions" (Ibid., 14). The Brookings Institution's report was still ultimately about predictions, claiming that approximately 25 percent of U.S. jobs will face "high exposure" to automation "in the coming decades," while "some 36 percent" of jobs "will experience medium exposure to automation by 2030" (Muro, Maxim, and Whiton 2019).

From the perspective of the average worker, the overall picture of the future of employment portrayed in these works is extraordinarily frightening, as it portends even greater levels of economic insecurity. The common thread throughout the reports on automation is that more education and training are always the best way workers can prepare for such economically devastating forces that lie ahead. As a result, this work has become a key part of the larger fantasy economy narrative and an important component of the education reform movement, as K–12 schools and higher education are instructed to provide students with the skills necessary to make them "robot-proof" in the marketplace.

Conclusion

With the ascendance of neoliberalism, wage stagnation and growing inequality have become entrenched in the American political economy. Having become apparent in the early 1980s, these trends became more pronounced over time. To justify growing inequality and stagnant wages for the majority, economic elites have drawn on human capital theory to create what I call the fantasy economy. In the political campaign that is the fantasy economy, the poor education and training of American workers has created a perpetually inadequate workforce, leading to widespread wage stagnation and growing inequality. I argue that the narrative of the fantasy economy has been extraordinarily difficult to alter because, by and large, this is the only narrative on education and the economy that Americans have heard. To be clear, there have been dissenting voices on all the specific claims about the deficiencies in the education system and workforce, many of which I discuss in Chapter 2. Yet one comprehensive empirical refutation of many of the key claims of the fantasy economy deserves mention here.

Perhaps the most significant counternarrative to *A Nation at Risk* and many of the core ideas that have become central to the fantasy economy was the Sandia Report. In the wake of the 1989 Education Summit of U.S. Governors commissioned by President George H. W. Bush, the Department of Energy's Sandia National Laboratories, under the direction of Energy Secretary James Watkins, produced an extensive report on the nation's education system. Michael A. Wartell and Robert M. Huelskamp discussed the report's findings in testimony before the U.S. House of Representatives Subcommittee on Elementary, Secondary, and Vocational Education of the Committee on Education and Labor on July 18, 1991 (Schneider and Houston 1993), and a substantially abbreviated version of Huelskamp's testimony was published two years later in the *Phi Delta Kappan* (Huelskamp 1993). But a 1991 article in *Education Week* stated that the Sandia authors could not be reached for comment and characterized the reaction to the report as an "uproar" (Miller 1991). The article quoted an anonymous source who said that the Sandia researchers "were told that it would never see the light of day, that they had better be quiet" (Ibid.). According to the article, "Sources in the research community said that the Sandia researchers have reported being berated and even threatened with the loss of funding by Administration officials" (Ibid.).

Thus, the report was not widely available until a version of it was published in 1993 in an academic journal, the *Journal of Educational Research*. The Sandia researchers addressed numerous indicators of the education system and qualifications of the workforce and found that, contrary to the rhetoric of *A Nation at Risk*, U.S. student performance had been relatively stable in recent decades. But perhaps the most interesting findings of the Sandia researchers involved the workforce and labor market. The report rejected the notion of a skills gap and cited primary educational attainment and labor market data in support of their argument. The Sandia authors also cited the findings of the NCEE's initial survey of U.S. employers that "only one in twenty employers believed that the skill requirements in the workplace would increase significantly during the decade of the 1990s" (Sandia National Laboratories 1993, 294). Significantly, the report also affirmed that "although the lack of skilled workers is often advanced by business leaders as a major problem, only 15 percent of those surveyed had difficulty filling skilled positions" (Ibid.). Finally, the Sandia Report argued what many scholars have documented since: that the nation was overproducing scientists and engineers. In an analysis of data from the National Science Foundation, the Sandia researchers found that nearly 40 percent of science and engineering bachelor's degree holders did not "pursue careers formally classified as scientist or engineer" and predicted that the "overage accumulates to over one million by the year 2010" (Ibid., 295).

The *Journal of Educational Research* included an introductory essay evaluating the report by education professor Lawrence C. Stedman (1993), who provided a mixed assessment. After describing the complex politics of the report's release during the George H. W. Bush administration, Stedman called the report "disappointing" and challenged the Sandia researchers' analysis of testing data (Ibid., 134). He concluded that there was "still a great need for fundamental school reform, and the Sandia report should not distract educators from that mission" (Ibid., 145). Despite the fact that the education reform movement was being built on claims of an underqualified workforce, Stedman refused to consider the Sandia researchers' analysis of the current and future educational needs of the labor market, saying he would "leave such areas as labor-force forecasts, educational expenditures, and projected demographics to the economists and futurists" (Ibid., 134).

The intrigue surrounding the Sandia Report is telling, seemingly reflecting the power politics at work in maintaining the sanctity of the fantasy economy's narrative regarding the nation's declining education system and workforce deficiencies, particularly in STEM fields. Eventually, empirical reality would make such claims much less controversial. Years later, public data and many scholarly works would dispel the myth of a shortage of STEM workers. Clearly aware of the limits of the STEM crisis narrative, business leaders eventually began framing increasing STEM education as a cure for poverty. But the report was produced in the years after *A Nation at Risk*, when the narrative of failing schools and a permanent skills gap was not yet fully established. Clearly powerful interests had major incentives to limit public and media consumption of a report produced by a federal agency that directly undermined the major claims of the emerging education reform movement.

In Chapter 2, I examine the key claims of the fantasy economy regarding education and the labor market. Using primary education and economic data supplemented by scholarly research, we can see that the tenets of the fantasy economy are much more a reflection of interest group politics than empirical reality.

2

Fantasy Meets Reality

Evaluating the Tenets of the Fantasy Economy

Everyone knows that the United States has long suffered
from widespread shortages in its science and engineering
workforce, and that if continued these shortages will cause
it to fall behind its major economic competitors. Everyone
knows that these workforce shortages are due mainly to
the myriad weaknesses of American k–12 education in
science and mathematics, which international comparisons
of student performance rank as average at best. Such
claims are now well established as conventional wisdom.
There is almost no debate in the mainstream. They echo
from corporate CEO to corporate CEO, from lobbyist to
lobbyist, from editorial writer to editorial writer. But what
if what everyone knows is wrong? What if this conventional
wisdom is just the same claims ricocheting in an echo
chamber? The truth is that there is little credible evidence
of the claimed widespread shortages in the U.S. science
and engineering workforce.
—Michael Teitelbaum, "The Myth of the Science
    and Engineering Shortage," *The Atlantic*

Introduction

This chapter examines the fantasy economy's overarching empirical claims
regarding the education system and workforce in relation to the labor
market. Using a combination of primary official data as well as scholarly research, I find that claims of a weak education system and underqualified labor force are either false or substantially misleading. Before
examining these claims, however, it is first necessary to document longer-
term demographic trends in the nation's schools and review historic patterns regarding student demographics and educational performance.

Demographics and Educational Performance

Approximately 90 percent of U.S. K–12 students attend public schools, and over the last several decades, public education has become increasingly racially diverse. In 2000, the population of school-age children was 62 percent white, 15 percent Black, and 16 percent Hispanic (National Center for Education Statistics 2019a, 26). By 2017, whites constituted 51 percent, Blacks 14 percent, and Hispanics 25 percent, while 5 percent of all school-age students were Asian (Ibid.). By the fall of 2019, roughly 10.4 percent of all public school students were English learners, and the home language for roughly three-quarters of these students was Spanish (National Center for Education Statistics 2022a). By 2028, as a percentage of all public school students, whites were projected to decline to 44 percent, Hispanics to increase modestly to roughly 28 percent, Blacks to be roughly 15 percent, and Asians to increase to approximately 6 percent, while students identifying as two or more races were expected to grow to over 5 percent (National Center for Education Statistics 2020a, 41). Recent official data also illustrates that roughly 67 percent of private school students were white (National Center for Education Statistics 2019b). Because of the disproportionately high percentage of white students in private schools, then, total K–12 enrollment for this group will likely remain very close to 50 percent in the coming years.

While the racial composition of U.S. students has changed considerably, poverty in the K–12 schools has changed little in recent decades and fluctuates with the overall poverty rate. According to the Department of Health and Human Services, 23 percent of children lived in poverty in 1964, prior to the full implementation of the Lyndon B. Johnson administration's social welfare policies (U.S. Department of Health and Human Services 2016, 2). By 2000, the percentage of children in poverty in public schools declined to 15 percent, but it increased to 21 percent by 2010, then declined to 18 percent by 2018 (National Center for Education Statistics 2020b, 5). In contrast, recent federal data showed that only 8 percent of all private school students were in poverty (National Center for Education Statistics 2019b).

A long line of research has documented racial and economic education achievement and attainment gaps[1] as well as the lagging academic performance of children whose home language is not English (U.S. Department of Education, n.d.). Educational achievement and attainment levels vary directly with income, and poverty is the biggest predictor of educational outcomes at the individual, school, and district levels. And because of the disproportionately high numbers of racial minorities in poverty, economic and racial disadvantages reinforce one another. In 2016, the child poverty rate for Blacks was 31 percent, 26 percent for Hispanics, and 10 percent for both whites and Asians (National Center for Education Statistics 2019a, 38). The racial achievement gap is driven by poverty.

Further, American students are much more likely to live in poverty than their counterparts in comparable countries, which is critical context for international education comparisons. In 2016, the average rate of child poverty for the thirty-six nations in the Organization for Economic Cooperation and Development (OECD) was roughly 13 percent (Organization for Economic Cooperation and Development 2019, 1). Only nine of the thirty-six countries had child poverty rates higher than those of the United States: China, South Africa, Brazil, Costa Rica, Turkey, India, Israel, Spain, and Chile (Ibid., 2). In the international context, researchers have examined how poverty affects a range of factors that influence educational performance. In 2017, scholars from the London School of Economics and Political Science compiled a systematic review of research examining the relationship between household financial resources and child outcomes among OECD countries over the last fifty years (Cooper and Stewart 2017). Outcomes examined included children's health; cognitive development; social, emotional, and behavioral development; home environment; and maternal mental health and health behaviors. The authors concluded that "the overwhelming majority of studies find significant and positive effects of income across the range of children's outcomes, including cognitive development and school achievement, social and behavioral development and children's health" (Ibid., 27). In an analysis of data from the Programme on International Student Assessment (PISA), researchers from the OECD found that the United States is one of six member nations in which socioeconomic level has a strong influence on student achievement and one in which schools are least effective in mitigating the negative effects of poverty on student performance (Lowell and Salzman 2007, 22–23).

While major reports such as *A Nation at Risk* and *Before It's Too Late* neglected to examine the well-established impact of student demographics on educational outcomes in any depth, in recent years, there has been an increasing recognition of how demographic variables affect achievement and attainment. But the removal of poverty as a causal factor in shaping educational outcomes has been the perennial political strategy of reformers in which elites continuously steer the conversation away from the overwhelming significance of income. As we will see in Chapter 4, the movement for school accountability was built largely on a sustained evasion of any acknowledgment of the impact of poverty on educational outcomes in a rhetorical campaign that focused on racial achievement gaps. Reformers framed the low achievement characteristic of high-poverty, disproportionately minority schools as the fault of schools and teachers. The more recent proliferation of the "no excuses" model of charter schools is another example of this approach. Charter school chains, including KIPP (Knowledge Is Power Program), Uncommon Schools, Success Academy, YES Prep, and Achievement First (Golann and Debs 2019) inherently downplay the long list of adverse outcomes associated with poverty by labeling them "excuses."

Further, by emphasizing the small number of high-poverty schools that "beat the odds" in terms of academic achievement, reformers suggest that all such schools could replicate these successes if they were run differently, with different teachers, different curricula, and so forth. The many books of Karen Chenoweth, a writer-in-residence at Education Trust, are representative of this approach (Chenoweth 2007, 2009, 2017; Chenoweth and Theokas 2011). In 2017, Bill Gates also implicitly revealed this line of thinking in a discussion of the racial achievement gap: "When disaggregated by race, we see two Americas. One where white students perform along the lines of the best in the world—with achievement comparable to countries like Finland and Korea. And another America, where Black and Latino students perform comparably to the students in the lowest performing OECD countries, such as Chile and Greece" (Gates 2017). For education reformers, addressing the issue of poverty directly or explicitly acknowledging its many adverse consequences would necessarily open the door to a discussion of income and wages. And in the shareholder economy of neoliberalism, labor is a cost to be minimized. Thus, in the fantasy economy, the focus must remain on the education system's role in both overcoming the historic effects of poverty and providing low-income students economic opportunity in the future.

With this knowledge of the relationship between student demographics and educational performance, I now turn to an analysis of two key empirical claims in the fantasy economy—the historically declining academic achievement of American students and the weak performance of U.S. students compared to those of other countries. This discussion, which draws largely on previously published work, finds that both claims lack merit. The overall performance of American students has remained relatively constant over the last several decades despite increasing racial and language diversity and chronically high child poverty rates. And popular international comparisons alleging the weakness of American education suffer from a range of logical flaws as well as decontextualized and misleading data.

The Illusion of Historically
Declining Achievement

One of the core beliefs in the fantasy economy is that American student achievement has declined over time. This claim, which is central to the skills gap narrative, has deep historical roots but was fully explicated in *A Nation at Risk*, and it assumes a golden age of American education that began to erode in the 1960s, a period during which, ironically, only half the population finished high school and just 10 percent received bachelor's degrees. Yet the proposition of historically declining achievement advanced in the report was based on little data. The National Assessment of Educational Progress (NAEP), created in 1969 and administered by the Department of Education, is considered the most definitive national data on student achievement. But the authors of *A Nation at Risk* opted not to use NAEP data in their analysis. Instead, the primary data that the report relied on was the Scholastic Aptitude Test (SAT). Specifically, *A Nation at Risk* cited the "virtually unbroken decline" in SAT scores between 1963 and 1980 (National Commission on Excellence in Education 1983, 8–9).

Yet as many analysts have pointed out, the number of total SAT test takers increased significantly during this period, and therefore the demographics of students taking the exam became much more representative of the broader population. As the number of test takers increased, long-standing patterns related to income and race affected national averages. For example, between 1960 and 1970, the number of students taking the SAT increased threefold (Owens 2015, 11), which substantially diversified the pool of test takers. While the number of Blacks taking the exam was in the 1 to 2 percent range in the early 1960s, by 1970, the percentage of test takers who were African American had risen to 8 percent (Ibid., 12), which affected average scores. An exam taken primarily by upper-income white students planning on attending elite colleges and universities became an exam for a broader cross section of American students. Thus, modestly declining SAT averages were quite predictable and should not be interpreted as an indicator of widespread declines in basic achievement. Consequently, one of the central assertions of *A Nation at Risk* was, at best, fundamentally misleading yet still became a cornerstone of the education reform movement.

While exams such as the SAT and ACT are taken by students planning to attend higher education, the NAEP is given to representative populations of all students and therefore better reflects achievement levels of the entire school system. In addition, we can assess long-term NAEP data to examine trends. Yet the Clinton administration's *Before It's Too Late* seized on the results from the 1996 NAEP, calling the preparation of American students in science and math "unacceptable" (National Commission on Mathematics and Science Teaching for the Twenty-First Century 2000, 7). Minorities of all students in grades 4, 8, and 12 performed at or above Proficient in mathematics and science (Ibid., 11). Additionally, more than one-third of American students scored Below Basic in math and science in 1996. On the surface, the 1996 NAEP testing results do not seem encouraging. But as Diane Ravitch (2013, 47) has pointed out, we must consider the qualitative descriptions of the NAEP's achievement categories to meaningfully interpret this data.

In the early 1990s, to improve public understanding of student performance, the NAEP established achievement levels, which included Below Basic, Basic, Proficient, and Advanced (Ibid., 46). Below Basic meant that students had a "weak grasp of the knowledge and skills" assessed, and, as Ravitch pointed out, this would be roughly equivalent to a grade of D or below on a traditional letter-grade scale (Ibid., 47). Reaching the level of Basic meant "partial mastery of prerequisite knowledge and skills that are fundamental for proficient work at each grade" (Ibid.), which translates into an average passing grade, likely in the C or B range. Proficient was defined as representing "solid academic performance for each grade assessed. This is a very high level of academic achievement. Students reaching this level have demonstrated competency over challenging subject matter, including subject-matter knowledge, application of such knowledge to real-world situations, and analytical skills appropriate to the subject matter" (Ibid.). This description sounds akin to a grade of B+ or in the A range. Finally, Advanced was defined as "superior level of academic performance," which only 3 to 8 percent of all students attain (Ibid.), which would be akin to a grade of A+. When using these definitions, a much different picture emerges: significant majorities of students—between roughly 57 and 69 percent of all students in fourth-, eighth-, and twelfth-grade science and math (National Commission on Mathematics and Science Teaching for the Twenty-First Century 2000, 11)—had achievement roughly equivalent to the C range or higher, while the remaining students achieved a grade akin to a D or below.

Further, the alarm raised over the 1996 NAEP data in *Before It's Too Late* also omitted the fact that scores reflected a pattern of improvement that had begun in 1990. Scale scores for fourth-, eighth-, and twelfth-grade students in math increased with each successive exam—1990, 1992, and 1996 (National Center for Education Statistics 1997, 25). Also, the percentage of students scoring Below Basic for all three grade levels in math also declined over time (Ibid., 47). Longer-term trends in reading scores further showed modest increases for nine- and thirteen-year-olds between 1990 and 1996, along with slight declines for seventeen-year-olds (National Center for Education Statistics 2000, vi). However, scores for all age groups in reading and math were higher in 1996 than when the assessment began in the early 1970s (Ibid., v, vi).

Results from the NAEP in the decades after 2000 further undermine claims that average student achievement is declining. The NAEP long-term trends assessment, which dates from the early 1970s, "contains large numbers of questions that have been used consistently for more than forty years" (Ravitch 2013, 51). The long-term trends in both reading and math for nine-, thirteen-, and seventeen-year-olds show increases between 1980 and 2012. While increases for seventeen-year-old students were modest, both nine- and thirteen-year-olds showed more significant increases (U.S. Government Accountability Office 2018, 23). And popular discussions of racial achievement gaps also typically fail to consider the fact that longitudinal NAEP data on scale scores from the early 1970s through 2020 in both math and reading reveals a narrowing of achievement gaps between both whites and Blacks and between whites and Hispanics at ages nine, thirteen, and seventeen (National Center for Education Statistics 2021a, 2021b). As Ravitch has argued, achievement gaps remain because all groups have improved their performance over the long term (Ravitch 2013, 57).

Finally, longer-term NAEP scale scores for reading and math from the 1990s through 2017 also show modest increases in average scores at most age levels in both subjects. For example, between 1998 (the first year that testing accommodations were permitted) and 2019, average scores in reading were relatively constant for students in grades 4 and 8, while decreasing modestly for students in grade 12 (National Center for Education Statistics 2020c). In math, from 1996 through 2019, average scale scores also increased for fourth and eighth graders, while scores remained relatively constant between 2005 and 2019 for twelfth graders as well (National Center for Education Statistics 2020d).[2] These longer-term increases should be understood against a backdrop of relatively constant rates of child poverty and steadily increasing racial and language diversity. Clearly, then, analysis of long-term average test scores since the early 1970s does not reveal a pattern of declining achievement.

While education critics typically cite test scores as evidence of a failing system, a variable rarely considered by reformers is the significant transformation of the coursework and curriculum of U.S. schooling over the past several decades. Overall, the curriculum has illustrated an increasing academic emphasis, which helps explain the longer-term trends in average testing performance. For example, there is ample evidence that students are taking more classes in math and science than previously. Between 1990 and 2009, the percentage of high school graduates who took coursework in all major advanced math and science classes increased, and for some courses the percentage increase was significant. In 1990, only 19 percent of graduates took biology, chemistry, and physics, but by 2009, 30 percent of graduates had taken all three of these courses. And in 1990, only 7 percent of American high school graduates took calculus, but by 2009, this number had increased to 16 percent (National Center for Education Statistics 2016c, 178).

Also, since the 1970s and 1980s, there has been a significant increase in the academic content of the lower grades in elementary school. The curriculum of many kindergarten classrooms today more closely resembles the curriculum of first grade not too many years ago. Comparing large, nationally representative data sets of kindergarten classrooms in 1998 and 2010, Daphna Bassok and her colleagues found that kindergarten teachers in 2010 had much higher academic expectations for children both before entering kindergarten as well as during kindergarten itself. In 2010, schools spent more time on advanced math and literacy, increased the amount of teacher-directed instruction and assessment, and devoted much less time to art, music, science, and activities chosen by the children (Bassok, Latham, and Rorem 2016). Whether this approach to kindergarten is beneficial for students in the long run is a matter of intense debate. Nonetheless, this transformation of kindergarten is further evidence of the increasing academic content of K–12 education. In sum, as Ravitch has concluded, "the difficulty and complexity of what is taught today far exceed anything the average student encountered in school decades ago" (2013, 45).

Tellingly, many years later, Jay Sommer, the only teacher on the National Commission on Excellence in Education, which wrote *A Nation at Risk*, admitted that the alarmist tone used in the final report was only intended to describe urban, high-poverty schools: "We were talking about inner-city schools . . . we left out the successes, and that was deliberate. I mean there is no comparison between an inner city school anyplace, in Chicago, and New Rochelle High School where I taught" (Owens 2015, 19). Sommer further affirmed that the commission "never intended its recommendations to be taken as dogma for every school or school system in America" (Ibid.). Thus, the schools that were at risk were high-poverty schools. But the Reagan administration and corporate education reformers had a much larger agenda in mind, and reports like *A Nation at Risk* and *Workforce 2000* became a call to arms for those advocating market-based education reforms.

The Flawed Logic of International Comparisons

Claims that tend to generate even more attention than those of historically declining achievement involve international comparisons showing American students underperforming the students of other nations. Since *A Nation at Risk*, international comparisons have been repeatedly linked to arguments about pending U.S. economic decline and have become a mainstay in the education reform movement. Several scholars have provided important context for such comparisons (Boe and Shin 2005; Ravitch 2013; Salzman and Lowell 2008; Teitelbaum 2014a). First, as discussed above, American students are much more likely to live in poverty than students in most comparable countries, and exams based on representative national samples will necessarily reflect the impact of poverty on achievement. Yet another problem with such comparisons is that averages of large data sets are often misleading because they tell us little about the distribution of observations within the data. Specifically, averages mask significant disparities within the data, including high performance in math and science among the top quartile and low performance among the bottom quartile. As Teitelbaum has concluded, "U.S. student performance in science and mathematics is unequal to a degree that may be unique among comparable countries" (2014a, 23). Inequality, then, must be at the center of any discussion of international testing comparisons. Moreover, it is especially ironic that many of the critics who argue for improved math and science education rely so heavily on overall averages given the substantial limitations associated with relying solely on statistical means of large data sets.

International comparisons present several other major problems. Analysts have often seized on the seeming decline in U.S. performance on the International Association for the Evaluation of Educational Achievement's (IEA) Trends in International Mathematics and Science Study (TIMSS) between eighth grade and the end of high school. For instance, *Before It's Too Late* pointed out that while U.S. fourth graders scored above international averages in both mathematics and science and eighth graders performed slightly above the international average in science and slightly below the international average in math, twelfth graders ranked near the bottom in both subjects among the twenty nations assessed in advanced math and physics (National Commission on Mathematics and Science Teaching for the 21st Century 2000, 10–11). However, as Erling E. Boe and Sujie Shin have articulated, one cannot automatically compare U.S. students to those abroad using the "end of secondary school" standard and assume that all students have received the same number of years of education. The number of years between eighth grade and the end of secondary school varies significantly across nations tested, ranging from roughly three years to nearly eight years (Boe and Shin 2005, 691).

Another problem facing those who decry U.S. performance on international assessments is the lack of participation by one of the country's biggest economic competitors, India, as well as the limited participation of China. India and China ranked 131st and 85th respectively on a recent United Nations Human Development Index (United Nations Development Programme 2019). There is considerable debate about the precise poverty rate in India, and in public discourse, the terms "poverty" and "extreme poverty" are often used interchangeably. By any reasonable standards, India's rate of poverty is quite high. But rather than use a subjective measure of poverty to assess the country's educational progress, I use the country's literacy rate as a proxy measure. According to a recent census by the Indian government, 27 percent of the country was illiterate, including roughly 32 percent of the rural population (Office of the Registrar General and Census Commissioner, India 2011, 46). Thus, if India administered a nationwide assessment representative of its population, its average academic performance would almost certainly be quite low, which is a substantial disincentive for the country to participate in international assessments.

Additionally, China's participation in international assessments, although expanded in recent years, has not come close to the levels of national participation of other nations, including the United States. In a discussion of the 2013 PISA results, education scholar Tom Loveless affirmed: "American press coverage—whether web-based, on television, or in old-fashioned print—will decry the mediocre showing of the U.S. and express astonishment at the performance of China. One problem. China does not take the PISA test. A dozen or so provinces in China take the PISA, along with two special administrative regions (Hong Kong and Macao). But journalists and pundits will focus on the results from one province, Shanghai, and those test scores will be depicted, in much of the public discussion that follows, as the results for China. That is wrong" (Loveless 2013). Yet the sheer sizes of both India and China, both of which are more than four times as large as the United States, enable the nations to produce large numbers of high-performing students. While not nearly as populous, the relative size of the United States also enables it to produce large numbers of high-performing students despite substantial inequalities within the school system. Analyzing PISA data from 2006, David Berliner calculated that the United States had 25 percent of the world's highest-performing students (scoring at levels 5 and 6), the greatest share of any nation in the world, followed by Japan, with 13 percent, and Germany and the U.K., both with 8 percent (Berliner 2011, 81). Clearly there is strength in sheer population size.

Population size and student demographics are also important context for evaluating the results of consistently high-performing nations, including Finland. Much has been written about the "Finnish Miracle" (Ripley 2014). Finland had 21 percent of its fifteen-year-olds in the highest categories on the 2006 PISA Science assessments, considerably higher than the 10 percent of U.S. students in these categories (Berliner 2011, 80). But as Berliner has pointed out (Ibid.), Finland has about 1.4 million children in school at all levels, and its child poverty rate is in the low single digits (Organization for Economic Cooperation and Development 2019), whereas the United States has over 70 million students in schools at all levels, with sizable numbers of public K–12 students in poverty. The United States, then, with its 10 percent of the highest achievers, has several million scientifically talented students, while Finland has a few hundred thousand. Although no one would argue that the United States should not aim to increase its percentage of students in the top categories in all subjects, considering aggregate data in addition to simple percentages makes it clear that the United States has a significant number of scientifically talented youth. In sum, a more comprehensive examination of educational data reveals a very different story than the conventional narrative of failing schools while also highlighting the impact of economic inequality and poverty on educational outcomes.

Increasing Educational Attainment in a Low-Education Labor Market

In addition to the proposition of failing schools, the other main claim underlying the fantasy economy campaign is that the supply of qualified workers is chronically insufficient. *Workforce 2000* is widely credited with creating the skills gap narrative, and in the decades since, several different strands of the skills gap have emerged. College completion efforts, typically led by foundations, stress a general need for more highly educated workers. Depending on the audience, these efforts are also framed in terms of the need for workers to merely attain post–high school education and training. Business and trade groups tend to focus more on increasing the supply of workers in STEM and technical fields. In all cases, however, workers are instructed to develop their skills through more formal education and training on the assumption that there are more than enough jobs to accommodate an increasingly educated and trained workforce. The widespread acceptance of the skills gap has created continuous political pressure on the educational establishment, which has led to the uncritical adoption of any programs that elites argue will improve the education system's ability to simultaneously meet the needs of employers and provide graduates more success in the labor market. Yet all claims about the qualifications of the labor force in relation to the requirements of the job market are ultimately empirical, and a close examination of these issues reveals that the education and skill levels of the labor force have been more than adequate for the supply of jobs for at least the last several decades.

Not long after the skills gap had become conventional wisdom, researchers demonstrated the misleading and erroneous claims articulated in the campaign's most influential document, *Workforce 2000*. In 1991, the Economic Policy Institute offered a comprehensive analysis of the report's major assertions and predictions (Mishel and Teixeira 1991). Lawrence Mishel and Ruy A. Teixeira, who relied heavily on official data, pointed out that the growth of skill levels required by the labor market was projected to slow. They further argued that "*at most*, 30 percent of the future labor force will need a college degree, up *from about 25 percent in the* mid-1980s" and that "employment projections suggest that there would be a surplus of college graduates" (Ibid., 2, emphasis in original), in a methodical refutation of the report's core claims. One year later, the U.S. General Accounting Office (GAO, renamed the Government Accountability Office in 2004) also published a report evaluating the claims of *Workforce 2000* and its companion report, *Civil Service 2000* (U.S. General Accounting Office 1992). The GAO concluded that "labor economists and other experts often disagreed with predictions that there will be widespread labor shortages and skills mismatches by the year 2000. Critics asserted that what labor shortages will occur will probably not be widespread but confined to certain industries, occupations, and locations" (Ibid., 3). Further, the GAO confirmed Mishel and Teixeira's analysis, concluding that labor economists "argued that the skill requirements of jobs will rise slowly, with fast growing/high-skill technical jobs compromising only 4 percent of all jobs by the year 2000" (Ibid.). In 2003, sociologist Michael Handel provided a comprehensive analysis of the skills gap literature. With respect to *Workforce 2000*'s major prediction of a high-education, high-skill job market, Handel concluded that "the Bureau of Labor Statistics (BLS) occupational projections and DOT [Dictionary of Occupational Titles] ratings the report used did not support such sweeping assertions." And regarding Johnston and Packer's assertion of low levels of workforce skills based on their analysis of test scores, Handel argued that "no subsequent research using BLS occupational data and DOT ratings supports these conclusions" (Handel 2003, 151).

To evaluate more recent claims of worker shortages and skills gaps, it is necessary to examine educational attainment patterns of both the population and the workforce, data that is tracked, respectively, by the Census and the Department of Labor. One of the most striking patterns over the last several decades has been the population's steadily increasing levels of educational attainment. Despite both chronically high child poverty rates and an increasingly diverse student population, today the United States has achieved nearly universal high school completion. In the middle twentieth century, a majority did not finish high school. For example, in 1940, only one-quarter of the population twenty-five and over had a high school degree (Ryan and Bauman 2016, 4). By 1970, this number had increased to roughly 52 percent (Bauman and Graf 2003, 4), and then by 2021, it had reached over 91 percent (U.S. Census Bureau 2022). Increases in post–high school attainment levels have also been significant. In 1940, only 5 percent of the population twenty-five and over had a bachelor's degree or higher (Ryan and Bauman 2016, 4). By 1970, almost 11 percent had acquired at least a bachelor's degree (Bauman and Graf 2003, 4), and by 2021, nearly 38 percent of the population twenty-five and over possessed at least a bachelor's degree (U.S. Census Bureau 2022). Attainment levels have also increased significantly at both the associate's and master's levels and above. In 2000, 6.3 percent of the population twenty-five and over reported that their highest educational attainment was the associate's degree (Bauman and Graf 2003, 2), and by 2021, this number had increased to 10.5 percent (U.S. Census Bureau 2022). Similarly, in 2000, just under 9 percent of the population twenty-five and older had received a master's degree or higher (Bauman and Graff 2003, 2), and by 2021, this number had climbed to 14.4 percent (U.S. Census Bureau 2022).

Educational attainment has also increased steadily among younger adults, ages twenty-five through twenty-nine, who have consistently higher levels of attainment than the general population. In 1940, under 40 percent of younger adults had a high school degree (Ryan and Bauman 2016, 4). After decades of steadily increasing attainment, by 2015, high school graduates in this age group increased to 91 percent (Ibid., 5), and the number became 94 percent by 2021 (National Center for Education Statistics 2022a). In 1976, 24 percent of adults between twenty-five and twenty-nine had at least a bachelor's degree, and by 2021, this number had reached 39 percent (Ryan and Bauman 2016, 5; National Center for Education Statistics 2022a). Clearly, Americans have pursued more formal education during a time of growing inequality.

While increases in educational attainment among the general population are significant, the attainment levels of the workforce are even more striking. Table 2.1 illustrates trends in the increasing educational attainment of the workforce over the past three decades, which are especially pronounced at the bachelor's and advanced degree levels. In 1992, bachelor's and advanced degree holders combined made up 26.5 percent of the workforce. Yet by 2016, nearly 39 percent of the labor force had at least a bachelor's degree. And the share of the labor force possessing only a high school degree or less has also declined consistently, with the total percentage of the labor force in these two lower-educational attainment categories declining from over 48 percent in 1992 to 33.5 percent by 2016.

The implicit economic promise underlying human capital theory is that the number of jobs requiring greater levels of formal education and training will increase as the population's educational attainment levels increase. From this perspective, underemployment is seen as a function of an individual's inferior education and training or personal qualities rather than a structural problem. The BLS has historically published detailed data on hundreds of individual occupations as well as the educational requirements of the entire labor market. In occupational profiles, this data includes wages, current and projected numbers of jobs as well as their geographic distribution, and the educational background of a

TABLE 2.1 HIGHEST LEVEL OF EDUCATIONAL ATTAINMENT OF THE WORKFORCE, 25 AND OVER, 1992–2016			
Highest Level of Attainment	**1992**	**2004**	**2016**
Less Than High School	12.6%	10.0%	7.7%
High School	35.6%	30.2%	25.8%
Some College or Associate's Degree	25.4%	27.5%	27.5%
Bachelor's Degree	17.2%	21.0%	24.2%
Advanced Degree	9.3%	11.3%	14.7%
Source: Brundage 2017.			

typical worker in each field. Many occupations have objective qualifications, often determined by policy or professional associations. But many jobs do not have formal educational credentials associated with them, and so the BLS uses several data sources to gauge the path of the typical worker in each occupation (Bureau of Labor Statistics 2021a).[3] The BLS then uses this data to aggregate the number of jobs in the labor market at each educational attainment level.

Table 2.2 illustrates recent official data on the educational attainment levels of the labor force and the distribution of employment by educational attainment level in 2019 and projected for 2029. Admittedly, the supply of and demand for specific types of workers varies by geographic location. However, the illustrated disparity between the population's historically high levels of educational attainment and the relatively low levels of education and training required by the labor market is striking and substantially undermines the promise of human capital theory. In 2019, while over 62 percent of jobs typically required a high school degree or no formal credential for entry, only about 32 percent of the labor force possessed these lower attainment levels. Further, the roughly 41 per-

TABLE 2.2 EDUCATIONAL ATTAINMENT OF THE LABOR FORCE AND EMPLOYMENT DISTRIBUTION OF THE LABOR MARKET BY TYPICAL ENTRY-LEVEL EDUCATION, 2019 AND 2029 (PROJECTED)

Educational Attainment Levels	Highest Educational Attainment of the Labor Force, 25 and Over: 2019	Employment Distribution by Educational Attainment: 2019	Employment Distribution by Educational Attainment: 2029 (Projected)
Less Than High School/ No Formal Credential	7.0%	23.8%	23.7%
High School Degree/ Equivalent	25.4%	38.3%	37.5%
Some College, No Degree	15.2%	2.5%	2.4%
Postsecondary Nondegree Award	*	6.2%	6.3%
Associate's	11.1%	2.2%	2.3%
Bachelor's	25.7%	22.6%	23.2%
Master's		1.6%	1.8%
Doctorate/Professional Degree	15.6%	2.7%	2.8%

Sources: Percentages for attainment of the labor force and projected 2029 employment distribution calculated from data in Bureau of Labor Statistics 2020, 2021b.
*The Current Population Survey does not have an educational attainment category for nondegree awards. According to a recent Occupational Requirements Survey, 5.8 percent of civilian workers had a certification requirement (Bureau of Labor Statistics 2021c).

cent of the labor force with a bachelor's degree or higher substantially outnumbered the 27 percent of jobs typically requiring these higher levels of attainment. This disparity is caused by the relatively large number of the highest-educated individuals in the workforce—the nearly 16 percent with a master's degree and above—seeking the less than 4.5 percent of all jobs typically requiring advanced degrees. In addition, the number of individuals with educational credentials in between high school and the bachelor's degree also substantially outnumbered jobs typically requiring these levels of formal education. Finally, as labor market scholars have long noted, the educational requirements of the labor market are expected to change little in the coming years.

In sum, the contrast between the educational attainment of the population and that required by the labor market clearly explains the underemployment of millions of workers at every level of education beyond the high school degree. Given the surplus of individuals possessing master's degrees or greater, millions of advanced degree holders are forced to compete for jobs typically requiring the bachelor's degree. As bachelor's degree holders are displaced by those with higher levels of education, they are then forced to accept jobs requiring less than a bachelor's. Ultimately, significant numbers of associate's and bachelor's degree holders as well as the roughly 15 percent of the workforce with some college but no degree end up working in the large, diverse group of jobs constituting approximately 60 percent of the labor market that typically require a high school degree or no formal credential.

Research on underemployment confirms this analysis. Estimates of the number of individuals with bachelor's degrees working in jobs requiring less than a bachelor's have ranged from roughly 25 percent (S. Rose 2017, 3) to well over 40 percent, particular among younger workers during recessionary periods (Abel, Deitz, and Su 2014, 4). The Federal Reserve Bank of New York has been at the forefront of research on employment outcomes for college graduates, and its data set begins in 1990. The Federal Reserve defines a job as a college job "if 50 percent or more of the people working in that job indicate that at least a bachelor's degree is necessary" (Federal Reserve Bank of New York 2022a). And since 1990, at any point in time, between approximately 32 and 35 percent of all individuals between ages twenty-two and sixty-five with bachelor's degrees were working in jobs typically requiring less than a bachelor's. The Federal Reserve also tracks this data among recent college graduates (ages twenty-two and twenty-seven), and underemployment rates for this group are even higher (Ibid.). And contrary to conventional wisdom, graduates in all the dozens of majors tracked by the Federal Reserve, including business-related fields, engineering, and technical fields, experience significant levels of underemployment (Federal Reserve Bank of New York 2022b). Some underemployed bachelor's degree holders eventually find employment commensurate with their education level. But, consistently, one-third do not, and this sizable minority should be understood as part of the collateral damage of the fantasy economy and a key variable explaining the politics of higher education today.

The ultimate justification for the education reform movement is the fantasy economy's conception of the labor market, one that continually attempts to distort what we see and experience every day—a predominantly low-wage, service-sector job market requiring little formal education. Additional data illustrating the real labor market can be found by looking at the most numerous jobs in the United States, outlined in Table 2.3. This list is dominated by low-education, low-wage jobs. And according to the most recent version of the Bureau of Labor Statistics' *Occupational Outlook Handbook*, only two of these jobs typically required any post–high school education—registered nurses and general and operations managers. The remaining jobs on the list typically required either no formal educational credential or a high school degree or equivalent for entry (Bureau of Labor Statistics 2022a).

In 1992, in *The Double Helix of Education and the Economy*, Sue Berryman and Thomas Bailey observed that "the ten occupations that are projected to add the most jobs to the economy by 2005, with the exception of registered nurses and general managers, all generally require low skills" (Berryman and Bailey 1992b, 31). Thirty years later, the edu-

TABLE 2.3 MOST NUMEROUS OCCUPATIONS AND MEDIAN WAGES, 2021		
Occupation	Number of Jobs: May 2021	Median Annual Wages: 2021
Retail Salespersons	3,693,490	$29,180
Home Health and Personal Care Aides	3,366,480	$29,430
Cashiers	3,318,020	$27,260
Fast Food and Counter Workers	3,095,120	$25,100
Registered Nurses	3,047,530	$77,600
General and Operations Managers	2,984,920	$97,970
Customer Service Representatives	2,787,070	$36,920
Laborers and Freight, Stock, and Material Movers, Hand	2,729,010	$31,230
Office Clerks, General	2,578,180	$37,030
Stockers and Order Fillers	2,451,430	$30,110
Source: Bureau of Labor Statistics 2021d.		

cational requirements of the most numerous occupations have changed little, despite the constant claims of education reformers.

Despite the substantial problem of underemployment among bachelor's and advanced degree holders today, for two reasons higher education has a strong disincentive to participate in a public discussion about this issue. First, economic insecurity is built into the structure of the contemporary university itself, as tenured or tenure-track faculty and administrators work alongside large numbers of equally credentialed faculty colleagues hired on a part-time, temporary basis and paid very low wages (Childress 2019). Thus, acknowledging the extent of the problem of underemployed, highly educated workers would require higher education to reflect on its own employment and wage practices. The degree to which elites seek to reframe any substantive discussion of the low wages and job insecurity of adjunct college faculty is evident in a recent *Biennial Report* of the Community College Research Center (CCRC) at Columbia University's Teachers College. The CCRC, an outgrowth of the Institute on Education and the Economy, receives a significant majority of its funding from private sources, a list that includes some of the biggest foundations and foundation- and corporate-funded education reform organizations, including the Gates, Lumina, Walton Family, and J. P. Morgan Chase Foundations, as well as the Education Commission of the States, Jobs for the Future, and Ascendium, among numerous other private organizations.[4]

In an article entitled "Why Adjuncts Are Crucial to the Push for Student Success," the CCRC acknowledged that part-time faculty make up a "staggering two thirds of all faculty at community colleges" (Community College Research Center 2019, 7). Yet the piece also stated the following: "Not every problem faced by adjunct faculty members requires a massive institution-wide overhaul to be solved. Sometimes, it's as simple as keeping a closet door unlocked a little bit later so instructors can get the office supplies they need. 'It would make a difference in people's professional lives if they had consistent access to white board markers,' C.C.R.C. Senior Research Associate Susan Bickerstaff said" (Ibid.). While Bickerstaff conceded the existence of a "two-tiered workforce . . . within a flawed system," the article concluded optimistically: "'I don't think anyone we interviewed is doing it for the money,' Bickerstaff said. 'They're doing it because they love teaching, they love the discipline, they love the college. They feel a commitment to the community college mission'" (Community College Research Center 2019, 7). This type of analysis implicitly minimizes the low wages and unstable employment of the large number of dedicated faculty who enable our higher education system to function.

But a more immediate reason for the silence of higher education on the problem of underemployment is the increasingly tuition-driven model on which higher education operates. Today, the success of nearly all colleges and universities—both public and private—is judged in terms of maximizing enrollment. This dynamic is particularly acute within public institutions, which educate over 70 percent of all students and have suffered decades of increasing public disinvestment. Thus, I suggest, higher education institutions are substantially disincentivized to meaningfully consider the real human cost of underemployed and low-paid graduates, most of whom carry substantial debt. At the same time, because higher education is routinely chastised for the poor labor market outcomes faced by many graduates, a more careful examination of the labor market is imperative.

The Myth of STEM Shortages

The analysis of STEM labor markets is somewhat complicated by the lack of an official definition of the term STEM. The most expansive definition of the term includes the social sciences. But counting social science fields as STEM defies common usage of the term, and STEM advocates do not appear interested in producing more sociology or political science majors. While there are obvious connections between health care and STEM fields, the STEM crisis literature repeatedly stresses the need to create more workers qualified in engineering and technology fields and says little if anything about addressing well-established needs among the skilled providers of health care, such as psychiatrists. Thus, the BLS considers health-care employment as distinct from STEM, which reflects both common usage and popular understanding of this concept.

The BLS definition of STEM includes all jobs in engineering and architectural fields, computer and mathematical fields, and all life sciences. The increasing emphasis on STEM education at all levels is based on the implicit assumption of the availability of a large and growing number of high-paying jobs in these fields. When we look at the labor market, however, a vastly different picture emerges. In 2020, according to the BLS, the jobs classified as STEM occupations represented roughly 6.7 percent of the total labor market (Bureau of Labor Statistics 2022b). And the BLS includes dozens of jobs in this category, including computer and mathematical occupations, architecture and engineering, life and physical sciences, managerial and postsecondary teaching, and sales jobs (Ibid.). But only some of these jobs are typically held by bachelor's degree holders, while many require either an associate's or advanced degree. Further, individuals in sales positions likely come from a variety of degree programs beyond traditional STEM fields. Hence, the percentage of all jobs in the labor market for STEM bachelor's degree holders is in the low single digits. Finally, the percentage of the workforce consisting of STEM jobs is expected to increase modestly by 2030 (Ibid.).

Data on the relatively low number of STEM jobs is illuminating. But in economics, a labor shortage exists when "the demand for workers for a particular occupation is greater than the supply of workers who are qualified, available, and willing to do that job" (Bureau of Labor Statistics 2019c). Therefore, examining the dynamics of labor markets involves looking at the supply of positions, the supply of qualified workers, and the wages offered. Depending on how broadly one defines STEM, researchers have found that American universities graduate anywhere from two to three times as many graduates in STEM programs as jobs available in these fields (Lowell and Salzman 2007; Salzman 2016; Xie and Killewald 2012). This necessarily results in large numbers of STEM graduates working in non-STEM occupations, a fact confirmed by several sources. For example, according to Daniel Kuehn and Hal Salzman, a 2012 report by the National Research Council on the STEM workforce for the Department of Defense found the "engineering, scientific, and technical workforce supply to be sufficient with the exception of cybersecurity experts, anthropologists, and linguists, for which the Department of Defense had unmet demand and difficulty recruiting" (Kuehn and Salzman 2018, 22). With liberal arts fields under constant attack in higher education, the Defense Department's need for more anthropologists and linguists is especially noteworthy. In 2014, the Census published survey data showing that 74 percent of those with a bachelor's degree in a STEM field were not employed in STEM occupations (U.S. Census Bureau 2014). In 2016, labor market scholar Hal Salzman testified to Congress that "only about a third of those with S.T.E.M. degrees are employed in S.T.E.M. jobs" (Salzman 2016, 1).

Data on engineering and technology labor markets also illustrates the relative oversupply of qualified workers in these fields. Between 1999 and 2013, "no more than about half of workers with a degree in engineering actually reported that they were working as engineers" (Kuehn and Salzman 2018, 18), and in 2018, Kuehn and Salzman found that among recent graduates with engineering degrees, about two-thirds said they worked in engineering or another STEM position (Ibid.). Also, the labor market for technology workers shows that many workers in the field lack formal educational credentials in either computer science or technology. Further, according to Salzman, only about one-third of technology workers have STEM degrees, roughly one-third do not have any four-year degree, and most are "in jobs that don't appear to require bachelors-level technology degrees" (Salzman 2016, 2). And the oversupply of advanced degree holders in many STEM fields, especially in the life sciences, has also become apparent. Because of the 30 to 50 percent of recent Ph.D.s unable to find full-time employment in their fields, the National Institutes of Health has established an $11 million program with seventeen universities to "develop alternative career paths for the nation's recent doctorates and postdoctoral Fellows" (Ibid., 1–2).

Historic data also suggests that the large supply of STEM-qualified workers relative to available positions is not a new phenomenon. A 1986 report by the National Academy of Engineering found that "evidence drawn from a variety of sources does not suggest pervasive or serious industrial shortages" (Kuehn and Salzman 2018, 22). A few years later, the Department of Energy's Sandia Report found that nearly 40 percent of natural science and engineering bachelor's degree recipients "do not pursue careers formally classified as scientist or engineer" (Sandia National Laboratories 1993, 295). Using National Science Foundation data as a benchmark, the Sandia Report further argued that the "NS&E (Natural Science and Engineering) pipeline is overproducing graduates every year" and that "the overage accumulates to over one million by the year 2010" (Ibid.).

Trends in wages for scientists and engineers also undermine any claims of shortages in these fields. In their 2012 book on the state of science in the United States, Yu Xie and Alexandra A. Killewald found that unlike other professions requiring high levels of education, such as medicine and law, "scientists' earnings have virtually stagnated after adjusting for inflation" (Xie and Killewald 2012, 130). And in a 2018 analysis of wage trends in engineering, Kuehn and Salzman found that "with only a few exceptions, median earnings levels have shown little wage growth over the past decade. The wage levels would suggest that only in a few fields has there been growing demand for engineers" (2018, 18). Wages for technology workers have stagnated as well (Salzman 2016). The exceptional case of petroleum engineers confirms the lack of any actual shortages across STEM fields in recent decades. Because of a wave of retirements and a lack of industry hiring in the aftermath of the oil boom of the 1970s and 1980s, in the early 2000s, the number of job openings began to exceed the number of qualified graduates (Lynn, Salzman, and Kuehn 2018, 249). This led to a significant increase in wages for petroleum engineers, which, in turn, caused more students to choose petroleum engineering as a field of study. Between 2003 and 2015, the number of bachelor's degrees in the field awarded by U.S. universities "more than quintupled"

(Ibid., 253). When oil prices declined in 2014 and 2015, industry cut its workforce, and the total number of petroleum engineering positions dropped from 38,500 in 2012 to 35,100 in 2014 (Ibid., 257). Lynn and his coauthors found that on balance, the case of petroleum engineers shows that "the U.S. education system and job market have been highly responsive economic forces, not the failures that alarmists have habitually portrayed" (Ibid., 260). However, even though the STEM labor force has been consistently more than able to meet the demand for jobs in these fields, colleges and universities instinctively compete to increase STEM programs while K–12 education has also prioritized the expansion of STEM curricula and programming.

The expansion of STEM programs has also been assisted by the wage stagnation across the rest of the labor market, particularly in the non-profit sector, where many non-STEM bachelor's degree holders find employment. For example, using a political science major to become a legislative staffer certainly did not immediately generate a high income in the 1980s and 1990s. But after years of austerity budgeting and increasing student loan debt, many young people of modest means simply rule out a major like political science because of the low wages in jobs typically held by graduates in this field. The same calculation is likely at work among college students when deciding whether to major in many other liberal arts fields. Enrollments in liberal arts disciplines are further weakened when we consider long-term data on wages. In the 1980s and 1990s, the economic costs of underemployment were not nearly as steep as they have become since. Wage stagnation and the decline of labor unions have made the prospect of underemployment simply too significant for most students. As a result, many young people likely do not pursue liberal arts majors simply because they believe that they cannot afford to do so, leaving disproportionate numbers of affluent students pursuing these areas of study. In sum, despite decades of an oversupply of STEM-qualified workers, STEM programs have become a significant beneficiary of wage stagnation and growing inequality.

In 2014, Michael Teitelbaum aptly summarized some of the myths driving education policy involving STEM in *The Atlantic* magazine as follows: "Everyone knows that the United States has long suffered from widespread shortages in its science and engineering workforce, and that if continued these shortages will cause it to fall behind its major economic competitors. Everyone knows that these workforce shortages are due mainly to the myriad weaknesses of America K–12 education in science and mathematics, which international comparisons of student performance rank as average at best. Such claims are now well established as conventional wisdom. There is almost no debate in the mainstream. They echo from corporate CEO to corporate CEO, from lobbyist to lobbyist, from editorial writer to editorial writer. But what if what everyone knows is wrong? What if this conventional wisdom is just the same claims ricocheting in an echo chamber? The truth is that there is little credible evidence of the claimed widespread shortages in the U.S. science and engineering workforce" (Teitelbaum 2014b). Yet despite the ready availability of data on science and engineering labor markets, reflexively increasing STEM education has continued to dominate both K–12 and higher education policy in recent years.

Labor Market Myths and Immigration Policy

Despite the lack of real shortages for workers in STEM fields, however, business interests have engaged in a constant political push for increasing the number of H-1B visas since the program's inception in 1990. The H-1B is a temporary work permit controlled by the employer, and it can be revoked at any time by terminating the employee. Former secretary of labor Ray Marshall described the employment relationship in the H-1B program as "indentured" (Hira 2018, 265). Yet the H-1B has become an important source of labor for U.S. employers in scientific and technology-related fields. For example, a recent report from the U.S. Citizenship and Immigration Services showed that roughly two-thirds of visa recipients have worked in computer-related occupations; 8 to 9 percent in architecture, engineering, and surveying occupations; over 5 percent in education; and roughly 4 percent in medicine and health occupations, with the balance scattered among numerous other fields (U.S. Citizenship and Immigration Services 2017, 13). Clearly, the dominant use of the visa is for technology workers. In recent years, the annual cap on H-1B visas has been 65,000, with an additional 20,000 for those individuals meeting the advanced degree exemption. However, universities, nonprofits, and governments are exempted from the annual cap as a result of the American Competitiveness Act of 2000, and these employers have accounted for approximately 10 percent of all H-1B visa applications in recent years (Ruiz 2017). Also, many employers use the H-1B as a temporary work permit only rather than a bridge to permanent citizenship for recipients (Hira 2018, 264). While the exact number of H-1B recipients in the United States at any one time is not known, estimates are "in the range of 650,000" (Ibid., 266).

The power of business interests' messaging has resulted in the widespread acceptance of two erroneous beliefs about the H-1B program, both of which work to the advantage of employers. First is the incorrect assumption that employers can only use the H-1B program if they cannot find domestic workers for the positions in question. In his detailed analysis of this perception, Teitelbaum has affirmed: "This is simply garbled reporting: such a requirement has never been part of the H-1B process. While we can never know why so many journalists have gotten this important point so wrong for so long, it may be due in part to credulous acceptance of statements to this effect by industry spokespeople or by other journalists" (Teitelbaum 2014a, 91). Another often-misunderstood fact of the program is that many H-1B visa recipients possess only a bachelor's degree. In recent years, the percentage of visa holders with a bachelor's degree has been roughly 45 percent (U.S. Citizenship and Immigration Services 2017, 10). As Hira has concluded, "The relatively low level of educational attainment is particularly surprising since much of the public discussion of H-1Bs presents them as recent advanced-degree graduates of U.S. universities" (Hira 2018, 278). These two major misconceptions about the H-1B program have disadvantaged STEM workers while benefiting employers and have significantly facilitated the STEM worker crisis narrative.

Skills Gaps in Manufacturing Employment?

The skills gap and associated worker shortage are also consistently invoked with reference to manufacturing employees, and these assertions have been used to justify decisions such as the relocation of manufacturing jobs overseas. Such claims are typically based on surveys of CEOs yet, as interest group activity, largely ignore objective labor market data provided by government agencies and scholars that contradicts this narrative. The most comprehensive scholarly study of the skills gap in manufacturing was based on extensive employer surveys and showed that there is little empirical support for any significant differential between the skills of the workforce and requirements of the labor market (Weaver and Osterman 2017). Andrew Weaver and Paul Osterman sent 2,700 surveys to a random sample of manufacturers, which yielded a response rate of nearly 36 percent. The survey assessed the degree to which manufacturers experienced long-term employee vacancies. Seventy-six percent of respondents reported no long-term vacancies among what were deemed "core workers," while less than 8 percent of employers reported long-term vacancies that amounted to less than or equal to 5 percent of their core workers. Thus, Weaver and Osterman concluded that "at most a quarter of manufacturing establishments show signs of hiring distress with regard to production workers" (Ibid., 288) and that the median manufacturer has zero core long-term vacancies. These figures contrasted greatly with the results of a widely cited survey produced by Deloitte and the National Association of Manufacturers in 2011 showing that 74 percent of manufacturers were experiencing a lack of skilled production workers and that the median manufacturer had vacancies equivalent to 5 percent of its entire workforce (Ibid.). Again, the gulf between interest groups' characterization of the labor market and that of more disinterested observers is vast.

Federal data on long-term trends in employment and wages in the manufacturing sector also undermine any claims of worker shortages. The number of manufacturing jobs has declined substantially in recent years. In 1990, nearly 12.7 million manufacturing jobs made up over 17 percent of the private-sector workforce. But by 2018, roughly 8.9 million manufacturing jobs made up just 8.5 percent of the total private-sector labor force (Harris and McCall 2019). In 1990, average hourly earnings for production workers in manufacturing were still greater than average hourly earnings of all private-sector workers. But by 2018, this was no longer the case, as average hourly earnings of private-sector workers exceeded those of production workers in manufacturing by 5 percent (Ibid.). While a few manufacturing industries have seen "strong earnings growth, many others have shown earnings increasing at a much slower rate than the overall private sector, with motor vehicles and parts demonstrating the most notable slowing" (Ibid.). Assertions of labor shortages in manufacturing do not withstand scrutiny when we consider the larger context of manufacturing employment in recent decades—a shrinking job sector characterized by stagnating wages within a growing, increasingly educated and trained population.

Further, close examination of the trade-group surveys cited as evidence of worker shortages faced by employers also reveals the logical problems with the worker-shortage thesis. Since 1997, the National Association of Manufacturers (NAM) has published quarterly surveys of CEOs of representative samples of manufacturing firms. In the first-quarter survey of 2019, during a period of very low unemployment, the NAM stated that "at 71.3 percent, the inability to attract and retain workers remained respondents' top concern for the sixth consecutive survey (Figure 3). The manufacturing industry's skills gap challenge is a longstanding problem, but one that has been made even worse by recent economic successes, including an unemployment rate near 50-year lows and a labor market with more job openings than people looking for work" (National Association of Manufacturers 2019, 2). Yet the same survey showed that roughly 90 percent of executives felt "somewhat or very positive" about their own company's outlook and concluded: "Clearly, manufacturers remain very optimistic about business conditions overall" (Ibid.). Further, CEOs expected employee wages to only increase 2.3 percent over the next twelve months (Ibid., 3), a number not substantially different from the current rate of inflation. Taken together, this data undermines the notion of any actual shortages of adequately skilled workers impeding the performance of manufacturers.

In 2020, with an unemployment rate hovering near 13 percent because of the COVID-19 pandemic, the second-quarter NAM survey affirmed that "despite moving workforce concerns out of the top spot, respondents continue to expect struggles in identifying workers over the longer term, especially as more Americans retire. Indeed, 50.5% of manufacturing leaders anticipate that difficulties in attracting and retaining employees will continue to be a challenge over the next 12 to 18 months once the COVID-19 crisis abates" (National Association of Manufacturers 2020, 2). The same survey showed that CEOs expected employees' wages to increase only 0.5 percent over the next year (Ibid., 3), well below the inflation rate and consistent with a large pool of available labor. In sum, I suggest that claims of worker shortages have effectively become part of contemporary business culture, echoed instinctively regardless of economic conditions or the qualifications of available workers. These claims reflect the economic interests of employers by intentionally steering the debate away from wage levels and, eventually, toward the educational establishment and workers themselves. Regarding recent assertions of the skills gap, as Ellen Ruppel Shell has argued: "But other than the say so of employers, there was little if any evidence to support the vague and slippery claim" (Ruppel Shell 2018, 163).

Where Are the Robots?

Finally, for decades, warnings of a future workplace increasingly dominated by robots and automation have received extensive attention and have been echoed in several recent commonly cited works (Frey and Osborne 2017; McKinsey Global Institute 2019; Muro, Maxim, and Whiton 2019). As a result of the popularity of such dire predictions, in 2019, at the request of Congress, the U.S. Government Accountability Office published a report entitled *Workforce Automation: Better Data Needed to Assess and Plan for Effects of Advanced Technologies on Jobs* (U.S. Government Accountability Office 2019). The report reviewed numerous existing federal data sets on employers and the labor force and found that there was no "comprehensive data on firms' adoption and use of advanced technologies" (Ibid., 13). Thus, the GAO found that there is no existing data that can be used to determine whether the job loss in certain industries is the result of automation or other factors. In recent decades, some of the most common reasons for domestic job loss include outsourcing, increasing consolidation of ownership, and trade.

For centuries, technology has made many processes more efficient and has often resulted in the loss of some types of jobs while adding others. However, except during recessions, the total number of jobs in the United States is always increasing. Technology, then, allows total job growth to continue while frequently lowering labor costs. Empirically, this is quite different from robots or automation simply replacing human jobs on a grand scale, a scenario that futurists have posited for decades. Thus, when Cathy Davidson claimed in *The New Education* that artificial intelligence and robots were poised to "do everything from drive our cars to fill out tax forms, it is not clear what new jobs will be created to offset the massive layoffs portended ahead" (Davidson 2017, 139), even if unwittingly, she was echoing a doomsday narrative that directs the discussion of economic opportunity squarely at the education system and skills of the workforce and away from employers and policy makers. Such claims, which have been advanced at least since the Reagan administration, have muddied the larger discussion of the loss of manufacturing jobs and the more direct causes of wage stagnation, including the decline of labor unions, a flat minimum wage, and a changing business culture that prioritizes the minimization of labor costs. Given the ever-increasing total number of jobs in our economy, such terrifying claims have little empirical basis, and the fact that the automation literature has evolved into essentially a permanent predication is revealing. Yet the frequent repetition of such claims has escalated the pressure on the education system to teach students to become "robot-proof."

Conclusion

This chapter has shown that the fantasy economy's major empirical claims regarding education and the workforce and labor market are not supported by the evidence. Some of these assertions, such as declining or mediocre educational achievement, are based on aggregate averages that fail to carefully consider the impact of chronically high poverty rates on educational performance. Further, when relying on government data and scholarly research, we discover that the labor market of the fantasy economy is largely an illusion. Claims of STEM labor shortages or worker shortages among either highly educated or manufacturing workers do not stand up to objective analysis. And predictions of massive waves of future automation of employment should be understood as a political tactic with little empirical or historical basis. Yet because these claims have been repeated by so many powerful individuals and institutions for so long, they have effectively become part of the conventional wisdom of the education reform movement.

Because so much of the data of the real economy and education system undermines the fantasy economy narrative, however, elites have used a range of misleading data techniques, including the creation of alternative data, to paint a picture of a high-education, high-skill labor market and education system in perpetual crisis. This misleading data and research campaign, which has relied on foundation and corporate funding, is the subject of Chapter 3.

3

Keeping Up the Fantasy

Misleading Research and Alternative Data

Thus, if used without proper adjustments, the B.L.S.
methodology can lead to a gross underestimate of
both current and future postsecondary-education
requirements of the labor market. . . . But if properly
adjusted, the official data show robust growth in the
demand for postsecondary education.
—ANTHONY CARNEVALE, "College for All?"
  Change Magazine

Introduction

As a political campaign, elites have used several misleading data and research techniques to paint a picture of a chronically failing education system and underqualified labor force. Some of the more common techniques,
such as the misuse of reliable data and the assertion of undocumented
claims, are standard interest group techniques. The most consequential
strategy, however, goes much further and has been central to both the
higher education and K–12 reform movements: the creation of alternative data. And I argue that because the claims of business interest groups
or foundations alone could not suffice in the battle to shape public opinion and policy, elites have funded university-based research institutes in
furtherance of this larger campaign.

 As part of a political campaign, much of this voluminous body of work
exists largely outside the world of peer review and has therefore received
virtually no scholarly scrutiny, enabling claims repeated endlessly to become conventional wisdom. Moreover, the public discussion of the relationship between education and the labor market also occurs within
the context of the credulous embrace of human capital theory. The desire
to believe in the necessary economic power of education within a high-
education labor market primes us to accept data and research purport-
ing to show the ever-increasing demand for highly educated workers. The

dominance of human capital theory has also enabled education policy to be immune from the ongoing debate about funded research and conflicts of interest that has taken center stage in the natural sciences and health care in recent years, a subject to which we now turn.

Conflicts of Interest in Research and Advocacy

Grounded in the pioneering work of social psychologist Robert Cialdini (2007), the scholarly research documenting the impact of unconscious biases on human behavior is extensive, and three sets of findings based on this research from the natural and health sciences are directly relevant to education research and policy. First, scholars have consistently shown that the findings of privately funded research overwhelmingly favor the interests of the funders. Research has also documented that despite believing otherwise, scientific professionals often cannot accurately discern biased information in marketing materials. And finally, scholars have shown that over time, scientific professionals become more committed to the goals of their funders.[1] Rooted in social psychology, this research assumes that those receiving funds—gifts—act in furtherance of the goals of their funders not because of any conscious intention to do so but rather because of the norm of reciprocity.

The emphasis on conflicts of interest in the sciences has led to the adoption of new practices and major public policies. Medical institutions and scientific journals now routinely require researchers and practitioners to disclose potential conflicts of interest, a practice that has also been widely adopted by social science journals. But the most significant policy resulting from the public debate about conflicts of interest has been the creation of the federal government's Open Payments website as part of the passage of the Affordable Care Act in 2009. Operated by the Center for Medicaid and Medicare Services, the site is a "national transparency program that collects and publishes information about financial relationships between drug and medical device companies (referred to as 'reporting entities') and certain health care providers (referred to as covered recipients'). These relationships may involve payments to providers for things including but not limited to research, meals, travel, gifts or speaking fees" (U.S. Centers for Medicare and Medicaid Services 2022).

Because foundations provide most of the funding for education-related research, the field has been largely insulated from the larger public discussion of conflicts of interest because within the academy, foundations have typically come to be seen as public interested. I argue that the separation of corporate interests from foundation giving has been accomplished through the creation of several organizations as well as decades of extensive foundation giving to higher education itself. But the economic self-interests of corporations and the wealthy are directly manifest in foundation giving in several ways. First, many concrete economic benefits accrue to those who create and contribute to foundations, including the reduction of income taxes for contributors; the possible avoidance of capital gains taxes for contributors; the ability to increase foundations' resources with tax-advantaged laws; and the possible reduction or elimination of estate taxes for contributors (Snow 2019). Foundation boards are also dominated by corporate elites, and no matter how public spirited these individuals are, their actions—as James Madison suggested in Federalist #10—will be shaped by their economic self-interest. Further, some of the most influential foundations active in education have their origins in corporations themselves, including several that have benefited disproportionately from the sale of educational products and services, curricular reforms aimed at creating specific types of workers, and the growth of the largely nonunionized service sector.

The Gates Foundation has origins in the wealth associated with Microsoft, one of the world's largest technology companies, which also has a significant interest in the labor supply. The Lumina Foundation, whose sole purpose is expanding post–high school education, was created in 2000 when USA Group, parent company of USA Funds, the country's "largest private guarantor and administrator of education loans" (Lumina Foundation for Education 2007a, 3), sold most of its operating assets to Sallie Mae for $770 million (Ibid., 4). In 2017, USA Funds relaunched as the Strada Education Network, a not-for-profit holding company (Columbo 2017), which, as of early 2021, had eight separate "affiliate organizations" in higher education services (Strada Education Network 2021). Most important, however, are the agenda-setting and framing functions advanced by foundations that implicitly advocate the major tenets of neoliberalism while making the K–12 and higher education systems responsible for creating economic opportunity and mitigating inequality. The Walton Family Foundation has its origins in the retail firm Walmart, which has been a significant beneficiary of a stagnant minimum wage, the decline of organized labor, and erosion of antitrust enforcement. In 2022, under the heading "Increase Achievement and Opportunity," the foundation's website stated that it was "embracing education as the engine of opportunity and a child's best chance at achieving the American Dream" (Walton Family Foundation 2022). In its Postsecondary Success program, in 2022 the Gates Foundation stated that the current economy "needs more educated workers than ever" (Gates Foundation 2022). The foundation's director of Postsecondary Success stated that he did not "want to get back to normal, because 'normal' in American higher education is not currently living up to its potential as an engine of equitable social and economic mobility" (Ibid.). Also in 2022, the Lumina Foundation stated: "The United States faces an urgent and growing need for talent. Many more people of all races, ethnicities, ages, and income levels will need college degrees, certificates, industry certifications, and other credentials of value to join or remain in the middle class" (Lumina Foundation 2022a). The implication of these types of statements is clear: it is the job of the education system to provide economic opportunity.

Numerous scholars have addressed foundations' growing influence in education policy, including their narrow focus on market-based policies and the lack of democratic accountability in a foundation-driven system (Callahan 2017; Hess 2005; Hess and Henig 2015; Kovacs 2011; Reckhow 2013; Reich 2018; Tompkins-Stange 2016). Political scientist Rob Reich (2018) has shown that foundations' ability to address inequality is limited at best. Some analysts have also focused on the Gates Foundation in particular, critiquing the misleading nature of the educational requirements of the labor market promulgated by Gates-funded education reform organizations (Kovacs and Christie 2011, 157). Teacher Anthony Cody's work provides what is likely the most far-reaching critique of the Gates Foundation's education agenda, including its overreliance on technology and lack of accountability. He offers a powerful perspective on the emphasis on quantitative data promulgated by reformers such as the Gates Foundation, labeling it a "cult of measurement" (Cody 2014, 148). Like Grubb and Lazerson's (2004) education gospel, Cody insightfully seeks to frame the discussion of economic opportunity and poverty well beyond the education system, which provides us with a foundation for reconsidering the role of education in a democratic society.

For two reasons, however, many social scientists are predisposed not to consider the most critical questions regarding foundation influence. First, the main tenets of the fantasy economy have been repeated so frequently within the education system itself that, I argue, most educators, including many well-meaning researchers immersed in their own scholarly literature, simply believe them. There *must* be an abundance of high-education jobs because, after all, we live in a knowledge economy. This framing also emphasizes the importance of educators, further disincentivizing them from critically considering the nature of the labor market.

In addition, many scholars have been significant beneficiaries of foundation giving, which provides even stronger disincentives from critical questions regarding foundations.

Frederick Hess, director of education policy studies at the American Enterprise Institute (AEI), is one of the leading scholars on foundations' role in education research (Hess 2005; Hess and Henig 2015) and has received millions of dollars in foundation grants over the course of his career, including several million from the Gates Foundation alone (Hess 2019). Hess's scholarly work on foundation influence in education policy directly reveals the tremendous influence of foundations, including their influence on research about foundations themselves. In *With the Best of Intentions* (2005), Hess acknowledged an "estimable collection of discussants and an audience packed with leading funders offered invaluable insights and comments to refine the analysis," and he thanks numerous specific foundation officials for their assistance (Ibid., vii–viii). In the 2015 volume, *The New Education Philanthropy*, Hess and Jeffrey Henig acknowledged receiving financial support from the William T. Grant, Spencer, and Ford Foundations (Hess and Henig 2015, 219). Many of the chapters implicitly accept the fantasy economy's high-education, high-wage labor market, with one chapter approvingly citing the Lumina Foundation's Jamie Merisotis's claim that "with experts predicting that nearly two-thirds of jobs will require some level of college-level learning by the end of this decade . . . it's clear that college attainment must increase dramatically" (Kelly and James 2015, 86–87).

However, this estimate presumably based on the data provided by Georgetown's Center on Education and the Workforce, an organization funded, in part, by the Gates and Lumina Foundations. Scholars are predisposed to believe in a high-education labor market, and therefore their citation of this data without knowledge of official data portraying a predominantly low-education, low-wage labor market is not surprising. Still, one the authors of this chapter also acknowledged receiving funds for higher education research from both the Gates and Lumina Foundations (Hess and Henig 2015, 200), further illustrating the extraordinary influence of the major funders of education reform on policy research and discussion. Ultimately, the fact that foundations can fund and shape research ostensibly addressing their own influence in education policy and research shows just how thoroughly they have reinvented themselves within the academy since the 1950s and 1960s as public-spirited organizations seemingly divorced from the interests of corporations and the wealthy.

To be sure, not all foundations have the same priorities, nor do they all necessarily assume that education alone is at the heart of economic opportunity. But as I show in Chapters 4 and 5, a relatively small group of influential foundations have been the primary funders of key reports and organizations advocating accountability and school choice, all of which have been built on human capital theory and the fantasy economy's strict emphasis on education's role in providing economic opportunity. In sum, once we expand the discussion of conflicts of interest to include the very terms of debate involving economic opportunity, we open the door to a much more comprehensive examination of the research and data driving education reform.

Framing the Issue through Misleading Data

The most influential reports that established the fantasy economy narrative were funded by the Reagan administration. *A Nation at Risk* and *Workforce 2000* were publicly funded but written by individuals selected by the Reagan administration, many of whom had ties to business and conservative organizations. All eighteen members of the commission that wrote *A Nation at Risk* "shared the common perspective that public schools were failing to meet the needs of America's students," and three of these individuals actively promoted tuition tax credits and school vouchers (Owens 2015, 7). Johnston and Packer's *Workforce 2000* was produced by the Hudson Institute, a futuristic, business-oriented think tank founded in 1961 by "Herman Kahn and colleagues from the Rand Corporation" (Johnston and Packer 1987). At the time of the report's publication, coauthor Johnston was the president of the corporate consulting arm of Hudson, and he had previously served as director of public policy research at the New York–based Conference Board, a "business research organization" (Ibid.). His background also included work on the 1976 presidential campaign of Jimmy Carter and positions in the Carter administration, as well as consulting work for the Ford Foundation and Labor Department (American Presidency Project 1979). In 1987, Johnston coauthored *Michigan beyond 2000*, also produced by the Hudson Institute, for the Republican-led Michigan State Senate, which argued that "high wages in the auto industry have spilled over into most other occupations and industries in the state, making the state less competitive with other regions of the country and world" (Johnston, Newitt, and Reed 1987, xvi). In 1982, Packer, who had received a Ph.D. in economics and was a former engineer, created Interactive Training, a firm that produced "interactive videodisc training courses (SKILLPACS) to teach basic workplace skills" (Johnston and Packer 1987). According to his biography in *Workforce 2000*, Packer worked in the Nixon administration's Office of Management and Budget, the Committee on Economic Development, the Senate's Committee on the Budget, and in the Carter administration's Labor Department (Ibid.).

A Nation at Risk and *Workforce 2000* reveal the extent to which elites have gone to present a view of the education system and labor market that advances a predetermined political and policy narrative. *A Nation at Risk* included little of the federal primary education and labor market data readily at its disposal, and official data was not cited as one of the commission's main sources of information (National Commission on Excellence in Education 1983). Rather, the report relied heavily on several dozen commissioned papers and testimony to paint a vivid picture of a failing education system and lay the groundwork for the education reform movement and skills gap campaign. With extensive quantitative data and figures throughout, *Workforce 2000* has the appearance of being more research based than *A Nation at Risk*. But careful examination of the report reveals its numerous flaws, including the lack of a bibliography and heavy reliance on the Hudson Institute itself as a data source. And as discussed in Chapter 2, the core prediction of an impending high-education, high-skill labor market of *Workforce 2000* has been discredited by several researchers.

Also, a significant error in the report was identified in 1990 by the *Washington Post*. In the third bullet point of the first page of the executive summary, the report stated that "only 15 percent of the new entrants to the labor force over the next 13 years will be native white males, compared to 47 percent in that category today" (Johnston and Packer 1987, xiii). But the *Post* story, which noted the outsize influence of the report, stated that the BLS published data in 1989 showing that white males would account for 31.6 percent of new labor force entrants in the coming years (Swoboda 1990). According to the *Post*, "As a result, over the last year, the Labor Department has been backing away from the Workforce 2000 projection. 'We're using the BLS numbers now,' said a Labor Department spokeswoman" (Ibid.). The *Post* article affirmed that further into the report, "authors correctly stated that 'white males, thought of only a generation ago as the mainstays of the economy, will comprise only 15 percent of the net additions to the labor force between 1985 and 2000.' . . . But somehow when the report's editors put together the executive summary—the easy reader for leaders of government and industry—the word 'net' was dropped, making the projection off by more than 100 percent" (Ibid.). In the *Post* article, an associate BLS commissioner in charge of employment projections called the mistake "incorrect labelling," while report coauthor Packer described it as an "editing error" (Ibid.).

Perhaps the most intriguing thing about *Workforce 2000*, however, is the fact that there were multiple different versions of the report published with identical text but different front and back covers.[2] What seems to have been the most common version of the report lists both Johnston and Packer as coauthors on the cover, has the Hudson logo on the cover, and has a blank back cover. But some published versions of the report do not list any named authors on the cover and have "U.S. Department of Labor" printed on the back. Despite these nontrivial differences, the contents of twenty unique versions examined were the same: title page, "About the Hudson Institute," acknowledgments, foreword, table of contents, list of tables, list of figures, and executive summary, followed by four numbered and titled chapters, for a total of 117 pages of text. And on the title page of each copy examined, Johnston and Packer are identified respectively as "Project Director" and "Co-Project Director" (Johnston and Packer 1987).

In addition, there are at least two partially declassified versions of the report available. One, dated October 10, 2012, has a cover labeled "Executive Summary" and lists William B. Johnston as the sole author. This version includes only some pages of the report and also includes several additional, annotated materials, including a 1986–1987 report from the BLS *Occupational Outlook Handbook*; one page from the *Statistical Abstract of the U.S.* with a handwritten date of 1988; several pages from the fall 1987 BLS *Occupational Outlook Quarterly*; and two pages from the *Congressional Clearinghouse on the Future* dated February 26, 1988, as well as articles from *The Futurist*, *Business Week*, and the *Montgomery Journal* and a book review from the *New York Times* (Central Intelligence Agency Library 2012). A second partially declassified version, dated April 15, 2013, also does not include the entire report, and omitted pages include those under the heading "Are Service Jobs Good Jobs?" which begins near the bottom of page 29 and ends on page 32 (Central Intelligence Agency Library 2013). The rationale for the publication of many different versions of the report—including some labeled "U.S. Department of Labor"—as well as for classifying materials related to *Workforce 2000* remain open questions.

According to the Department of Education's Education Resources Information Center (ERIC) database, *Workforce 2000* was published in June 1987 (Education Resources Information Center 1987), and footnote 2 on page 96 directs the reader to a "technical appendix for details of the methodology employed in these projections" (Johnston and Packer 1987, 96). Yet the technical appendix was not included in any published version of the report I was able to locate (including both partially declassified versions). In 1991, Mishel and Teixeira stated that the technical appendix "was not distributed with the original report and is not widely available" (Mishel and Teixeira 1991, 14). Written by Matthew P. Jaffe, the appendix includes the Hudson logo on the cover and is dated December 1987 (Jaffe 1987). Mishel and Teixeira's 1991 analysis of the appendix concluded that the Hudson Institute's figures indicated a "quite modest" increase in skill levels for the labor market and that the "five most highly skilled occupational groups" would account for "just 10.6 percent of new jobs" between 1984 and 2000 and would only account for "6.1 percent of the job pool" by 2000 (Mishel and Teixeira 1991, 14, 15).

In 1997, the Hudson Institute's Carol D'Amico discussed the impact of *Workforce 2000* in the journal *Employment Relations Today*. She affirmed: "Although 'think tanks' seldom produce bestsellers, Workforce 2000 proved the exception to the rule. Its sales approached 80,000 copies." She argued that the report "placed the terms 'skills gap' and 'workplace diversity' on the national agenda" (D'Amico 1997, 1), and she praised the accuracy of the report's prediction of the high education and skill levels associated with the future labor market. D'Amico was also concerned about the supply of skilled workers and critical of "generous Social Security benefits and pension plans—combined with high marginal tax rates on retirement income," which, she argued, "have encouraged men to leave the labor force beginning at age 55" (Ibid., 5). At the same time, she appeared optimistic and argued that the trend was "beginning to reverse itself in the late 1990s due to less enticing retirement benefits and a greater share of workers in professional occupations (where continued work is generally more attractive than in most blue-collar jobs)" (Ibid.). D'Amico coauthored the Hudson Institute's *Workforce 2020* (Judy and D'Amico 1997). She became assistant secretary of the Office of Vocational and Adult Education in the George W. Bush administration and was executive vice president of Ivy Tech Community College (a chain of community colleges in Indiana) and executive vice president of the Strada Education Group (Strada Center for Education Consumer Insights, n.d.).

In addition to *Workforce 2000*, the Reagan administration's National Institute of Education (NIE) funded research for the skills gap campaign. As described in a 1982 *Education Week* article, Reagan removed the "entire 15-member National Council on Education Research, the N.I.E. policy-making body whose members are supposed to serve staggered, three-year terms," and appointed officials who had worked on his

1980 presidential campaign (E. White 1982). A Reagan-appointed dep-
uty director of the institute who had assumed the director's duties stated
that the agency's research agenda needed to be "redirected," while the
newly appointed director of planning and program development, a former
Heritage Foundation policy analyst with no experience in educational
research, said he was "steering the institute away from a 'socio-legal agenda,' and toward the 'foundations of American education'" (Ibid.). The
piece also pointed out that the "N.I.E. has begun research on politically
sensitive issues from a decidedly conservative perspective" (Ibid.). And
in 1985, the NIE awarded Columbia University's Teachers College a $4
million grant (equivalent to well over $10 million in 2022) to "study the
relationship of education to employment, economic growth, and productivity" (*Columbia University Record* 1985, 1). Columbia was one of
ten U.S. educational institutions chosen for such a grant (Ibid.). Originally called the Center for Education and Employment (Ibid.), the grant
became the foundation for the Institute on Education and the Economy.
The same year the IEE was initially funded, 1985, the NIE was abol-
ished, and its functions were placed in several other agencies within the
Department of Education (National Archives and Records Administration 1995).

Sue Berryman was appointed to lead the new research institute. Berryman, who had a Ph.D. and had written several reports for the Rand
Corporation, was described in a Columbia University campus news article as a "nationally recognized social scientist and public policy analyst" (*Columbia University Record* 1985). The same article also stated
that Berryman would be joined at the new IEE by "senior staff of the
American Enterprise Institute for Public Policy Research" (Ibid.). Teachers College president Michael Timpane affirmed that the new research
center would "study the relation of education to people's success in the
workplace, and also education's changing role in a time of rapid technological development," and would "be a focal point for national concerns in both the education and business communities." Among other
emphases, the institute would examine "successful careers of blacks and
women" and aim to reach multiple audiences, including the "general public, educators, government officials on local, state, and national levels,
businesses of all sizes, and minority and other special interest groups"
(Ibid., 7).

The Institute on Education and the Economy was formally established
in 1986 and in relatively short order became an important player in the
skills gap campaign. It produced a steady stream of work on the labor
market and education, including reports, academic and popular articles,

conferences, and "specifically tailored publications" (Institute on Education and the Economy, n.d.). The IEE hosted "meetings with professionals in industry, academia, and the world of education" and described one of its functions as helping "businesses articulate their workforce problems to educators and policy leaders who are trying to improve schools" (Ibid.). The 1989 *New York Times* cover story on the skills gap highlighted the work of the new institute and included quantitative data provided by Columbia's Thomas Bailey, who stated that "new opportunities for workers with no more than a high school degree are falling sharply" (Fiske 1989b). Bailey became director of the IEE in 1992, founded the Community College Research Center in 1996, and was named president of the university's Teachers College in 2018 (Teachers College, Columbia University, n.d.).

The IEE's mission statement affirmed that the "foundation of this focus was articulated in *The Double Helix of Education and the Economy* . . . which analyzed the relationship between changes in the economy and the need for a fundamental rethinking of our educational system" (Institute on Education and the Economy, n.d.). This public campaign was clearly very costly, and after its initial public funding, the IEE received funding from numerous foundations and corporations, including the Pew Charitable Trusts, Alfred P. Sloane Foundation, William T. Grant Foundation, Rockefeller Foundation, Russell Sage Foundation, Carnegie Corporation, the American Express Company, Edna McConnell Clark Foundation, Joyce Foundation, Frederick Schultz, the Howard Heinz Endowment, the Rand Corporation, the Eisenhower Center for the Conservation of Human Resources, Citicorp, Ball Foundation, G. Victor and Margaret D. Ball Foundation, the Robert and Terri Cohn Family Foundation, and the Spencer Foundation (Berryman and Bailey 1992b, ii; Institute on Education and the Economy 1995, 3; Institute on Education and the Economy, n.d.). The IEE also received funding from the U.S. Department of Education's Office of Educational Research and Improvement (the successor to the NIE), the U.S. Department of Labor, the National Council for Vocational Education, the National Assessment for Vocational Education, and Columbia University's Teachers College (Berryman and Bailey 1992b, i). *The Double Helix of Education and the Economy* argued both prongs of the skills gap campaign—that the skills necessary for jobs historically requiring little formal education were increasing and that the occupational structure overall was shifting toward high-education employment.

As Chapter 2 outlined, the total number of jobs in all STEM fields combined is quite small. But the Clinton administration's *Before It's Too*

Late, produced in 2000 by the National Commission on Mathematics and Science Teaching for the 21st Century, painted a misleading picture of the labor market as possessing large numbers of jobs in these fields (National Commission on Mathematics and Science Teaching for the 21st Century 2000, 12–13). *Before It's Too Late* also included claims about the labor market at odds with official data and scholarship. For example, the report stated that "'knowledge work' is replacing low-end, low-wage jobs" (Ibid., 13). The authors further asserted the remarkable claim that in "1950, 80% of jobs were classified as 'unskilled'; now, an estimated 85% of all jobs are classified as 'skilled'" (Ibid.). And the example provided was machine tooling, which now required "sophisticated skills, commonly including computer programming and knowledge of calculus" (Ibid.). The sources for these two claims, however, were an interest group representing community colleges (the American Association of Community Colleges) and an interview with the director of public relations of the Association for Manufacturing Technology as cited in a chapter in a then-forthcoming volume to be published by the Brookings Institution (Ibid., 43). Like *Workforce 2000*, the report also fell back on the concept of productivity and claimed that recent "productivity gains are unsustainable without a workforce sufficiently educated in the sciences and mathematics" (Ibid., 12).

While much of the work of the fantasy economy exists outside peer review, many major economists have presented misleading analyses of educational attainment data in highly influential scholarly works. In their widely cited book *The Race between Education and Technology* Claudia Goldin and Lawrence F. Katz (2008) argued that inequality decreased for much of the twentieth century because the supply of educated workers increased with advances in technology. Thus, they posited, inequality had increased in recent decades because of a slowing rate of increase in educational attainment levels. Hence, they advocated policies to "increase the growth rate of U.S. educational attainment and the relative supply of college workers" (Goldin and Katz 2008, 350). But like much of human capital theory, this analysis cannot be sustained when relying on official labor market data, which illustrates widespread underemployment in a predominantly low-education, low-wage labor market. And on the book's last page, Goldin and Katz acknowledge that "no longer does having a high school or a college degree make you indispensable, especially if your skills can be imported or emulated by a computer program" (Ibid., 353).

Another influential book rooted in human capital theory, *Crossing the Finish Line*, by William Bowen, Mathew Chingos, and Michael

McPherson (2009), draws heavily on Goldin and Katz's work and takes this argument a step further. In 1989, Bowen, an economist and former president of Princeton University, coauthored *Prospects for the Faculty in the Arts and Sciences*, which had predicted a shortage of college faculty in the humanities and social sciences until well into the twenty-first century (Bowen and Sosa 1989). *Crossing the Finish Line* focuses again on the rate of increasing educational attainment levels as opposed to overall levels of attainment. The book further distorts attainment rates by relying on college-degree completion rates only among twenty-five- to twenty-nine-year-olds, failing to consider that the percentage of the population over twenty-five with bachelor's and advanced degrees has steadily increased for several decades. Citing Goldin and Katz, Bowen, Chingos, and McPherson claim that "in recent years, growth in the supply of college-educated workers has been sluggish and has not kept up with increases in demand—especially increases in the demand for individuals with strong problem-solving skills and degrees from the more selective undergraduate programs and leading professional schools" (Ibid., 5–6). Yet Bowen and his colleagues pay scant attention to the real economy, including the widespread underemployment of bachelor's and advanced degree holders and a labor market dominated by low-education, low-wage jobs. As a result, they argue that racial and economic inequality are best addressed solely by increasing college attainment rates among racial minorities and the disadvantaged, a position substantially at odds with official labor market and educational attainment data.

Economists' misleading analyses of educational attainment has also been evident at the highest levels of economic policy making. In 2008, Federal Reserve chair Ben Bernanke, ignoring historically high rates of attainment as well as consistently high levels of underemployment among college and advanced degree holders, argued that the "best way to improve economic opportunity and to reduce inequality is to improve educational attainment and skills of American workers" (Bowen, Chingos, and McPherson 2009, 1). In a 2019 network news interview, Federal Reserve chair Jerome Powell linked the trend of declining labor force participation with the complexities of a high-technology workplace that "requires rising skills on the part of the people" (CBS News 2019). He also pointed to the slowing rate of increase in educational attainment as a cause of a lack of workforce participation (Ibid.). But such analyses fail to consider how the proliferation of low-education, low-wage jobs in the real economy serves as a major deterrent to would-be workers while framing the discussion of economic opportunity primarily in terms of education.

Corporate Funders and Advanced Statistics:
The Robots Are Always Coming

As we saw in Chapter 2, there do not appear to be any comprehensive data sets on the historic replacement of jobs in the United States by automation or robots. Thus, the most widely cited literature on automation, which is funded largely by corporate interests, consists almost entirely of predictions based on high-level statistics. Frey and Osborne's 2017 article in *Technology Forecasting and Social Change* is at the center of this debate. Frey is the Oxford Martin Citi Fellow at Oxford University, where he "founded the programme on the Future of Work with support from Citigroup" (Frey 2019). Osborne is professor of machine learning in the Department of Engineering at Oxford University and has received grants from several corporations and foundations (Osborne 2021). The 2019 Brookings report on automation repeatedly affirms the organization's independence. For example, the report states that Brookings is a "nonprofit organization devoted to independent research and policy solutions," that "its mission is to conduct high-quality, independent research," and that it is "committed to quality, independence, and impact in all of its work" (Muro, Maxim, and Whiton 2019, 106). The report was produced by Brookings's Metropolitan Policy Program, and the authors acknowledged the "generous support of this analysis and our metropolitan advanced economy work more broadly" from several major corporations, foundations, and individuals, including the Arconic Foundation, Bank of America, the Central Indiana Corporate Partnership and BioCrossroads, Microsoft, Mario Marino, Antoine van Agtmael, and the Metropolitan Council—a "network of business, civic, and philanthropic leaders" (Ibid.). And McKinsey, whose 2019 report *The Future of Work* predicts the possibility of significant future workplace automation, is one of the largest corporate consulting firms in the world.

Even though corporate elites and futurists have made automation predictions for several decades, Frey and Osborne reject the prospect of historically based empirical research. Rather, they argue that their work focuses on "technology that is in only the early stages of development. This means that historical data on the impact on the technological developments we observe is unavailable" (Frey and Osborne 2017, 265). They take issue with the BLS workforce projections because they are based on "what can be referred to as changes in normal technological progress, and not on any breakthrough technologies that may be seen as conjectural" (Ibid.). Their approach, then, results in future predictions built on high-level statistics. The McKinsey and Brookings reports are also focused on predictions. Presumably intended for a larger audience, both reports are full of the highest-quality graphics and less advanced quantitative methods. These reports also illustrate the self-referential nature of the information infrastructure of the fantasy economy. In multiple instances, the Brookings report cites its own analysis of others' data. For example, they cite "Brookings analysis of BLS, Census, EMSI, Moody's, and McKinsey Data" multiple times (Muro, Maxim, and Whiton 2019). McKinsey also cites its own reports many times, and six of the consultant's previous reports appear in the report's bibliography (McKinsey Global Institute 2019, 113). In the end, I suggest that the automation literature has effectively become a permanent prediction funded substantially by corporate interests. This work relies heavily on quantitative data, yet this data is not typically based on historical evidence. And more education and training are consistently elites' preferred solution to this purportedly looming catastrophe for workers.

Alternative Data on the Educational Requirements of the Labor Market

During the Great Recession, elites initiated a more comprehensive higher education reform agenda, including an emphasis on significantly increasing college completion and post–high school education and training as the cure for economic inequality. This agenda was given a major boost in 2006 by the Bush administration's report on U.S. higher education, which reinforced the assumption that education beyond high school was the only path to economic opportunity and stability yet also maintained that higher education required substantial reforms. The report acknowledged the financial support of the Lumina Foundation, IBM, Microsoft, the National Center for Public Policy and Higher Education, and the University of Texas System (Secretary of Education's Commission on the Future of Higher Education 2006, iv). The National Center for Public Policy and Higher Education was established in 1998 and received "continuing, core financial support from a consortium of national foundations," including "The Pew Charitable Trusts and The Ford Foundation" (National Center for Public Policy and Higher Education, n.d.). The same year, the Community College Research Center (CCRC) supplanted the IEE at Columbia University.

But I argue that elites had a major data problem obstructing a higher education reform agenda, which became evident in a debate regarding the National Center on Education and the Economy's 2006 report, *Tough*

Choices or Tough Times. In 2007, the journal *Phi Delta Kappan* hosted a forum about the report, which included articles from the Economic Policy Institute's Lawrence Mishel and Richard Rothstein and the NCEE's Marc Tucker, among others. In questioning the report's analysis of the relationship between increasing academic standards and the educational requirements of the labor market, Mishel and Rothstein argued that the NCEE "provides no justification for contradicting the Bureau of Labor Statistics (BLS) projection that fewer than one-third of future jobs will require college degrees at today's lower standard. The BLS also expects not more than another quarter or so of new jobs to require some college training" (Mishel and Rothstein 2007, 31). They went on to conclude that the "middle class, in short, is threatened not by lack of skills but by poor pay for skilled jobs. Social and economic policy reform, not school transformation, must be the remedy for this middle class squeeze" (Ibid.). In response, Tucker said that the commission that produced the report advocated "greatly increasing the quality and quantity of well-educated high school students in the workforce, but we said nothing about how many of them should go on to college. So, whether or not our recommendations differ from the B.L.S. projections is hard to say" (Tucker 2007, 52).

In 2007, the Ford Foundation provided Georgetown University a grant of $300,000 to "conduct research and policy analysis on changing educational and training requirements for the labor market" (Ford Foundation 2007). The same year, the Lumina Foundation—one of four foundation funders of the NCEE's report and a funder of the Bush administration's *A Test of Leadership*—gave Georgetown a $450,000 grant to "conduct research on the relationship between higher education and the economy, including projecting the supply and demand for college-educated workers" (Lumina Foundation 2007b). Washington figure Anthony Carnevale was Director, Labor Market and Economic Study, at the NCEE when *Tough Choices or Tough Times* was published (New Commission on the Skills of the American Workforce2011b), and in 2007, *Community College Journal* (a publication of the American Association of Community Colleges) published an article by Carnevale, who was identified as research professor and director of the Global Institute on Education and Work at Georgetown University (Carnevale 2007, 27). The same issue of the journal also included a news item about the Lumina Foundation's appointment of Jamie Merisotis as its new CEO (*Community College Journal* 2007, 8).

The project of creating alternative data on the educational requirements of the labor market took a major step forward in early 2008 when Carnevale, again identified as director of the Global Institute on Education and the Economy at Georgetown, published an article challenging the BLS methodology in *Change: The Magazine of Higher Learning* (Carnevale 2008). The piece had extensive quantitative data, including four figures, all of which cited author's analysis of official data sources and data from McKinsey but included no bibliography. And Carnevale concluded: "Thus, if used without proper adjustments, the BLS methodology can lead to a gross underestimate of both current and future postsecondary-education requirements in the labor market. Unfortunately, these errors cascade down through official state and local data, because all states and local authorities use the BLS model and none of them, as far as I know, corrects for educational growth in occupational requirements. But if properly adjusted, the official data show robust growth in the demand for postsecondary education" (Ibid., 27). In a 2019 conversation with Carnevale, Lumina's Merisotis recounted a lunch meeting between the two roughly ten years earlier as follows: "You, you [Carnevale] said to me that 'We have a data problem in this business. We have a problem on both sides of the equation, on the education side and on the workforce side. And if we can figure out how to create more open data and how to bring these data sets together, we'll actually have a powerful story to tell about this integration of learning and working that's taking place in society right now'" (Lumina Foundation 2019).

In 1993, Merisotis cofounded the Washington-based Institute on Higher Education Policy (IHEP; Lumina Foundation 2022b), a corporate- and foundation-funded "nonpartisan nonprofit research, policy, and advocacy organization committed to promoting access and success in higher education for all students, with a focus on students of color, students from low-income backgrounds, and other historically marginalized populations" (Institute for Higher Education Policy 2022a). In its first several years, the IHEP co-published several reports with the Education Resources Institute (TERI), which called itself "the largest not-for-profit guarantor of U.S. private education loans" (Reuters 2008). With titles such as *Now What? Life after College for Recent College Graduates* (1997a), *College Debt and the American Family* (1995), *Graduating into Debt: The Burdens of Borrowing for Graduate and Professional Students* (n.d.), *Life after Forty: A New Portrait of Today's—and Tomorrow's—Postsecondary Students* (1996), and *Taxing Matters: College Aid, Tax Policy, and Equal Opportunity* (1997b), these reports discussed the financial situation faced by college graduates and suggested ways that policy makers could ease the student loan debt burden.

In *Now What?* published in 1997, the IHEP and TERI relied on BLS data on the educational requirements of the labor market and included a full-page table replicating the 1995 BLS projections. This data showed that in 1994, roughly 30 percent of all jobs typically required post–high school education, and this number was projected to increase marginally by 2005 (Education Resources Institute and Institute for Higher Education Policy 1997, 18). The report identified a handful of the fastest-growing occupations for bachelor's degree holders (Ibid., 19) yet also acknowledged "areas of concern," including the growing debt facing college graduates as well as the fact that a "large percentage of recent college graduates live at home with their parents, potentially adding to the financial burdens of their parents' generation" (Ibid., 7). But the report also stressed the skills gap, arguing that "some employers express dissatisfaction with the training and skills levels of those who have just graduated from college" (Ibid., 7). *Now What?* was "prepared under the direction of Colleen O'Brien, Managing Director of The Institute for Higher Education Policy, with assistance from Katheryn Volle, Alisa Federico, and Jamie Merisotis at The Institute, and Ted Freeman and Tom Parker at TERI" (Ibid.).

After the initial grants by Ford and Lumina, in May 2008, the Gates Foundation gave Georgetown nearly $3 million to "support a project aligning education and training systems with career requirements to increase opportunity for low and moderate income youth" (Gates Foundation 2008a). In a December 2008 press release, the foundation described its new college completion campaign, including the creation of Georgetown's Center on Education and the Workforce, as follows: "The Georgetown University Center on Education and the Workforce ($2.9 million over 4 years) is dedicated to expanding merit-based opportunity for all by aligning education and workforce demands. Using a market-driven, empirically-based approach, the Center conducts research and provides information and in-depth analysis that informs education and labor-market decision makers in three core areas: jobs, skills, and people. The Center is founded by leading labor economist Anthony Carnevale and provides support on a national and state level" (Gates Foundation 2008b). In 2009, the CEW received a second grant from Lumina for over $2.5 million "to conduct and disseminate research on the relationship between higher education and the economy, including projecting the supply and demand for college-educated workers" (Lumina Foundation 2009). The CEW's original mission statement used language nearly identical to parts of the 2008 Gates press release but added that the new center was funded by both Ford and Lumina as well: "The Georgetown University Center on Education and the Workforce is dedicated to expanding merit-based opportunity for all by aligning education and workforce demands. Using a market-driven, empirically-based approach, the Center conducts research and provides information and in-depth analysis that informs education and labor-market decision makers in three core areas: jobs, skills and people. The Center, founded by leading labor economist Anthony Carnevale, is a unique collaboration between Lumina Foundation for Education, Ford Foundation and The Bill & Melinda Gates Foundation" (Center on Education and the Workforce 2009).

As part of Georgetown University (Carnevale 2021), the CEW has no independent tax documents or articles of incorporation, and, as of 2022, its website stated that it was "funded by generous grants from its partner foundations: the Bill & Melinda Gates Foundation, Lumina Foundation, JPMorgan Chase, Ascendium Education Group, The Joyce Foundation, and The Annie E. Casey Foundation" (Center on Education and the Workforce 2022a). The CEW promotes its influence in the media, Capitol Hill, and beyond, and its reports are ubiquitous in the higher education policy ecosystem. Before the CEW, Anthony Carnevale's lengthy Washington career included work for several firms with interests related to education, including ten years as vice president for public leadership with the Educational Testing Service from 1996 to 2006, director of human resource and employment studies at the Committee for Economic Development (the "nation's oldest business-sponsored policy research organization"), and ten years as founder and president of the Institute for Workplace Learning, which "worked directly with a consortia of private companies to develop high performance work systems and to develop more effective work and training systems" (Center on Education and the Workforce 2022b).

In June 2010, citing the "poor quality" of official data (Carnevale, Smith, and Strohl 2010a, 1), the CEW published its first projections of jobs and education requirements of the labor market. The projections were accompanied by a fifty-six-page Technical Summary, authored by the same three individuals but also acknowledging "design and methodological contributions by Avinash Bhati" (Carnevale, Smith, and Strohl 2010b, 1). Bhati was the founder of the firm Maxarth, which recently stated that it provides "creative data and analytical solutions for real-world problems and opportunities" (Maxarth 2022). The Technical Summary also cited Bishop and Carter's (1990, 1991) earlier critiques of BLS methodology, which were supported by funds from the Center for Advanced Human Resource Studies (Cornell University), the Center on the Educational Quality of the Workforce (University of Pennsylvania), and a New York State Fellowship for Minority Graduate Students (Bishop and Carter 1991, 37). One of Bishop and Carter's pieces was published in the Communications section of the BLS *Monthly Labor Review* (Ibid.), and the other was a paper entitled "The Worsening Shortage of College Graduate Workers," in which the authors acknowledged that the paper had not "undergone formal review or approval of the faculty of the ILR [Industrial and Labor Relations] school. It is intended to make results of Center Research, conferences, and projects available to others interested in human resource management in preliminary form to encourage discussion and suggestions" (Bishop and Carter 1990). The CEW published updated projections in 2013 running through 2020 (Carnevale, Smith, and Strohl 2013a).

The CEW's projections advance both prongs of the skills gap—that high-education jobs are increasing at a faster rate than the BLS projects and that educational and skill requirements of many historically low-education jobs are increasing as well. And the overall picture of the labor market painted by the CEW is substantially different from the one long illustrated in official data. As noted above, the CEW's 2010 projections asserted that in 2007, roughly 59 percent of all jobs were "available for workers with postsecondary education" and projected that by 2018, "about two-thirds of all employment will require some college education or better" (Carnevale, Smith, and Strohl 2010a, 14). The CEW further projected that by 2018, "63 percent of job openings will require workers with at least some college education" (Ibid., 13). Yet as noted previously, contemporaneous data from the BLS showed that only about 31 percent of all jobs in 2008 required any post–high school education and training, and the agency projected little increase in educational requirements by 2018 (Bureau of Labor Statistics 2009). The 2013 CEW projections had a similarly optimistic assessment of the educational needs of the labor market, with the organization projecting that by 2020, "65 percent of all jobs in the economy will require postsecondary education and training beyond high school" and that 65 percent of all job openings would require post–high school education as well (Carnevale, Smith, and Strohl 2013a, 1).

The substantial discrepancy between the CEW's data and that of the BLS necessitates a discussion of the BLS methodology, which the CEW found flawed. As discussed in Chapter 2, the agency uses multiple methods to ascertain the level of education and training most workers would need to enter an occupation (Bureau of Labor Statistics 2021a). The BLS projects jobs, not the educational requirements of jobs. It only adjusts educational requirements for an occupation if typical education levels of incumbents change, requiring a reclassification. It is conceivable, therefore, that if the labor market gets to a point where, for example, a typical worker in food services has at least an associate's degree, then the BLS could reclassify the occupation of food-service workers as typically requiring an associate's degree for entry to reflect this change. Thus, if the educational attainment levels of the population continue to increase, the agency's aggregate data on the educational requirements of the labor market could change even as the distribution of jobs remains roughly the same.

A significant problem with the logic of the CEW's projections is the conflation of the educational attainment of the population with the educational requirements of existing jobs. The Technical Summary for the CEW's projections claims that the BLS "**systematically under-predicts the demand for postsecondary education and training**" (Carnevale, Smith, and Strohl 2010b, 3, emphasis in original). To make this case, the authors argued that while the most recent BLS projections showed that 25 percent of all jobs in 2006 would require postsecondary degrees, "34.3 percent of the labor force actually had postsecondary degrees and awards. . . . This 9.3 percentage point differential represents 12.3 million workers with postsecondary education above B.L.S. forecasts" (Ibid.). But the educational attainment levels of the population are certainly not synonymous with the educational requirements of the entire labor market.[3] According to federal data, the U.S. labor force is highly educated and dispersed across a large and diverse labor market dominated by what are understood as typically low-education, low-skill jobs. But conflating the population's aggregate educational attainment levels with the educational requirements of the labor market has both enabled the uncritical acceptance of the CEW's alternative data and allowed the organization to largely avoid discussing the significant problem of underemployment in its work.

The CEW's alternative data showing a disproportionately high-education labor market has been disseminated in other ways too, including being cited by the funders of this data in popular business books. In 2015, Lumina's Merisotis published *America Needs Talent: Attracting, Educating, and Deploying the 21st-Century Workforce*, in which he labeled the nation's public education system "abysmal" (Merisotis 2015, 20). He cited the CEW data several times without mentioning the much less encouraging federal data on the educational requirements of the labor market. For example, Merisotis stated that "by 2020, the center [CEW] says, that 65 percent of *all* U.S. jobs will require a postsecondary credential" (Ibid., 21, emphasis in original). He further maintained that Lumina's goal of "ensuring that 60 percent of Americans hold a high-quality postsecondary degree, certificate, or other credential by 2025—was based on the projections that the Georgetown Center had done showing how big of a gap the U.S. had to narrow in order to address its talent needs" (Ibid., 23). The discussion of the CEW in the book's acknowledgments was as follows: "Heartfelt thanks to Tony Carnevale at the Georgetown Center for Education and the Workforce whose high-quality work is reflected throughout the book, including in many of the original data analyses highlighted in the text and graphics" (Ibid., 197). Regarding the state of higher education, Merisotis concluded: "But let's not kid ourselves: America's higher education system is indeed in need of an overhaul" (Ibid., 65).

In early 2020, as noted above, the *Chronicle of Higher Education* confirmed that the CEW's alternative data had indeed become conventional wisdom: "'By the year 2020, nearly two-thirds of all jobs will require postsecondary education and training.' Anyone who's been to a higher-ed conference or read a book on the topic in the past decade has no doubt heard some version of that prediction—some of us to the point of numbness" (Blumenstyk 2020). According to the article, the "center considers a position a bachelor's-level job if most of the people with that job have a bachelor's degree and they get paid more than those who don't have the degree" (Ibid.). The article did not mention the substantially different official data regarding educational levels required by the labor market produced by the BLS—which presumably the author was not aware of—nor did it identify the CEW's funders. Regarding the organization's projections for 2020, the CEW's Nicole Smith stated: "People have become more educated than we expected" (Ibid.). This is accurate: the educational attainment levels of the population have continually increased. But again, the population's educational attainment levels are certainly not synonymous with the education levels required by the labor market. The article went on to point out that "for 2027, the center will predict 70 percent of all jobs will require some education beyond high school" (Ibid.).

The same year, Merisotis published *Human Work in the Age of Smart Machines*, in which he again cited the CEW's data several times. According to Merisotis, the "Great Recession has been described by the U.S. labor economist Anthony Carnevale as a 'smart bomb targeting low skill jobs'" (Merisotis 2020, 15), a politically wise framing yet one seemingly divorced from the realities of the labor market revealed in official data. In the acknowledgments, Merisotis again thanked individuals from the CEW (Ibid., 175–177). On several occasions, CEW authors have also written chapters for edited volumes that relied on the CEW's own alternative data on the educational requirements of the labor market without mentioning the substantially different official data on the critical issue

(Carnevale and Rose 2012; Carnevale and Smith 2016a, 2016b; Carnevale, Smith, and Strohl 2013b). The epigraph of one of these essays succinctly affirms one of the fantasy economy's overarching goals: "**The New Consensus: Postsecondary Education is the Legitimate Arbiter of Economic Opportunity**" (Carnevale, Smith, and Strohl 2013b, 93, emphasis in original). This consensus is a political statement that, I argue, depends on creating the perception of a labor market dominated by jobs requiring post–high school education and training.

The perception of a high-education labor market can also be seen in major education policies. In 2018, California created an online community college based on an estimate of the educational requirements of the state's labor market largely similar to the assessment of the CEW. The rationale for the new online community college was that "sixty percent of jobs in the state require some sort of training beyond high school, but the majority of Californians ages 25 to 34 do not have even an associate degree" (Fischer 2018). Yet the California Employment Development Department's employment projections through 2028 undermined the notion of a high-education labor market. The list of occupations with the most job openings through 2028 was dominated by low-education, low-wage jobs, including food preparation and service workers; personal care aides; retail sales staff; laborers; cashiers; waiters and waitresses; janitors and cleaners; office clerks; stock clerks and order fillers; and customer service representatives (California Employment Development Department 2021).

The interest group role played by the CEW was evident in early 2020 when two federal studies documenting the troubling economic outcomes for significant numbers of college graduates received major media coverage. On January 11, 2020, the *Washington Post* published a column (Singletary 2020) about a study by the Federal Reserve Bank of St. Louis that suggested that "college and postgraduate education may be failing some recent graduates as a financial investment" (Emmons, Kent, and Ricketts 2019, 297). On February 13, Carnevale published a response that fell back on a comparison of median incomes for those with a bachelor's degree to those without and mentioned CEW projections that by 2027, "about 70 percent of jobs will require a college credential" (Carnevale 2020a). He further affirmed that "raising alarms about the value of college because graduates aren't able to accumulate wealth more quickly is like saying the graduation party was ruined because the champagne wasn't cold enough" (Ibid.). At the same time, Carnevale sought to keep the political pressure on higher education, arguing that "improvements are long overdue in the way colleges operate. Colleges need to do many things, including becoming more efficient and transparent and partnering with like-minded institutions to offer innovative, student-friendly educational options. That will make them better run and, we hope, less expensive. This would be good for all college students" (Ibid.).

Shortly thereafter, *Inside Higher Ed* published an article about a new study from the Federal Reserve Bank of New York's ongoing research on employment outcomes among college graduates, which highlighted that 41 percent of recent college graduates were underemployed (Redden 2020). Not long after, in the *CEW Quarterly*, Carnevale sought to reframe the debate by emphasizing the continuing economic promise of higher education and criticized the research methods of underemployment studies:

> When unemployment levels fluctuate for recent college graduates, the value of a college degree is questioned. Even though the bachelor's degree continues to be the gold standard for entry into the middle class, rising college costs and student debt make college easy prey for reporters and their editors. There's always a market for articles about how college graduates are in trouble, especially in recessions. . . . Methodologies used to calculate underemployment study the educational levels listed in job ads (half of which don't report educational requirements), misuse entry-level education requirements to define demand, or fail to consider wage premiums. All of these approaches understate the value of college. . . . College graduates at age 22 do have higher unemployment rates than all workers, but unemployment rates decline sharply within three years. That's just the nature of being a recent graduate—a lot of churn between graduation and the seven months that follow. And when the economy is doing well, people spend time seeking jobs. Today's unemployment rate is at historically low levels (4%)—a true employee's market. New graduates can shop around until they find a job that matches their salary requirements and preferred work environment. (Carnevale 2020b)

Such an assessment dismisses the lived reality of millions of underemployed and underpaid bachelor's and advanced degree holders in furtherance of a higher education policy agenda built on the flawed assumption that increasing college attendance can remedy the decades of wage stagnation faced by most workers. In the end, I maintain that the CEW's alternative data on the educational requirements of the labor market is fundamental to both higher education and K–12 reform today because official data shows the low-wage, low-education labor market of the real economy. But the widespread, uncritical acceptance of the CEW's alternative data, within the context of high levels of underemployment and wage stagnation experienced by bachelor's and advanced degree holders, has created the perfect storm, as higher education is unable to rebut popular calls for major structural changes.

Cliff: A Very Steep, Vertical, or Overhanging Face of Rock, Earth, or Ice

The most recent predicted crisis facing higher education is also based on alternative data—the threat of plummeting future college enrollments frequently referred to as the demographic cliff. In the natural world, a cliff is a vertical or near-vertical drop, and falling off a cliff would likely lead to an individual's death. Thus, that this term has uncritically entered the lexicon of a tuition-driven higher education establishment is extraordinarily significant. Further, the demographic cliff should be understood within the larger fantasy economy narrative positing a chronically failing education system and perpetually underqualified workforce. Firmly grounded in human capital theory, the demographic cliff literature implicitly holds higher education responsible for graduates' labor market outcomes well beyond its control. Ultimately, the effectiveness of this predicted crisis in shaping mainstream discussion and policy both illustrates and reinforces higher education's structurally weak political position.

It is imperative that we assess the demographic cliff narrative in historical context. As the skills gap was created during a period of rapid deindustrialization and middle-class job loss, the demographic cliff has evolved into a dominant narrative during a period of modestly declining higher education enrollments from their historic highs during the Great Recession (National Center for Education Statistics 2022b). Further austerity measures forced public higher education to cut faculty and staff, thereby making it even more tuition dependent. The demographic cliff literature, however, assumes the inevitability of austerity rather than treating taxing and spending decisions as political choices (Grawe 2018, 2021a). As a result, the policy options discussed in this debate focus almost exclusively on various ways to maintain and increase enrollments, including the expansion of online education, the sale of numerous products and services aimed at improving enrollments, the elimination of programs, and even the prospect of closing campuses. Making public higher education less tuition dependent and thereby less adversely impacted by enrollment fluctuations is implicitly ruled out. Ultimately, the assumptions, language, and policy prescriptions of the demographic cliff are steeped in the contours of neoliberalism.

However, unlike the CEW's claim that "about two-thirds of all employment will require some college education or better" (Carnevale, Smith, and Strohl 2010, 14), the demographic cliff cannot be captured in a concise, quantitative slogan. Rather, current and projected higher education enrollments consist of a vast number of data points that change every year, and so any significant trends—should they exist—must be captured in purely qualitative terms, hence the critical importance of the term "demographic cliff." And the evolution of this concept in the education reform literature has occurred over several decades. In the report of the first Commission on the Skills of the American Workforce in 1990, the National Center on Education and the Economy warned that in the absence of major education reforms, the country was "headed toward an economic cliff" (National Center on Education and the Economy 1990, 8). This analysis was consistent with both *A Nation at Risk* and *Workforce 2000*, the latter of which also stressed the prospect of future demographic crises adversely affecting the labor force and economy. In 1991, the Western Interstate Commission for Higher Education (WICHE) and the College Board published *The Road to College*, an outgrowth of WICHE's high school graduate projections project, which was "supported by The College Board, the Lily Foundation, and the Teachers Insurance and Annuity Association" (Western Interstate Commission for Higher Education and the College Board 1991, vii). The report projected high school graduates by race and ethnicity for the fifty states through 1995 and, because of racial changes in the population, concluded that "higher education institutions in the United States will be faced with dramatic demographic changes before the end of the century" (Ibid., 1). This framing was subsequently echoed by the higher education press in an article entitled "Study Predicts Dramatic Shifts in Enrollments," in which a College Board official expressed concerns about minority students' lack of preparation for entering the workforce (Evangelauf 1991). Despite this warning, however, by the late 1990s, total enrollment in higher education began a steady increase that continued until the Great Recession (National Center for Education Statistics 2021c).

In 2013, the cliff metaphor appeared in a news article about WICHE's newest projections of high school graduates. The article, entitled "The Pupil Cliff" (Kiley 2013), discussed the organization's most recent report, and Deborah A. Santiago, cofounder and vice president for policy and research at Excelencia in Education, stated: "How do we use this data to compel action? We always talk about these trends in terms of natural disasters—a tsunami of students, a cliff—but we're not doing a damn thing about it" (Ibid.). Concerns over potentially declining numbers of students for higher education institutions and future workforce needs were again raised by WICHE's president Joe Garcia and the CEW's Nicole Smith in a 2016 article about WICHE's 2016 projections (Seltzer 2016).

However, Nathan Grawe's 2018 book, *Demographics and the Demand for Higher Education*, fully embraced the cliff narrative and took it to new levels. As noted previously, research by the National Center for Education Statistics published in the years leading up to Grawe's book projected relatively constant numbers of high school graduates as well as modestly increasing higher education enrollments over approximately the next eight years (National Center for Education Statistics 2014, 8, 20; 2016a, 14, 24; 2016b, 14, 24; 2017b, 14, 24). But Grawe did not cite either the federal projections of high school graduates or higher education enrollments in creating his model of future college-going students (Grawe 2018). Rather, he relied heavily on the projections of high school graduates provided by WICHE. And when considering WICHE's recent projections, he maintained that "total numbers of students are headed toward a cliff" and speculated that the "coming contraction in higher education may be proportionately larger than that in high school graduates" (Grawe 2018, 19). Like that of the CEW, Grawe's work became widely cited in the higher education literature, which embraced the narrative reflexively (*Chronicle of Higher Education* 2019; Grawe 2021a).

Founded as an interstate compact in the 1950s, WICHE received funding from numerous foundations and corporations as it expanded (Abbott, n.d., 282), and a recent annual report listed the organization's numerous funders, sponsors, and partners, which included major foundations such as Gates and Lumina along with many firms in educational services (Western Interstate Commission for Higher Education 2019, 26–27). Over the years, the organization has also had important connections to other influential higher education nonprofits. In 1989, it created the WICHE Cooperative for Educational Technologies (WCET), which recently described itself as "the leader in the practice, policy, & advocacy of digital learning in higher education" (Western Interstate Commission for Higher Education Cooperative for Educational Technologies 2022). WCET and WICHE "serve as the intermediary organization for the Every Learner Everywhere Network," a Gates-supported initiative that "advocates for equitable outcomes in U.S. higher education through advances in digital learning" (Every Learner Everywhere 2022). In addition, the National Center for

Higher Education Data Systems (NCHEDS) began in 1969 as the "Management Information Systems program at the Western Interstate Commission for Higher Education (WICHE)" before becoming an independent nonprofit in 1977 (National Center for Higher Education Management Systems 2022). Formed in 1954, the State Higher Education Executive Officers Association (SHEEO) "serves the chief executives of statewide governing, policy, and coordinating boards of postsecondary education and their staffs" (State Higher Education Executive Officers Association 2022a), and SHEEO, WICHE, and the NCHEDS share a building in Boulder, Colorado (State Higher Education Executive Officers Association 2022b).

In recent years, WICHE has worked in "five primary focus areas," including finance and affordability; access and success; workforce and society; technology and innovation; and accountability. And the organization defines accountability as "striving to ensure that students receive an education that is valuable to them and that government is receiving a strong return on its investment" (Western Interstate Commission for Higher Education 2022). WICHE has published updated projections of high school graduates roughly every four years, and many of them have been sponsored by the College Board and ACT, which as the two firms responsible for the primary college entrance exams have a significant stake in higher education enrollments. The 1998 projections were a "joint publication" of WICHE and the College Board and also acknowledged the support of the James Irvine and W. K. Kellogg Foundations (Western Interstate Commission for Higher Education and the College Board 1998). Subsequent editions acknowledged the support of both ACT and the College Board (Western Interstate Commission for Higher Education 2003, xi; 2008, xi; 2012, ix; 2016, ix), while the 2020 projections acknowledged support from the College Board (Western Interstate Commission for Higher Education 2020).

Making very long-term population or enrollment projections is difficult. In their 2019 ten-year projections for public school enrollments in Wisconsin, researchers from the University of Wisconsin, Madison's Applied Population Laboratory concluded: "As with nearly all types of forecasts, dependability in these enrollment projections decreases over time" (Applied Population Laboratory, University of Wisconsin, Madison 2019, 8). Grawe's initial projections, published in 2018, went through 2029, and his updated projections, published in 2021, run through 2034 (2021b). WICHE's 1998 projections went fourteen years (through 2011–2012) (Western Interstate Commission for Higher Education and the College Board 1998, 8), but by 2020, it had increased the length of its projections to seventeen years into the future (Western Interstate Commission for Higher Education 2020, 1). Over the last several years, the National Center for Education Statistics' projections have been roughly eight years each.

The title of Grawe's second book, published in 2021, *The Agile College: How Institutions Successfully Navigate Demographic Changes*, succinctly implies the policy recommendations of the demographic cliff narrative, which had been firmly established as conventional wisdom. Yet Grawe appeared to delay the onset of the demographic cliff: "A brief increase in births in 2014 portends a temporary and incomplete recovery in 2031 and 32, before the onset of continued decline in 2033" (Grawe 2021a, 7), twelve years from the book's publication. Thus, I maintain that the demographic cliff narrative is showing signs akin to the automation literature that instructs educators to make their students "robot-proof" in the present because of waves of automation-induced job loss that have become, in effect, a permanent prediction. And the merits of permanent predictions, of course, can never be evaluated. Nonetheless, cash-strapped colleges and universities are being instructed to address a predicted future enrollment collapse *now*. Because of the structurally weak political standing of higher education, this framing necessarily facilitates further budgetary austerity and the implementation of major policy changes advocated by corporate interests.

During the Great Recession, higher education enrollments peaked, and they declined somewhat between 2015 and 2019 (National Center for Education Statistics 2021c). In 2020, the National Center for Education Statistics (NCES; 2020a, 13, 21) published updated projections, which foresaw relatively constant numbers of both high school graduates and higher education enrollments through the late 2020s. The projections received little attention, however, because by this time, the demographic cliff narrative had become entrenched. Subsequently, in 2022, the NCES projected gradually increasing high school graduates through the middle to late 2020s, followed by a modest decline, as both WICHE and Grawe had also previously projected (National Center for Education Statistics 2022c). But, more importantly, the NCES also projected that higher education enrollments would be relatively constant throughout the 2020s, with very slight increases projected by 2030 (National Center for Education Statistics 2022b). Thus, according to the NCES projections, there was not anything close to an enrollment cliff facing higher education as far as its data went into the future, roughly eight years.

This should hardly be surprising, however. In our low-wage economy, the public well understands that higher education may represent their only shot at any economic opportunity. Moreover, the U.S. population is growing, and poverty—a consistently strong predictor of higher education attendance—is relatively constant, fluctuating with aggregate economic conditions. Given this context, the notion that significantly declining numbers of people would choose to attend higher education is counterintuitive at best. To be sure, a handful of states have experienced declining numbers of high school graduates, but even this trend can only be seen if one begins the analysis relatively recently. Cliff advocates will continue to seize on these isolated data points the same way that for decades K–12 education reformers have focused almost exclusively on decontextualized testing data based on statistical means as prima facie evidence of a declining U.S. school system.

Business interests have predicted a future demographic crisis in the United States for decades, one that has yet to happen, and in recent years, this crisis has been applied to higher education in the form of the demographic cliff. Like the educational requirements of the labor market, the demographic cliff relies on alternative data despite the long-standing availability of federal projections of education statistics. And the uncritical acceptance of both pieces of alternative data simultaneously reveals and reinforces higher education's structurally weak political position, making it largely powerless to fend off radical changes.

Conclusion

Privately funded data and research, a large percentage of which is not peer reviewed, has been critical to the fantasy economy campaign. Yet because of the reflexive acceptance of human capital theory, questions about the conflicts of interest inherent in an education policy ecosystem funded substantially by private interests with policy agendas have not received meaningful attention. But we must expand the definition of conflicts of interest beyond the sale of products and services to include the terms of debate established by the elite-led education reform movement, which focuses exclusively on education's role in economic opportunity. Corporations and the wealthy have a tremendous interest in maintaining this framing of economic opportunity because it takes the basic characteristics of neoliberalism as a given and places all attention on the education system and individual workers.

The research and data techniques used in this campaign reflect those used by other interest groups, including undocumented or misleading claims (many of which originated with other interest groups); the disproportionate reliance on commissioned research in high-profile reports; the far-fetched predictions of reports such as those of *Workforce 2000*; the recurring use of predictions as in the automation literature; and the creation of alternative data even when official data on similar phenomena is available. Rather than being caricatured as some sort of conspiratorial plot, however, this campaign should simply be understood as a product of our interest group–driven political system.

Without question, the data and research campaign of the fantasy economy has been extraordinarily effective. In the same 2019 discussion between Lumina's Merisotis and the CEW's Carnevale mentioned earlier in this chapter, Merisotis posed the following question: "Tell me a little bit about, sort of, where do you think we are in terms of the data questions. Have we, have we, made progress in helping people understand more about why these two systems (education and the workforce) are integrated?" Carnevale offered a lengthy response, which included his assertion that because of the work of the CEW and others "I think, in a sense, the check is in the mail. That is, I think we've made the case. You can't find—hard to find, you can find—hard to find a politician who stands in front of a room nowadays and doesn't say that people need some form of formal preparation beyond high school in order to get a good job" (Lumina Foundation 2019).

As a political organization, Carnevale judged the CEW's success in political terms, and his assessment is entirely correct. Because of the low wages associated with the large number of low-education jobs in our economy, most politicians would not dare to publicly state that one would not need post–high school education to obtain a good job. Carnevale's assessment, then, underscores the significance of the CEW's alterative data that in 2020, "nearly two-thirds of all jobs will require postsecondary education and training." Also in 2019, the BLS published data showing that in 2016, only roughly 37 percent of all jobs typically required any post–high school education, and the agency again projected little change in the educational requirements of the labor market through 2026 (Bureau of Labor Statistics 2019b). Yet again, official data continued to show a very different labor market than alternative data and also showed consistently high rates of underemployment among bachelor's degree holders (Federal Reserve Bank of New York 2022a). In the end, however, it would be very difficult to exercise any political pressure on higher education by relying on this type of official labor market data.

The community of scholars is uniquely positioned to interrogate the data and research that is regularly presented as ironclad evidence of various educational and labor market trends. Indeed, critical analysis is the essence of scholarship, and careful examination of the flood of literature funded by private interests and promoted by education reformers is even more pressing given the increasingly precarious political situation in which higher education finds itself. Admittedly, such a research agenda will be extraordinarily difficult given the lavish foundation funding of the academy itself and individual scholars. The transformation of the perception of foundations' motivations for education philanthropy has origins in the 1960s and is a subject taken up in Chapter 4.

4

The Fantasy Economy's
Overarching Goal

Educational Accountability

It is, of course, this very separation of knowledge and
consequent retreat, from social reality and social
conscience that has aroused the young, and which has
shaken the confidence in education of those who make the
decisions in terms of the universities' and colleges' future.
—GEORGE W. BONHAM, *Inside Academe*

Change will occur when there's both a policy structure
that encourages it and permits it, and when individual
educators, parents, and others see the change as theirs.
—KATI HAYCOCK, *Education Week*

Introduction

Chapter 4 traces the origins of educational accountability to the 1960s,
when corporate America became increasingly dismayed at events in both
K–12 and higher education and created institutions to advance its interests through foundation giving. Subsequently, foundations became the
main vehicle for corporate education reform on the basis of a purported
separation of foundation giving from the interests of corporations and
the wealthy. While originally motivated by opposition to striking K–12
teachers and political activities on college campuses, corporate interests
would come to argue that education's shortcomings were responsible for
the inequality brought on by neoliberalism.

The concepts of free markets, technology, and data have been central
components of the political movement for school accountability. Accountability itself reflected market-based thinking, as schools would be expected to not only overcome the adverse effects of poverty on students'

current academic performance but also be responsible for their future economic status. Thus, the accountability movement depended increasingly on the theme of technology to advance a picture of an increasingly complex, high-education labor market. Finally, by the middle 1990s, the concept of data had become an indispensable piece of the accountability campaign and the broader education reform movement. But the data allowed into the discussion was tightly controlled as reformers presented a misleading version of the labor market and education system to justify the adoption of accountability policies.

And while accountability appeared popular as an abstract principle, generating support for concrete accountability policies based on standardized testing faced major opposition and therefore required a more carefully crafted political campaign, which included creating what appeared to be a diverse ideological base of support. As a result, elites created high-profile Washington-based groups funded by a relatively small number of the same foundations and business interests and featuring many of the same individuals. The racist rhetoric of the culture of poverty would be jettisoned, and by the 1990s, reformers built a campaign around the achievement gap, which was blamed entirely on the schools. Despite the apparent popularity of this messaging, however, the historical accident of 9/11 was necessary to compel enough members of Congress in both parties to drop their objections and pass No Child Left Behind. Not long after passage, many clearly foreseeable implementation problems became apparent in the new testing and accountability system, which led reformers to initiate a campaign for the Common Core. And during the Great Recession, corporate reformers began the push for higher education reform, which included accountability, a subject I return to in the Epilogue.

"Funding Would Not Be an Issue": *Change* Magazine and the American Association for Higher Education

In the 1960s, increasing numbers of young people attended newly built public colleges and universities across the country, which presented a multitude of new opportunities for business interests. College campuses became an important source of the political unrest of the era as well, which made business interests uneasy. In April 1965, the Ford Foundation and the American Council on Education summoned sixty higher education leaders and journalists to a meeting in rural Virginia (Marchese and Miller 2018, 18). At the time, Ford was the "academy's most influential funder, and its leaders had an agenda" (Ibid.). According to Ted Marchese and Margaret A. Miller, "while higher education had become an industry, its infrastructure for communication was cottage era" (Ibid.). Thus, higher education needed a "first-rate newspaper (like the Wall Street Journal), a magazine of thought (like the Atlantic or Harper's), and a book publisher devoted to issues of practice (like Prentice Hall or McGraw-Hill)" (Ibid.). Significantly, meeting attendees were reportedly also told that "funding would not be an issue" (Ibid.). One of the products of this meeting was *Change: The Magazine of Higher Learning*, launched in January 1969 with significant additional funding from the Esso Education Foundation (Ibid., 19). In December 1969, the Esso Education Foundation's chairman stated that "these are critical times for higher education. Colleges and universities are being called upon to not only provide education for unprecedented numbers of students, but to provide a new, more meaningful type of education. With our programs, we hope to encourage and, more especially, facilitate the constructive change that is so vital if our institutions of higher learning are to meet the needs of the present and challenges of the future" (University of Dayton 1969). Presumably, then, *Change* would work toward these goals. Shortly thereafter, the *Chronicle of Higher Education* (which received grants from the Ford and Carnegie Foundations), began publication, and Jossey-Bass publishers was established (Marchese and Miller 2018, 18).

George W. Bonham, the inaugural editor of *Change*, envisioned the magazine as a "'marketplace for innovation' that would stimulate educational reform" (Marchese and Miller 2018, 19). Contributors were deeply troubled by the turbulent political events on college campuses and believed that higher education lacked intellectual diversity and was largely disconnected from real-world events. Sociologist and Catholic priest Andrew M. Greeley's disdain for higher education was palpable: "Having failed to run the university well, it [the academy] now assumes the right to be permitted to run the rest of society" (1972, 98). *Change* identified faculty as the primary barrier to reform and as insufficiently respectful of business. Greeley protested that "anyone who is engaged in educational reform efforts (which do not involve closing down class and sending faculty and students off to the barricades) realizes that the real barrier to educational reform is the faculty" (Ibid., 101). David Riesman claimed that faculty's "scorn for business as usual is often an implicit attack on businessmen, made by people who regard their own occupation or source of income as somehow more pure" (1972, 112). And as if delivering a message directly from the magazine's funders, Bonham ominously discussed the problems of higher education as defined by *Change*: "It is, of course, this very separation of knowledge and consequent retreat, from social reality and social conscience that has aroused the young, and which has shaken the confidence in education of those who make the decisions in terms of the universities' and colleges' future" (Bonham 1972, 10). Still, he found reason for hope because "beneath all of this turmoil, there now emerges a new spirit on our campuses and a new resolve to successfully deal with our young, with each other and life, in quite new and more honest ways. These new pathways remain blurred and still unconnected. Yet, they are being forged in the minds and hearts of many remarkable men and women on campuses all over the country. Some day they will all connect and transform higher learning into something quite remarkable and more essential to national life" (Ibid., 11). With the generous backing of Ford and Esso, *Change* saw itself as a central player in the transformation of higher education.

A few years later, in 1969, striking schoolteachers led to the creation of the American Association for Higher Education (AAHE). Until the 1960s, the National Education Association (NEA) was a Washington-based group representing both educational administrators and teachers, and the Association of Higher Education (AHE) represented higher education institutions from within the NEA. In 1992, Charlene White, the executive secretary of the AHE and AAHE for forty-two years, explained that the AHE separated from the NEA and became the AAHE because the "N.E.A. began acting more and more like a union. They were encouraging striking schools, and they wanted higher education to do the same thing" (1992, 12). But the members of the AHA who "were close to the association—who came to the conference regularly and that sort of thing—did not agree with that at all" (Ibid.).

According to White's account, after a dispute about this issue between the AHA and the NEA in early 1969, the NEA informed the AHA that its funding would be cut off by May 31 (C. White 1992, 12). The AHA began soliciting contributions and, fearful of being expelled from the NEA offices before May 31, changed its name to the American Association for Higher Education (AAHE) and filed incorporation papers on February 27, 1969 (American Association for Higher Education 1969), just one month after the launch of *Change* magazine. The AAHE hired a consulting firm to handle the donations, which were mailed to a post office box (C. White 1992, 12). White recalled that the newly formed group sent proposals to foundations and corporations, stated that the AAHE "got a surprising amount of money to get started and keep us going," and mentioned two foundations in particular—Ford, which gave "something like $50,000 to start, and Carnegie gave us a big sum of money, too" (Ibid.). She further affirmed: "We always felt that part of the reason was that foundations agreed with us that you didn't get ahead by striking and keeping students out of school, you did it in other ways" (Ibid.). According to White, "about three hundred people" became life members in the AAHE as well, providing a major source of revenue (Ibid.).

The AAHE's articles of incorporation stated the ten "purposes and objectives" of the new nonprofit corporation, a list that, I argue, illustrated corporate elites' priorities and long-term goals for education reform. The AAHE would "identify and analyze critical issues, trends, and developments in higher education and to seek constructive solutions to important problems" and provide "organized focus and leadership for the varied interests, institutions, and efforts of higher education" (American Association for Higher Education 1969). Like *Change*, the AAHE echoed elites' displeasure with higher education faculty and administrators and would "encourage the improvement of the qualities and competencies of professional people in all areas of higher education, and to improve the conditions of effective performance" (Ibid.). The AAHE would also "assist in the collection, organization, and dissemination of valid and useful information on current issues in higher education" (Ibid.). Significantly, the AAHE also established two pillars of the subsequent education reform movement by promoting increasing rates of college attendance and desiring "to assist in coordinating the efforts of educational institutions and agencies at all levels" (Ibid.), thereby linking K–12 and higher education reform. And rather than using the terminology of business or labor, the articles of incorporation stated that the AAHE would "provide for liaison and cooperation of higher education with state and national governmental agencies and with foundations" (Ibid.).

The creation of the AAHE and *Change* marked important milestones in the implementation of corporate America's education reform agenda. And in 1983, the two entities joined forces, as the AAHE assumed responsibility for the content of the magazine, and for the AAHE, "Change became an important member benefit" (Marchese and Miller 2018, 19). By this time, mainly through their extensive giving, foundations had largely redefined themselves as independent charitable supporters of higher education, a goal that has been more difficult to accomplish in K–12 education reform because of the larger presence of teachers' unions.

Our Children's Crippled Future and *Unfinished Business*

With *Change* magazine and the AAHE advancing corporate interests in higher education in the 1970s, the nascent standards movement focused its efforts on K–12 schooling. The theme of low-income children as victims of the school system was fully developed in 1977 in *Our Children's Crippled Future: How American Education Has Failed*, published by the Hudson Institute's Frank E. Armbruster (1977). In 1972, Armbruster's roughly 450-page volume, *The Forgotten Americans: The Values, Beliefs, and Concerns of the Majority* (Armbruster 1972), sought to outline the contours of American public opinion on numerous contemporary issues, including many cultural issues. And *Our Children's Crippled Future* was rooted in the racialized culture of poverty: "Many a pupil from core-city sections of our large cities brings to school the feeling that he is highly unlikely to suffer any consequences for breaking rules or, for that matter, the law. Permissive schools merely reinforce this feeling and 'prove' again that only the naïve do things the hard way—by the rules. Very soon the cynical student is 'hustling' and 'shaking down' smaller and weaker students for whatever he can get. If he is cross-bused into a nonslum school, he is likely to feel like a bear dropped in a tub of honey—until the local children learn to stop bringing lunch money or valuables to school, stop using the rest rooms, and do anything else needed to stay out of his path" (Armbruster 1977, 162).

For Armbruster, rather than offering a needed corrective to the culture of poverty, the schools were adopting approaches that prevented many low-income children from succeeding. He also was deeply bothered by the content of popular culture. Armbruster articulated a brief preview of the skills gap campaign, arguing that "in our growing service-industry oriented economy, the gap between types of available jobs is great and is directly related to education" (Ibid., 132). But his educational standard for employability in the new labor market was relatively low, depending on simple literacy and the ability to do "basic math problems" (Ibid.). A major theme of Armbruster's was the promulgation of the view that students' educational achievement was entirely divorced from their socioeconomic background, which became a foundational assumption of the education reform movement. He was therefore intolerant of educators' claims that the "causes of the problems, which educators cannot possibly compensate for, lie outside the school: the home, the parents, the environment, television, anything but the educators" (Ibid., 193). In the end, Armbruster advocated for accountability measures based on standardized testing results and strongly opposed those who questioned the supremacy of quantitative data by suggesting "that the youngsters have gained so many 'unmeasurable' but much more valuable benefits from school" (Ibid.). If test scores were seen as inadequate, teachers, administrators, and district budgets should face tangible consequences.

But when *A Nation at Risk* (*ANAR*) was published in 1983, the emerging education reform movement was not yet fully committed either to Armbruster's formulation linking students' educational achievement solely to the activities of schools or to the high-education, high-skill labor market of the fantasy economy. The report included a carefully worded acknowledgment of the many external forces impeding the educational performance of low-income students: "That we have compromised this commitment is, upon reflection, hardly surprising, given the multitude of often conflicting demands we have placed on our Nation's schools and colleges. They are routinely called on to provide solutions to personal, social, and political problems that the home and other institutions either will not or cannot resolve. We must understand that these demands on our schools and colleges often exact an educational cost as well as a financial one" (National Commission on Excellence in Education 1983, 6). And although *ANAR* suggested that the decline of manufacturing was related to what the report saw as the decline of schools, it also implied some skepticism about the high-education, technology-based labor market that would become boilerplate among education reformers just a few years later: "Learning is the indispensable investment required for success in the 'information age' we are entering" (Ibid., 7).

Such equivocations, however, would not enable the exclusive emphasis on education's role in providing economic opportunity or the sweeping education policies reformers sought, including testing and accountability. As a result, elites began to hone a message implicitly drawing on Armbruster's work that focused exclusively on the schools' role in creating economic opportunity in a high-technology, high-education labor market, and quantitative data became an increasingly important part of this campaign. Signs of this approach were evident in a 1988 report by California's Achievement Council, *Unfinished Business: Fulfilling Our Children's Promise*, by Kati Haycock and Susana Navarro. The authors acknowledged the financial support of the ARCO Foundation for the report as well as for general support for the Achievement Council, which was created in 1983. The report also acknowledged numerous other "major contributors to the Achievement Council," including the William and Flora Hewlett Foundation, Ahmanson Foundation, San Francisco Foundation, Irvine Foundation, David and Lucille Packard Foundation, Stuart Foundation, Joseph Drown Foundation, Wells Fargo Foundation, and Ralph Parsons Foundation, as well as AT&T and the California Casualty Insurance Group (Haycock and Navarro 1988).

Published when deindustrialization and the loss of middle-class jobs were front-page news as well as the subject of a growing body of influential scholarship (Wilson 1987), *Unfinished Business* included a significant amount of data and made the case for holding schools accountable not only for students' academic performance but also for their future economic opportunities, a framing that, I argue, necessarily depended on the emerging skills gap narrative. Haycock and Navarro directly addressed growing inequality under the heading "Widening Gap between Rich and Poor" and even quoted a state report that concluded that 60 percent of California's families "have either barely regained their 1977 status after suffering a loss of prosperity or have lost ground steadily" (Haycock and Navarro 1988, 7, 8). But the authors assumed that the distribution of jobs as well as wage rates was inevitable, stating that the "number of living-wage blue collar jobs in this State has fallen dramatically and will continue to decline. Those jobs that remain have neither wages nor benefits sufficient to support an individual, let alone a family" (Ibid., 4). Growing inequality was linked exclusively to education, and according to Haycock and Navarro, without significant increases in higher education attainment, especially among racial minorities, "many jobs requiring college education will go begging, and many California employers may have to consider moving out of the state. . . . At the same time, many of the young people who could fill those professional level jobs will themselves go begging" (Ibid.).

Significantly, Haycock and Navarro also dropped the blunt racism of appeals rooted in the culture of poverty. Rather, seemingly influenced by the arguments of scholars such as William Julius Wilson in *The Truly Disadvantaged* (1987), they affirmed that the "effects of this kind of poverty can crush the spirit and blot out any hope of escape" and that many residents of poor neighborhoods "become overwhelmed by a pervasive sense of hopelessness" (Haycock and Navarro 1988, 22). At the same time, however, they tried to evoke white fears, warning that "our society will become increasingly divided, with a well-educated minority, composed primarily of Whites and Asians, dominating the upper tiers, while a poorly educated majority, composed primarily of Latinos and Blacks, remains at the bottom" (Ibid., ii). For Haycock and Navarro, California "seems headed down a deadly path. Not, perhaps, by deliberate choice, as much as by the absence of long-range policy making. Each year, we will spend more and more on the consequences of our failure to educate young people. More corrections and probation costs. More police and welfare costs. More indigent health care and low-income housing subsidies. . . . All of these will place ever greater demands on the economic system, which will itself be seriously weakened by the dearth of well-educated workers. And the more we spend on the consequences, the less we will have left for schools, creating a vicious cycle of failure" (Ibid., 4, 5). Yet I argue that this fear-based approach had limited political support and, like the cultural commentary of earlier reformers, would eventually also be de-emphasized to advance school accountability.

"Deep Concern for How Well Economically Disadvantaged Children Were Faring in the Public Schools"

By the time the George H. W. Bush administration took office in 1989, reformers had begun to sharpen their messaging for educational accountability, which stressed expanding opportunities for the poor within a high-education, technologically sophisticated labor market. Corporate elites mobilized, and the Business Roundtable published *Essential Components of a Successful Education System*, which declared that "our nation's public kindergarten through 12th grade education system is in crisis—over one-fifth of our students fail to graduate from high school and those who do often lack the skills to succeed" (Business Roundtable 1989, 3). Schools should receive "rewards for success, assistance to improve and penalties for failure," but the group of executives also maintained that "health and other social services are sufficient to reduce significant barriers to learning" (Ibid., 7, 8). Presumably, then, existing social welfare policies were sufficient to enable the education system to overcome the obstacles posed by economic hardship. At the same time, President Bush sought to create a "kinder, gentler" America while declaring himself the Education President, and the skills gap theme became omnipresent, effectively replacing the culture of poverty in elite discourse regarding economic opportunity. Bush emphasized the need to overhaul the entire education system and in September 1989 called an Education Summit of the nation's governors, which included closed-door sessions on both K–12 and higher education.

The *New York Times'* front-page article on the skills gap published two days before the Bush Education Summit vividly captured the new business-driven messaging. While several CEOs said their firms could not find enough qualified workers, a clear theme of the piece was elite concern for the plight of the disadvantaged. Therefore, the political target was the school system, not the poor or uneducated. The Institute on Education and the Economy's Sue Berryman said that the "well educated face a future of expanding job opportunities and rising wages . . . while those not well educated face a future of contracting opportunities and poverty" (Fiske 1989b). She further maintained that "our least advantaged students are now drowning in 10 feet of water instead of 15 feet of water, but they're still drowning. . . . Lots more are drowning in five feet" (Ibid.). Berryman's politically sophisticated framing clearly implied that it was the education system's job not only to overcome the effects of poverty but to provide a decent income for all.

By 1990, the country continued to lose industrial jobs, and education reformers stepped up their campaign in Washington for school accountability. However, the campaign needed the appearance of a diverse coalition to reach enough Democrats and Republicans in Congress for passage. In 1990, the Achievement Council's Kati Haycock moved to the Children's Defense Fund (CDF). Established in 1973, the CDF focused on a variety of issues affecting children's well-being, including family income and employment, childcare, health, youth development, housing and homelessness, and vulnerable children and families, as well as education (Children's Defense Fund 1991). In a 1990 interview, Haycock identified her two main goals for the organization. She sought to "bring more cohesion to the CFS's [sic] planning process" and "to put education way up on the CDF's agenda" (Stevens 1990). Haycock wanted the CDF to "move from an agenda that's about preventing damage to kids—keeping them safe and healthy—to an agenda that produces achievement" (Ibid.). In the interview, she elaborated on the rationale for a focus on education: "Our future competitiveness rests absolutely on our ability to make [low-income minority] kids capable of being as productive as everybody else" (Ibid.). More specifically, Haycock affirmed: "We need an accountability system. There have to be clear rewards and penalties. We need to identify schools that are much further away than others from achieving and provide them with a lot of help. And we need to give teachers ongoing support" (Ibid.). She also stated that her interest in the plight of racial minorities stemmed, in part, from her own ethnic background: "Part of it was also my own heritage: my maternal grandmother is Mexican-American. So I grew up with a sort of bi-cultural existence. Although I do not look Hispanic and do not claim to be Hispanic in any formal way, at school [I noticed] discrimination against those who looked and acted Mexican-American and I kept wondering, why do people treat them like this? Why not me? Because I don't look Mexican-American?" (Ibid.).

Yet the Children's Defense Fund remained focused on a variety of public policy issues, and Haycock's stay there was short lived.

Also in 1990, the AAHE took a major step toward advancing school accountability through the creation of a "special project to encourage colleges and universities to support K–12 reform efforts" (Education Trust 1997a), which was aided by a $1.5 million grant from the Pew Charitable Trusts (Pitsch 1991). Originating in the wealth created by the Sun Oil Company, Pew was founded in Philadelphia in 1948 and had a history of funding right-wing organizations within a culture of secrecy (Rottenberg 1991; Williams 1991). For example, in the 1940s, company vice president Joseph N. Pew contributed $3,000 to help establish the isolationist newsletter *Human Events* (S. Diamond 1995, 24). In the 1950s, J. Howard Pew was a trustee of the Foundation for Economic Education, a libertarian organization founded in 1946 (Ibid., 27–28). In 1950, the latter Pew also provided $50,000 to the Christian Freedom Foundation to launch *Christian Economics*, a free weekly publication sent to more than 175,000 Protestant clergy across the country (Ibid., 98–99). By the 1960s, J. Howard Pew was also a leading sponsor of anti-communist broadcasts that included themes such as "opposition to foreign aid, the United Nations, the Supreme Court, labor unions, medicare, and 'forced integration'" (Ibid., 52). According to the *New York Times*, J. Howard Pew was also a "friend of Robert Welch, the John Birch Society's founder," and, "while he denied membership in the society, he is listed as having served on the editorial advisory board of the Society's publication, American Opinion, and was a stockholder of Robert Welch, Inc., the society's publishing arm. He supported right-wing causes, and entertained Billy Graham and Barry Goldwater" (D. Diamond 1981). As late as 1979, Pew insisted its "grantees not reveal the source of their funding" (Williams 1991, 20), was not listed in telephone books until 1980, and did not publish a complete annual report until 1986 (Rottenberg 1991, 138).

In the early 1990s, however, Pew promoted a new, more progressive public image. *Foundation News* stated that Pew had "eliminated almost all of their right-wing grantmaking" and hired an "activist, socially liberal executive director and top program staff" (Williams 1991, 20), while *Town and Country* noted that the organization had hired a "Sixties-liberal former nurse" as executive director (Rottenberg 1991, 138). The *Town and Country* article argued that the new Pew organization had "clearly rejected at least one tenet of the old Pew family faith: distrust of government," and cited its partnership with the Philadelphia public schools and other public agencies as evidence of this shift in orientation (Ibid., 219).

In the same article, however, Andy Pew affirmed: "If Uncle Joe and Uncle Howard were sitting here today . . . they'd approve of the direction we've taken" (Ibid.). I suggest that by emphasizing education reform in high-poverty schools, Pew was implicitly endorsing the free markets of neoliberalism, which viewed market-based solutions to education as necessary and, more significantly, assigned the creation of economic opportunity solely to the education system.

Beginning in 1990, Pew's newly appointed program director for education, Robert Schwartz, initiated several major projects with Pew's support, including the NCEE's National Alliance for Restructuring Education; the University of Pittsburgh's Learning Research and Development Center's New Standards; Jobs for the Future's National Youth Apprenticeship Initiative; the AAHE's Community Compacts for Student Success; the Pew Network for Standards-Based Reform at the Education Development Center; the Compact for Faculty Diversity at WICHE; and Preparing Future Faculty at the American Association of Colleges and Universities (Schwartz 2011, 1). In 1989, Pew had also funded the Philadelphia Schools Collaborative with an initial grant of $8.3 million (the 2022 equivalent of roughly $20 million) to restructure twenty-two of the city's comprehensive high schools (Rottenberg 1991, 138). Along with the Business Roundtable, Pew had become a significant force in the education reform movement.

In 1990 Kati Haycock also became a key player in the newly created Commission on Chapter 1. The privately created commission, which had no official status, consisted of twenty-eight "educators, child advocates, researchers, and other concerned individuals," all of whom shared a "deep concern for how well economically disadvantaged children were faring in the public schools and how well they were being served by Chapter 1 of the Elementary and Secondary Education Act of 1965, the largest program of federal assistance to the schools" (Commission on Chapter 1 1992a, v). The commission explicitly relied on the Business Roundtable's *Essential Components of a Successful Education System* to "help structure" its work (Rhodes 2012, 108). By this time, the roundtable's larger agenda revolved around the "constant maximization of shareholder returns" (J. Hacker and Pierson 2016, 179). A footnote in the commission's final report stated that the group was an "independent body not affiliated with any other organization" while acknowledging the financial support of two organizations, the Edna McConnell Clark and John D. and Catherine T. MacArthur Foundations (Commission on Chapter 1 1992a, v). Commission chair and Steering Committee member was David Hornbeck, codirector of the National Alliance for Restructuring Education and senior policy adviser for the Business Roundtable (Ibid., ii). Other commission members included the AAHE's Haycock (also on the Steering Committee), as well as individuals from numerous education reform organizations, such as the NCEE's Marc Tucker, William Kolberg from the National Alliance of Business, and Susana Navarro, formerly of the Achievement Council, among several others. The commission's attorneys were William L. Taylor and Dianne Piche' (Ibid., ii–iii).

While Jesse Rhodes labels Hornbeck a civil rights entrepreneur (Rhodes 2012, 78), his background shows an individual allied with the education reform movement led by corporate elites and foundations. After serving as Maryland's state superintendent of education, he had numerous positions, including as president of the Council of Chief State School Officers; as a member on the boards of *Education Week* and the National Center on Education and the Economy; and as chairman of the board of the Carnegie Foundation for the Advancement of Teaching (Hornbeck and Salamon 1991, x; *Maryland Manual On-Line*, n.d.). His 1991 coedited book *Human Capital and America's Future* was funded by the Ford, Carnegie, and William T. Grant Foundations (Hornbeck and Salamon 1991, vii) and included chapters by *Workforce 2000*'s coauthor Arnold H. Packer as well as a chapter coauthored by Anthony Carnevale. In the book's final chapter, Hornbeck repeated many familiar business claims about the increasing complexity of the labor market and, regarding the education system, affirmed that "unprecedented and profound change is necessary" (Ibid., 363).

By 1992, Haycock had become the director of the AAHE's schools-college collaboration, and the Commission on Chapter 1 published Interim and Final Reports. The Interim Report acknowledged in a footnote that commission member Bella Rosenberg of American Federation of Teachers disagreed with "several analyses and recommendations" (Commission on Chapter 1 1992b, 4). In the Final Report, the authors attributed lower academic achievement among minority and low-income children to the schools. Because one of the main audiences of the education reform movement has been educators themselves, however, the commission also argued that "while thousands of dedicated Chapter 1 professionals and paraprofessionals were providing extra services to students who needed help mastering the basics, the rules of the game changed" (Commission on Chapter 1 1992a, 4). The report then advanced the skills gap narrative: "Basic skills no longer count for as much as they once did. To find a secure place in the increasingly competitive and technological international economy, young people must be able to think, to analyze, and to communicate complex ideas" (Ibid.). The commission stated that while government would "invest heavily" in school staff, it would also hold them "accountable for results" (Ibid., 7).

The new schools-college collaboration at the AAHE was the driving force behind the Commission on Chapter 1, "provided a home and staff support for the commission during a second, 'public education' phase of its work," and distributed more than thirty thousand copies of its final report (Haycock and Hornbeck 1995, 81). The report received major press coverage and was reprinted in full in *Education Week*, the *AAHE Bulletin*, and *Basic Education* (Ibid.). In the March 1993 *AAHE Bulletin*, Haycock discussed the work of the "independent commission" and suggested ways AAHE members could act on the ideas of the report, including communicating directly with their members of Congress as well as with Senator Ted Kennedy and Representative Bill Ford or hosting a "community-wide meeting" (Haycock 1993, 7). David Hornbeck went on to be superintendent of the Philadelphia School District in 1994, charged with administering the Pew grant to restructure district high schools. In a book chapter he coauthored with Haycock one year later, the two implicitly suggested that the commission's role was to set the policy agenda: "The point was to get people thinking and talking about the education of poor children" (Haycock and Hornbeck 1995, 81), and by this measure, the commission clearly succeeded.

"We Can't Go at the Public through C-SPAN"

Despite these efforts, there was little evidence that public support for concrete accountability policies based on testing was increasing, a problem that reformers were keenly aware of. As a result, in 1993, with support from the John D. and Catherine T. MacArthur Foundation (Walsh 1993), *Education Week* ran a special series entitled "From Risk to Renewal," which included a roundtable of "11 of the nation's leading education reformers" (*Education Week* 1993b). All participants "agreed in principle that America's schools must be changed in substantial ways and that incremental change will not suffice" but "diverged on the specifics of how to best accomplish that transformation" (Ibid.). The group included Hornbeck; Christopher T. Cross, also from the Business Roundtable as well as a former official in the George H. W. Bush administration; Haycock; Patricia Graham, president of the Spencer Foundation and professor of history of American education and former dean of the Graduate School of Education at Harvard; Richard P. Mills, Vermont education commissioner and chairman of the Coordinating Council for the National Alliance for Restructuring Education; Governor Roy Romer of Colorado;

Robert F. Sexton, executive director of Kentucky's Pritchard Committee for Academic Excellence; and several other education professors and administrators (Ibid.).

The roundtable provides a rare glimpse into the thinking that informed the political strategy used in the campaign for school accountability. Haycock maintained that the group was "pretty close to agreement on policy issues, and now we need to begin to figure out the very much more complicated task of getting thousands of communities across the country to take ownership of these ideas" (*Education Week* 1993a). Hornbeck pointed out that a "major barrier to getting systemic reform" was public opinion. Polling showed that the public was not satisfied with the education system overall but had favorable views of their own schools (Ibid.). Kentucky's Sexton pointed out that surveys from his state showed that local decision-making and "'accountability,' as the polling firms phrased it," were the most popular elements of school reform, whereas the least popular was assessment and testing (Ibid.). This presented a significant problem since the accountability framework established by business interests was built on standardized testing. Yet as Mills insightfully observed, "We have real communication skills in this country, through advertising and through political campaigns. We can't go at the public through C-SPAN. The general public doesn't watch C-SPAN" (Ibid.). Haycock stressed that "change will occur only when there's both a policy structure that encourages it and permits it, and when individual educators, parents, and others see the change as theirs" (Ibid.), indicating that the campaign should be substantially directed at the education establishment. She offered insight as to how to change public opinion on such a grand scale, saying, "That only occurs around small tables, and the process of creating ownership ought to get at least as much attention from strategists as the process of creating a rational policy structure" (Ibid.). Thus, the group agreed that a more compelling message and broad-based public relations campaign was required to increase support for what the unnamed *Education Week* participant identified as the "genuinely radical change that is being called for" (Ibid.).

The Business Roundtable's Cross said his organization had created an advertising campaign that was "being sent to every T.V. and radio station and newspaper in the country. The objective is to raise public awareness about the need for change in education" (*Education Week* 1993a). Hornbeck even suggested that reformers consider hiring Democratic political strategist James Carville and argued that the group should approach "this communication problem the way serious Presidential candidates approach winning an election, we would do it both on the street and on the airwaves simultaneously" (Ibid.). However, the Spencer Foundation's Graham suggested that elites would impose testing and accountability even in the absence of public support: "We are trying to get people to make a very unpleasant, to many, transition from something that's been pleasant to something that will be good for them and that they will learn to love" (Ibid.). And by comparing school accountability to the anti-smoking campaign that ultimately changed the habits of the middle class and affluent but not those with lower income, Graham also maintained that "this time we can't ignore the poor" (Ibid.). Reformers, then, had to at least attempt to sell school accountability to the disadvantaged.

Another article in *Education Week*'s series on reform profiled the Business Roundtable's efforts in Flint, Michigan, the subject of Michael Moore's documentary *Roger and Me* (Walsh 1993). While the emerging narrative of the skills gap campaign linked manufacturing-job loss to the education system, the Flint article quoted John Austen, the executive director of the Flint Roundtable, who stated that the public was "way behind" and had "an outdated set of perceptions about the global economy" (Ibid.), implicitly suggesting other possible reasons for the region's economic problems. In a lengthy article, *Education Week*'s Mark Walsh made a limited attempt at probing the dominant narrative linking the loss of industrial jobs with the education system by quoting one union worker, described as an "activist," who wondered: "'If they've got problems with the way the American workforce is educated, then why are the industries looking to move to Mexico? . . . I can't believe the people there are better educated. That's cheaper labor, though'" (Ibid.). Walsh did not pursue this line of reasoning with any of the elites interviewed, however.

The Flint article in *Education Week* also included a discussion about the public relations campaign that business groups were engaged in to push educational accountability. Specifically, the article mentioned the Business Roundtable's "Keep the Promise" campaign built on the theme that "the nation has promised each child a future, and schools must improve to follow through on that obligation" (Walsh 1993). An executive from Young and Rubicam, the advertising agency hired to create the campaign, "concluded it would be very hard to get the majority of Americans to care about education reform. . . . But it would not be hard to get them to care about children. We had to humanize the issue" (Ibid.). Thus, the first television advertisement in the "Keep the Promise" campaign focused on Baby Jessica, the infant who was rescued from a well in Texas in 1987, in which the narrator stated: "No country comes to the aid of a child the way we do. . . . Imagine if the same effort that went into saving that little child in Texas went into keeping the promise that every child in America gets the best education" (Ibid.).

Still, the political difficulties associated with the educational accountability policy sought by elites were on display during President Clinton's first term. In 1994, two pieces of education legislation passed—*Goals 2000* and the *Improving America's Schools Act*, which included the reauthorization of Title I education funding. But under the reauthorization, states were given the "freedom to design their own standards, assessments, and accountability systems" (McGuinn 2006, 98). Passing accountability policies through the implementation of federal education funding remained a major challenge.

Race, Data, and the Emergence of Education Trust

Since the late 1960s, elites had prioritized the linkage of higher education and K–12 reform efforts, and in 1996 the AAHE's project on school-college collaboration was officially incorporated as the nonprofit Education Trust (Education Trust 1996a), led by Kati Haycock. While Education Trust became known for its efforts to promote K–12 reform, it also maintained that "higher education is in at least as much need of improvement as is K–12" (Education Trust 1997a). The group's original policy agenda consisted of several items, including establishing high standards for all students, kindergarten through college; replacing "watered-down instruction" with "rigorous and challenging classes for all students"; preparing all teachers and higher education faculty to teach to high standards; shifting most decision-making away from "central school district bureaucracies to principals, teachers, and parents at the school building level"; and giving more authority for improving student outcomes in higher education to "department or cross-disciplinary faculty teams" (Ibid.). Education Trust was also created to advance educational accountability, including the implementation of standards that were linked to "consequences for teachers, schools and students" (Ibid.). Further, Education Trust argued that "effort and accomplishment must be recognized and rewarded; extra help must be provided to those who need it; and change must be assured in schools that resist improvement" (Ibid.).

But because it was a political organization advancing school accountability and targeting high-poverty schools, the demographic composition of Education Trust's leadership mattered. AAHE president Russ Edgerton had hired Haycock to lead the schools-college collaboration in the early 1990s, and in 1998 he recalled that he didn't "know where her [Haycock's] deep commitment to minority access and equity comes from . . . but it's down to her toes" (Chenoweth 1998, 16). Author Karin Chenoweth referred to Haycock as "one of four daughters born to a Mexican immigrant father who was a cottage cheese truck driver and an Anglo, stay at home mother" (Ibid.). According to Chenoweth, by "genetic quirk, she inherited her blue eyes and blond hair from her mother's side of the family" (Ibid.). This was a different account of Haycock's ethnic background than the one Haycock provided in the 1990 interview when she was at the Achievement Council (Stevens 1990). Chenoweth went to work for Education Trust in 2004 (Chenoweth, n.d.) and subsequently authored several books on education reform.

In recent decades, Education Trust has typically been characterized as a progressive, truth-telling advocacy group. Journalist Dana Goldstein argued that Education Trust was a "totally new kind of progressive advocacy group, one that unapologetically used test scores—long considered suspicious on the Left—to argue that education, especially better teachers, could effectively fight poverty" (Goldstein 2014, 183). Political scientist Patrick McGuinn has called Education Trust a "minority advocacy" group (2006, 171) and an "anti-poverty" group (2013, 232). And while the political scientist Rhodes concedes that Education Trust represented one segment of the civil rights community, he identifies Haycock and the group as "civil rights entrepreneurs" (2012, 18). However, Rhodes also quotes a Heritage Foundation official who claimed that "many educational conservatives 'thought the Education Trust was great' due to its unwavering emphasis on accountability for results" (Ibid., 141). In 2022, Education Trust described itself as follows: "Fierce advocates for the high academic achievement of all students—particularly those of color or living in poverty"—and affirmed it is "Equity-Driven," "Data-Centered," and "Student-Focused" (Education Trust 2022a).

Education Trust did not acknowledge any funders in one of its first major publications, *Education Watch*, which was released in 1996. And according to the Education Department's Education Resources Information Center (ERIC), the copyright holder (Education Trust) "did not provide funding statements or indication that there is a sponsoring agency" (Education Resources Information Center 2021). The lengthy report had no discussion of the group's origins, stating only that it was "created to promote high academic achievement for all students, at all levels, kindergarten through college. While we know that all schools and colleges could better serve their students, our work focuses on the schools and colleges most often left behind in efforts to improve education: those serving low-income, Latino and African American students" (Education Trust 1996b). In March 1997, the group's website identified external funders for programs administered by Education Trust, including Pew Charitable Trusts, the U.S. Department of Education, and the Dewitt Wallace Reader's Digest Foundation (Education Trust 1997a). The 1998 profile by Chenoweth identified the Ford, Knight, and Annie E. Casey Foundations and the Carnegie Corporation as early funders. But the piece also stated that Pew "provided The Education Trust with most of its money in the early years and continues to support it," and also mentioned a $3.5 million grant from the DeWitt Wallace Readers Fund (Chenoweth 1998, 17). Rhodes stated that the group's beginnings can be traced to securing "stable funding from philanthropies such as the Ford Foundation, the Carnegie Corporation, and the Hewlett Foundation" (2012, 141). Numerous other organizations were acknowledged as funders in the group's early publications, and by 2022, the organization listed several dozen individual funders, including many of the most influential foundations active in education reform (Education Trust 2022b).

In January 1997, Russell Edgerton left the AAHE "to join the Pew Charitable Trusts" (*Chronicle of Higher Education* 1997). But the name Russ Edgerton appears on Education Trust's 990 tax forms from 1999 through 2004 as one of the organization's five highest-paid employees other than officers, directors, and trustees, and several of these years he is identified as "Forum Director" (Education Trust 1999, 2000, 2001, 2002, 2003a, 2004). Pew's education director, Robert Schwartz, was also a board member for Education Trust from 1997 through 2013 (Ibid. 1997b, 1998a, 1999, 2000, 2001, 2002, 2003a, 2004, 2005, 2006, 2007, 2008, 2009, 2010, 2011, 2012, 2013). In addition, Schwartz was the founding president of Achieve, a nonprofit created in 1997 by the "nation's Governors and corporate leaders to provide advice and assistance to states on standards, assessments, and accountability issues, and public advocacy for education reform" (Schwartz 2011, 1). Tax records show that Pew and six corporations were the only contributors of $5,000 or more to Achieve in 1998, with Pew pledging $450,000 (Achieve 1998).[1] Clearly, Pew was a driving force of the campaign for school accountability.

I argue that no organization has been more responsible for advancing the political power of the concept of data than Education Trust. The 1998 profile emphasized that Haycock had to "convince people—particularly people in the school systems—of how serious and dire the situation is. Her instruments of persuasion and change are data, data, and more data" (Chenoweth 1998, 14). And its regular publication, *Education Watch*, "served as the basis of Haycock's 'data shows'" (Ibid.). These reports were mainly collections of official data on education and the economy supplemented by some secondary literature. But the framing of the necessity of major education reform in the inaugural edition of *Education Watch* made whatever data followed of secondary importance:

> Education matters. To the nation, it means having the human capital to keep our economy vibrant and competitive, and a citizenry equipped to participate responsibly in the democratic process. Education also matters to the individual. More education converts into more personal income, greater employability and less dependency. For many Americans, education offers a weapon against poverty and the effects of racism.
>
> Education matters to a greater extent now than at any time in our history. The world is entering a technological age that could well exceed the impact of the Industrial Revolution. Knowledge in some fields is doubling almost every year, while our capacity to disseminate new information expands exponentially. Success in this new age is awarded to individuals who have enough knowledge to negotiate the information explosion and the skills necessary to adapt well to constant change. (Education Trust 1996b, 3)

In addition, the report advanced perhaps the most urgent and comprehensive articulation of the skills gap narrative ever to appear in a major publication:

> In today's market, it takes more than a general high-school education to provide an individual with a reasonable amount of economic security. The factory job that in the last half century raised the blue collar worker into middle class prosperity has been redefined as a high-skilled occupation. The Big Three motor companies—once the symbol for offering relatively high pay for low skills—now want entry-level workers who show competency with algebra, geometry, and computers in addition to the ability to solve problems and think creatively and independently.
>
> The need for high-skilled workers has put an unprecedented premium on a college education. Today's college graduate can expect to earn *twice* the wages of a high-school graduate and nearly *triple* those of high-school drop out. College-educated workers are also more able to hold a job that supports a family; not only are their earnings higher, their chance of being unemployed is half that of a high-school drop out. And what students learn really mat-

ters: among individuals with the same level of educational attainment, those with more highly developed skills earn significantly more. (Ibid., emphasis in original)

Finally, *Education Watch* framed the importance of major education reform in terms beyond those of previous reports such as *A Nation at Risk*:

> More than economic security alone is at stake. The continuation of a civil and democratic society is becoming a greater challenge as the issues we face as voters grow more complex and our concerns more diverse. The shrinking world is more than just a metaphor, for we daily conduct business with people and cultures from across the globe by means of high-speed travel and electronic communications, as well as face to face in our neighborhoods. Society needs an informed populace prepared to handle the ambiguity of modern life, to accept differences among us, and to seek out solutions to our common problems. (Ibid.)

Contrasted with much of the rhetoric of Columbia's Institute on Education and the Economy, the language in *Education Watch* was created to be noticed. In fact, versions of these claims are still commonplace today in business interest groups' accounts of the educational requirements of the labor market. Technological advances created an information explosion that was making the workplace continually more complex. Despite such rapid change, American workers were simply not keeping up, and, presumably, auto workers' lack of knowledge in advanced math and computers and their inability to solve problems or work independently and creatively were the reasons for the loss of domestic manufacturing jobs. While references to insufficient knowledge of algebra and geometry would eventually be largely abandoned by reformers, in 1996, such claims were new and met with little skepticism by the mainstream.

Yet in political terms, the reference to racism and reliance on data were the most important components of *Education Watch*. Earlier reformers rooted in the culture of poverty had minimized or denied racism and often invoked coded racist appeals in the larger discussion of economic opportunity. Thus, ET's assertion that "for many Americans, education offers a weapon against poverty and the effects of racism" was a distinctly different approach for education reformers and helped solidify the organization's progressive reputation. The report also had extensive official data for the nation and all fifty states. However, unlike previous reports by reformers, it contained no extended discussion of wage stagnation and growing inequality. Rather, *Education Watch* included numerous figures that, predictably, showed the association between greater education levels and higher income. The overall message of *Education Watch* was a simple one: economic stability and mobility depended solely on one's ability to obtain post–high school education, and the report stressed the importance of obtaining a college degree. Because the K–12 education system was the primary barrier impeding the economic opportunities afforded to disadvantaged students, then, accountability policies were necessary. In sum, the description of the educational and skill levels required by the labor market combined with the mere acknowledgment of *any* racism within the context of dozens of pages of data made Education Trust a powerful force in the school accountability movement.

After the publication of *Education Watch* in 1996, Education Trust further distanced itself from the culture-of-poverty thesis that focused on the behavior of the poor themselves and emphasized the new framing of these issues by holding schools responsible for the academic achievement of lower-income students and, in turn, for their future economic opportunity. At a press conference on December 3, 1998, Haycock maintained that "despite mythology to the contrary, it is neither poverty nor single-parent homes nor a lack of 'cultural sensitivity' that causes the low achievement that has gripped these communities for so long, but horribly prepared teachers, pathetically low level curriculum, and no standards" (Education Trust 1998b). The ultimate rationale for education reform was the purportedly high-education, high-skill labor market. Haycock asserted that providing a challenging curriculum for only some students "may have made sense in an industrial era" but no longer made sense "when almost all of our young people need postsecondary education" (Ibid.). A gifted political actor, Haycock ratcheted up the pressure for accountability that same year by provocatively claiming that the "polls among Black folk around vouchers versus public education are an indication that you cannot continue screwing a whole bunch of people and have them not catch you at it and decide the game is so rigged that they may not continue to play" (Chenoweth 1998, 14).

Another organization that played a key role in creating the impression of a racially and ideologically diverse coalition behind school accountability was the Citizens Commission on Civil Rights (CCCR), which scholars have labeled a "minority advocacy" group (McGuinn 2006, 171) and a "civil rights" organization (Rhodes 2012, 18). The CCCR was established in 1982, and according to its articles of incorporation, it was created, in part, "to act as an independent, bipartisan organization to educate the public and promote public awareness of federal civil rights policies" and to "advocate new policies so the nation can move forward and deal constructively with the vast amount of unfinished business on the civil rights agenda" (Citizens Commission on Civil Rights 1982, 1–2). Toward this end, during the 1980s and 1990s, the CCCR published edited volumes with chapters by law professors and lawyers addressing multiple civil rights issues, such as housing, affirmative action, K–12 and higher education, criminal justice, voting rights, and social welfare, and the Ford Foundation was acknowledged as a funder of these reports.

In 1999, however, the CCCR published two different types of reports focusing only on education, the first of which was entitled *Title I in Midstream: The Fight to Improve Schools for Poor Kids*. *Education Week* covered the report in a story entitled "Civil Rights Group Decries Implementation of Title 1" (Robelen 1999). *Title I in Midstream* focused entirely on school accountability and provided an extended articulation of the rationale outlined in the Commission on Chapter 1's 1992 report. *Title I in Midstream* acknowledged funding from the same two foundations who funded the Commission on Chapter 1—Edna McConnell Clark and John D. and Catherine T. MacArthur—as well as the Spencer and Annenberg Foundations (Yu and Taylor 1999a, 5). Three individuals involved in the Commission on Chapter 1—all of whom Rhodes labels as "civil rights entrepreneurs" (Rhodes 2012, 140)—were also instrumental in creating *Title I in Midstream*. Diane Piche' was listed as project director, Phyllis P. McClure provided assistance, and William L. Taylor was a coeditor of the report (Yu and Taylor 1999a, 3). The same year, the CCCR also published *Title I in Alabama: The Struggle to Meet Basic Needs*, with the same three individuals in the same roles as well as the same four acknowledged funders (Yu and Taylor 1999b, 5). While not acknowledged as a funder of these reports, the Ford Foundation was the only acknowledged funder of another 1999 CCCR volume that followed the pattern established in the organization's previous reports by addressing several different policy areas (Yu and Taylor 1999c, 5). Ultimately, *Title I in Midstream* and *Title I in Alabama* contributed to the critical political task of creating the appearance of a diverse coalition behind the foundation- and corporate-driven accountability movement.

Compassionate Conservativism and the Texas Miracle That Wasn't

In 2000, Texas governor George W. Bush, the son of President George H. W. Bush, became the Republican candidate for president. While his father declared himself the Education President, the younger Bush affirmed he was a compassionate conservative, and education reform was a major issue in his 2000 presidential campaign, in which he stressed school accountability. In a speech to the Latin Business Association in September 1999, Governor Bush discussed the school system's role in discrimination against minority students: "Now some say it is unfair to hold disadvantaged children to rigorous standards. I say it is discrimination to require anything less—the soft bigotry of low expectations. . . . It is a scandal of the first order when the average test scores of African-American and Latino students at age 17 are roughly the same as white 13-year-old's. Whatever the cause, the effect is discrimination" (*New York Times* 1999). In a speech to the NAACP in July 2000, Bush made a similar argument, again invoking one of the most effective rhetorical weapons in the campaign for accountability: "And I will confront another form of bias: the soft bigotry of low expectations" (*Washington Post* 2000). Bush went on to advocate for a testing and accountability system and assert that "the role of education is to leave no child behind" (Ibid.).

During the campaign, Bush also frequently discussed what became known as the "Texas Miracle" in education, involving the significant improvement of the academic achievement of the state's racial minorities since the introduction of a high-stakes testing and accountability system in the early 1990s. The City of Houston was often singled out as an example of a large urban district that turned around its high-poverty, low-performing schools, and former Houston superintendent Rod Paige was appointed as President Bush's first secretary of education. The Texas Miracle was built on quantitative data, but a close examination of the data significantly undermined the miracle story. As the social psychologist Donald T. Campbell posited several decades ago, the *"more any quantitative social indicator is used for social decision-making, the more subject it will be to corruption pressures and the more apt it will be to distort and corrupt the social processes it is intended to monitor"* (Campbell 1979, 85, emphasis in original). When high stakes are attached solely to quantitative metrics, incentives to game the system are essentially built in, and the purported Texas Miracle appears to have been a function of these perverse incentives.

The most comprehensive empirical examination of the Texas Miracle was provided by Walt Haney, professor of education at Boston College and senior research associate at the college's Center for the Study of Testing Evaluation and Educational Policy, in a lengthy peer-reviewed study published in 2000 (Haney 2000). He acknowledged the financial support of his employer, Boston College, for providing him a sabbatical, and he stated flatly that "no corporations, foundations or anonymous donors have supported the research reported here" (Ibid.). Haney found numerous problems with claims of a Texas Miracle, including that the passing scores set by the state for the Texas Assessment of Academic Skills (TAAS) were "arbitrary, discriminatory and failed to take measurement error into account" (Ibid.). He further found that only 50 percent of minority students had been progressing from ninth grade to graduation since the implementation of the exam, and by the late 1990s, nearly 30 percent of Black and Hispanic students had to repeat ninth grade (Ibid.). Haney also found that "cumulative rates of grade retention in Texas are almost twice as high for Black and Hispanic students as for White students" (Ibid.). And Texas student performance on the NAEP during the 1990s further undermined any notion of a statewide Texas Miracle (Ibid.). Shortly after the Haney study, scholars from the Rand Corporation also found significant discrepancies between NAEP results for Texas students and state testing data during the 1990s in an analysis that contributed to more doubt about the miracle narrative (S. Klein et al. 2000).

But during the presidential campaign, the miracle myth largely persisted, and support for school accountability among key players in Washington grew. By this time, major business interests were advocating forcefully for high-stakes testing and an accountability policy implemented through federal education funding. The main organized interests questioning this approach were teachers' unions, but any critiques of accountability proposals were drowned out by the larger narrative of a high-education, high-skill labor market. Although educational attainment rates were at all-time highs and roughly one-third of bachelor's degree holders underemployed, education reformers had successfully framed the mainstream debate about inequality as a problem rooted in the schools. By the time of the 2000 election, the stories of plant closings, the offshoring of employment, the steady decline of organized labor, persistent wage stagnation, and the abundance of low-education, low-wage service-sector jobs were transformed into the fantasy economy narrative of failing schools and a chronically underqualified workforce in a high-education, high-skill economy. Bush lost the popular vote but won the White House because of the infamous *Bush v. Gore* Supreme Court ruling. While making some inroads with Hispanic voters because of several issues, Bush failed to make any progress among Blacks, receiving only 10 percent of the African American vote. Clearly the Black community did not see that the problems faced by high-poverty schools would be solved by school accountability policies.

National Tragedy Pushes Accountability over the Finish Line

Shortly after Bush took office, legislative proposals for school accountability took shape, and business interests engaged in a "massive lobbying blitz" (Rhodes 2012, 152) in Congress while continuing to publicly advance arguments in support of school accountability based on arguments rooted in free market principles and technological supremacy. For instance, the Business Coalition for Excellence on Education argued that "in a world of global competition and rapid technological advances, U.S. schools must prepare all students for the challenges of the 21st Century" (Ibid., 153). According to Rhodes, business leaders understood standards, testing, and accountability as "the ticket to renewed worker productivity and economic growth" (Ibid., 14). But these arguments had been advanced for decades and were contradicted by official data. Data from the BLS showed that total labor productivity and output had increased between the 1980s and 1990s (Sprague 2017). A long-term comparative analysis by the BLS also concluded that domestic manufacturing output grew at a faster rate than in several other regions of the world in the 1990s, and that U.S. output also grew at a faster rate in the 1990s than during the years before 1973 (Cobet and Wilson 2002, 60). Finally, real gross domestic product was also on a consistently upward trajectory throughout the 1990s. Thus, the argument about lagging productivity in the years leading up to No Child Left Behind was misleading at best. Yet despite increased growth and productivity, inflation-adjusted incomes for a substantial majority of the population remained mostly flat and income inequality continued to increase.

In March 2001, the CCCR published another report advocating school accountability entitled *Closing the Deal*, which acknowledged the funding of the John D. and Catherine T. MacArthur, Spencer, and Ford Foundations (Citizens Commission on Civil Rights 2001, 1), signaling Ford's public endorsement of the school accountability agenda. By this time, the CCCR's visible role in the Washington debate helped solidify the perception that accountability was supported by a diverse coalition. The conservative Thomas B. Fordham Institute even affirmed that the report was "published by a (left-leaning) private outfit called the Citizens' Commission on Civil Rights" (Thomas B. Fordham Institute 2001). Dropping the culture-of-poverty framing and focusing on education as the primary method of addressing poverty and providing economic opportunity—which, historically, was a conservative ideological position—had come to be seen as ideologically progressive. Thus, the CCCR and Education Trust placed substantial political pressure on Democrats in Congress to support accountability.

By the summer of 2001, the House and Senate had passed different versions of the school accountability bill, and a congressional conference committee was created to reconcile the 2,750 differences between the two versions of the legislation (Rudalevige 2003, 41). According to conventional standards, negotiations were extraordinarily confidential, as members of the conference committee "limited their own interaction with lobbyists, and directed their staffs not to discuss the details of the legislation with interest group representatives" (Rhodes 2012, 153). The lengths to which congressional negotiators went to maintain secrecy is understandable given the fact that there is little evidence that the public was any more favorable toward the institutionalization of a standardized testing regime in 2001 than it had been in 1993, when the *Education Week* roundtable conceded that there was little support for testing. Given its unpopularity, then, standardized testing was largely omitted from the political campaign, and even the word "accountability" was de-emphasized, as reformers focused on defeating the achievement gap, which was blamed entirely on the schools.

The conference committee was in the process of negotiating the multitude of differences between the House and Senate versions of the bill on September 11, 2001, and the events of that fateful day proved sufficient to put school accountability over the finish line. But a lack of appreciation of this unique historical context has also helped reinforce the narrative that school accountability legislation had far more political support than the evidence indicates. Rather, in the wake of this momentous national trauma, which led to an all-consuming debate about terrorism and the prospect of U.S. military retaliation, policy makers were under tremendous pressure to unify the nation. While the extraordinarily unique context presented an incredible opportunity for accountability advocates, it also mandated a temporary change in messaging. Just ten days after the tragedy, in majestic prose, Haycock assured the education community that her organization's scheduled November conference would go on as planned. She further linked the group's cause not only with the future of the nation's children but with America itself: "Simple defiance, however, is not all this is about. As our national leaders turn their attention to strengthening America's ability to deter threats to our democracy from abroad, it is essential that we rededicate ourselves to strengthening the foundations of our democracy here at home. . . . Our work together—the work of both raising overall achievement and closing, once and for all, historic gaps between groups—is hugely important both to America's children and to her very future" (Haycock 2001).

Hence the September 11 attacks and resulting patriotism "arguably helped move the conference proceedings to their conclusion" (Rhodes 2012, 153), as members of both parties dropped various objections to the bill, allowing for its lopsided final passage. Given this context, few Americans or major media outlets were paying close attention to the details of a law that would henceforth fundamentally change the daily operations of public schools throughout the country. When he signed the legislation on January 8, 2002, President Bush still enjoyed an artificially inflated approval rating of roughly 80 percent (Gallup, n.d.). At the signing ceremony at a high school in Hamilton, Ohio, Bush was flanked by two students, both of whom were African Americans, along with several congressional leaders and the education secretary, former Houston superintendent Rod Paige (A. Klein 2015). The popular title of the legislation, "No Child Left Behind," appears to have its origins in the early 1990s with the Business Roundtable's "Keep the Promise" television campaign, featuring the rescue of Baby Jessica from a well in Texas (Walsh 1993).

As a reauthorization of the 1965 Education Act, No Child Left Behind was the codification of an accountability framework implemented through the administration of Title I funds. While the framework was developed by business interests, the law's theoretical foundations resided in principal agent theory, which suggested that supervisors—principals—need to monitor the activities of employees, who act as their agents. Because agents could not be trusted, they needed to be motivated with rewards and punishments. Reformers reasoned that because public school educators typically enjoyed greater job security than most employees, they had to be compelled to change their ways, and accountability was the vehicle to bring about this compliance. The implementation of standardized testing data as the primary evidence of achievement in an accountability-based system—an approach advocated by the Hudson Institute's Armbruster in 1977 and subsequently by the Business Roundtable—was the mechanism by which school accountability would be implemented.

The new testing regime involved annual assessments in reading and math in grades 3 through 8 and at least once in grades 10 through 12. Students would be also tested in science at least one time in each of three periods: grades 3 through 5, 6 through 9, and 10 through 12. Because of the political challenges associated with creating national standards, states were charged with creating standards and assessments, and all students were required to participate in testing, regardless of disabilities or limited English proficiency. Testing results would be made public and disaggregated by subgroups, including major racial and ethnic groups, low-income students, students with disabilities, and students with limited English proficiency. To make Adequate Yearly Progress (AYP), individual schools and districts were required to meet annual targets for each subgroup. If a school did not make AYP for multiple years, it faced increasingly punitive accountability measures, ranging from identification as in need of improvement to the provision of student transportation to a district school that was making AYP and to mandatory provision of supplemental educational services. If a school continued to not make AYP for a fourth consecutive year, its home district was required to implement one of several potential corrective actions, including the replacement of relevant school staff; implementation of a new curriculum; a decrease in the school's management authority; the appointment of an outside expert; an extension of the school day or year; or restructuring. All schools that missed AYP for a fifth consecutive year faced restructuring, which included one of the following: reopening the school as a charter school; replacing all or most of the school's staff; contracting with a private firm to manage the school; turning operation of the school over to the state; or some other form of major restructuring of the school's governance. No Child Left Behind also required all teachers to be highly qualified, and schools were mandated to use effective methods and instructional strategies grounded in scientifically based research. Considering the totality of the law, then, No Child Left Behind clearly represented the "genuinely radical change" identified in the 1993 *Education Week* roundtable sought by reformers.

Backlash and the Common Core

Not long after passage, however, it became clear that most Americans did not know much about the specific changes that No Child Left Behind would bring to public education. In 2003, only about one-third of Americans said they knew enough about No Child Left Behind to have an opinion, and "the more parents learned about N.C.L.B., the less they liked it" (Hess and Eden 2017, 6). Even before full implementation, accountability supporters felt compelled to engage in damage control while simultaneously defending specifics of the law. In April 2003, Education Trust posted a report on its website entitled *ESEA: Myths versus Realities* (Education Trust 2003b), and Kati Haycock's testimony to the

Republican-controlled House Subcommittee on 21st Century Competitiveness of the Committee on Education and the Workforce in May reflected reformers' growing defensiveness. Haycock appeared to ridicule a well-regarded work of social science: "Studies like the so-called 'Coleman Report' issued in 1966 indicated that schools accounted for very little in the equation of academic achievement. More recent research has, however, turned these understandings upside down. . . . And the thing that matters most is good teaching" (Haycock 2003, 55). Summarizing some research on the effects of teachers on achievement, she affirmed that improving teacher quality was the difference between "a 'remedial' label and placement in the accelerated or even gifted track. And the difference between entry into a selective college and a lifetime working at McDonald's" (Ibid., 57). Given the abundance of low-wage jobs in food services, this framing holds schools responsible for structural labor market realities.

On July 11, 2003, the *New York Times* published a front-page story on a Texas state audit of the Houston School District, which had received a $1 million prize from the Broad Foundation as the best urban district in the country in 2002. Based on records of sixteen middle and high schools, the state review found that while district officials had reported that only 1.5 percent of its students had dropped out during the 2001–2002 school year, the actual number was likely much higher because "more than half of the 5,500 students who left in the 2000–01 school year should have been declared dropouts but were not" (Schemo 2003). The state audit recommended that the rankings of fourteen of the sixteen schools examined be lowered from best to worst and that the whole district be ranked "unacceptable" (Ibid.). Secretary of Education Rod Paige, the former superintendent of the Houston School District, "declined to directly address questions about the undercounting of dropouts" for the article (Ibid.). Rather, a spokesman said that "'Dr. Paige has a very strong record of success in education reform in Houston' and had 'promoted a culture of accountability'" (Ibid.). Like Haney and the Rand researchers, the article brought attention to the perverse incentives associated with high-stakes quantitative metrics, and while the Houston scandal "was not—as they say in the news business—a story with legs" (G. Anderson 2007, 106), it contributed to the growing unpopularity of a law that many still had little knowledge about.

And as No Child Left Behind was fully implemented, several other foreseeable negative consequences of attaching high stakes to quantitative metrics became apparent, including the practice of teaching to the test and the decline of instruction in subjects like social studies and the arts.[2] The law's perverse incentives also led to several cheating scandals in schools in cities including Atlanta, New York, Philadelphia, and Washington, DC (Chen 2020), and by 2006, many other implementation problems had become apparent. For example, a growing number of schools did not make AYP because one subgroup within the school, often students with disabilities, did not make sufficient progress, which triggered sanctions. The tutoring provisions for schools not making AYP were also not being implemented universally, mainly because of a lack of funding. And in many cases, local officials in cash-strapped cities used failure to make AYP as an excuse to close underperforming high-poverty schools with declining enrollments (Kraus 2013). All these issues contributed to No Child Left Behind's unpopularity with Black voters despite the accountability movement's steadfast cultivation of Black support. In 2004, Bush was reelected but increased his share of the Black vote only marginally, to 11 percent.

Yet perhaps the most far-reaching problem resulting from the new accountability law was the creation of substantially different standards among the states, which, as Ravitch has noted, "led to vastly inflated claims of progress and confusion about standards, with fifty standards for fifty states" (Ravitch 2010, 101). These differences were the impetus for the creation of the Common Core State Standards, the origins of which can be found in the American Diploma Project, founded in 2001 with the support of Achieve, Education Trust, the Thomas Fordham Foundation, and the National Alliance of Business (Achieve 2008, 1). In political terms, as Deborah Duncan Owens has argued, Education Trust's support of the American Diploma Project was the most important: "When the E.T. put their name on the A.D.P., and all of the resulting reports that ended up creating the new curricular standards as well as supporting Draconian accountability and assessment measures, for lawmakers this only validated that these education reform efforts covered the entire spectrum of American society" (Owens 2015, 161).

The American Diploma Project's report *Ready or Not: Creating a High School Diploma That Counts* was supported by a grant from the William and Flora Hewlett Foundation and relied on the work of Anthony Carnevale and Donna M. Desrochers, researchers at the Educational Testing Service (American Diploma Project 2004, 105). Carnevale and Desrochers used BLS and Department of Education data to "define the relationship between education employment and earnings" (Ibid.). They divided the labor market into three categories: "Highly Paid, Professional Jobs," "Well-Paid, Skilled Jobs," and "Low-Paid or Low-Skilled Jobs" (Ibid.). According to the report, "factors such as entry level salary; provision of benefits; and opportunities for further career advancement, education and training were all considered in the creation of these job categories" (Ibid.). The year was 2004, and Carnevale and Desrochers defined the earnings range for the "Well-Paid, Skilled Jobs" category from $25,000 to $40,000; and for the "Highly Paid, Professional Jobs" category $40,000 and higher (Ibid.). According to the report, these two top tiers "are the jobs that pay enough to support a family well above the poverty level, provide benefits, and offer clear pathways for career advancement through further education and training" and, critically, "represent 62 percent of *all* jobs over the next 10 years" (Ibid., emphasis added).

The subsequent 2005 National Education Summit on High Schools was sponsored by Achieve and the National Governors Association "in partnership with the Business Roundtable, the Education Commission of the States and the Hunt Institute" (Achieve and National Governor's Association 2005), and Bill Gates gave the keynote speech. Emphasizing his foundation's commitment to advancing equity around the world, Gates (2005) stated that "here in America, we believe we can do the most to promote equity through education." He affirmed that he was not at the conference to "pose as an education expert" (Ibid.). Rather, he headed a corporation and a foundation, and both these positions gave him a "perspective on education in America," which left him "appalled" (Ibid.). He argued that "America's high schools were obsolete" because "even when they're working exactly as designed—cannot teach our kids what they need to know today" (Ibid.). Gates emphasized the adoption of new technology as the key to improving education: "Training the workforce of tomorrow with the high schools of today is like trying to teach kids about today's computers on a 50-year-old mainframe. It's the wrong tool for the times. Our high schools were designed fifty years ago to meet the needs of another age. Until we design them to meet the needs of the 21st century, we will keep limiting—even ruining—the lives of millions of Americans every year" (Ibid.). Comparing U.S. schools to what he had seen abroad, Gates said he was "terrified for our workforce of tomorrow" (Ibid.). He bemoaned the fact that workers with only a high school education earned "on average—about twenty-five thousand dollars a year. For a family of five, that's close to the poverty line" (Ibid.). He emphasized college attendance as the key to providing economic opportunity for the disadvantaged and implored: "For the sake of our young people and everyone who will depend on them—we must stop rationing education in America" (Ibid.). Again, this type of analysis assumes that there are plenty of jobs for those with college degrees and that all jobs requiring bachelor's degrees or greater pay middle-class wages, neither of which can be supported by official labor market and educational attainment data.

Also in 2005, the American Association for Higher Education disbanded. A report in *The Chronicle of Higher Education* stated that AAHE's work is "well known in higher education, thanks in part to the group's magazine, *Change*" (Bartlett 2005). AAHE president Clara Lovett added that the organization's most important accomplishment was the "early support of student-learning assessment" (Ibid.). As suggested above, higher education assessment was necessarily dependent on the success of the skills gap campaign, while it also reflected the assumptions of the larger narrative about education's role in providing economic opportunity and mitigating inequality. The legacy of the AAHE, however, is about far more than assessment. One of the organization's original goals of increasing higher education attainment rates had become a central component of education reformers' larger strategy. But I suggest that the most important contribution of the AAHE was its creation of what became Education Trust, which began in 1990 as the AAHE's "special project to encourage colleges and universities to support K–12 reform efforts" (Education Trust 1997a). Thus, I argue, the ascendance of Education Trust into a major national organization meant that the AAHE was simply no longer needed. A few years after its initial dissolution, the AAHE was transformed into an organization called the American Association for Higher Education and Accreditation (AAHEA), an "educational/accreditation organization, A Faith-Based 501-C3 Organization since 1969" (the year the AAHE was incorporated; American Association for Higher Education and Accreditation, n.d.). But the new organization bore little resemblance to the organization reformers created in reaction to striking schoolteachers in 1969.

Toward the end of President Bush's second term, No Child Left Behind remained unpopular. As criticisms of the law mounted, the Citizens Commission on Civil Rights' executive director Diane Piche' defended accountability and high-stakes testing in *Education Next* and argued that it should be viewed alongside other major civil rights laws designed "to promote equity and opportunity in the public schools" (Piche' 2007, 59). Claiming that No Child Left Behind "may be the most vilified act of Congress in modern times," she affirmed: "My civil rights colleagues and I fought for some of its tougher provisions" (Ibid.). The same year, the CCCR published another report, *Fresh Ideas in Collective Bargaining: How New Agreements Help Kids*, which acknowledged the financial support of the Gates Foundation as well as the National Council on Teacher Quality for "their hard work in creating the data base" (Taylor and

Rosario 2007). In 2007, the National Council on Teacher Quality stated that it "received all of its funding from private foundations," one of which was the Gates Foundation (National Council on Teacher Quality 2007). By this time, William Taylor was chair of the CCCR, and Piche' was executive director (Taylor and Rosario 2007). But tax records show that Piche' was the CCCR's only paid employee listed under current officers, directors, trustees, and key employees, with a salary of $62,686 (Citizens Commission on Civil Rights 2007).

Along with defending an unpopular law, reformers continued their mission to bring the Common Core to fruition. In the summer of 2008, Gene Wilhoit of the Council of Chief State School Officers and David Coleman of Student Achievement Partners personally lobbied Bill and Melinda Gates for funding for the political campaign for the Common Core (Layton 2014b). Shortly thereafter, the Gates Foundation contributed over $200 million to the Common Core campaign, which involved grants to numerous organizations across the country, including the national teachers' unions and business groups (Ibid.), making meaningful debate effectively impossible. The same year, Achieve published *Out of Many, One: Toward Rigorous Common Core Standards*, which acknowledged the "generous support" of the Gates Foundation for the report and for the "broader work of the American Diploma Project" (Achieve 2008, 28), giving the Common Core additional momentum.

When President Bush left office in early 2009, "NCLB had turned from a shining bipartisan achievement to a tarnished bipartisan albatross" (Hess and Eden 2017, 6). The CCCR published another report with the group Education Reform Now that adopted a much more aggressive tone against teachers' unions, stating that "at times, the union opposition to reform has become vehement" (Taylor and Rosario 2009, 6). The same year, states were incentivized to adopt the Common Core State Standards through the Obama administration's Race to the Top initiative, and after considerable controversy, forty-one states and the District of Columbia adopted the standards. In 2015, amid the continuing popular backlash against No Child Left Behind, Congress and the Obama administration passed the Every Student Succeeds Act (ESSA), which left in place the same general testing and accountability framework implemented through Title I funds but gave states increased latitude in shaping accountability systems. In 2017, Achieve published *Twenty Years of Driving Student Success* (Achieve 2017). On the cover, under a photograph of a group of predominantly minority students, the report stated: "The era of abundantly available middle-class jobs for unskilled workers is over. The future, indeed the present, demands that our young people be equipped with the skills, knowledge, and habits of mind to succeed" (Ibid.). The report went on to affirm that business leaders "routinely face a shortage of qualified candidates for jobs they need to fill" (Ibid., 2). Once again, the focus turned to the skills gap and the purportedly high-education, high-skill economy.

Conclusion

The educational accountability movement has origins in the 1960s, a time of major political upheaval. During this period, the National Educational Association supported striking K–12 teachers, which led to the formation of the American Association for Higher Education, and *Change* magazine was first published a few years later. The AAHE and *Change* sought to fundamentally reshape the direction of education, and both received extensive foundation support. Because foundations had been understood as reflecting corporate interests, however, I argue that it became politically necessary to redefine the image of foundations as charitable donors distinct from the interests of corporations and the wealthy. These efforts were largely successful, and therefore it would eventually become politically acceptable for foundations to be the primary acknowledged funders of major reports and organizations advocating significant education reforms, including accountability.

Yet as the participants in the 1993 *Education Week* roundtable concluded, passing an accountability system based on standardized tests required a fundamentally different political campaign. By this time, accountability supporters had already begun to reformulate and extend Armbruster's emphasis on low-income students as victims of the schools. The new message of reformers, which effectively dropped the culture-of-poverty framing, was fully articulated by groups such as Education Trust. In this framing, racism was acknowledged, but primarily as an effect of past policies, and the concept of data became paramount. The ultimate justification for reform was an increasingly detailed account of the educational and skill requirements of the labor market. The racial achievement gap, according to reformers' emerging narrative, was caused by the schools—not by economic disadvantage—and therefore, school accountability policies were necessary to provide low-income minority students access to economic opportunity in what was perpetually described as a high-education, high-skill labor market. I argue that this was the business establishment's political response to and justification for the wage stagnation and increasing economic inequality brought on by neoliberalism—to make the debate about economic opportunity solely a debate about education. Despite the appearance of a diverse base of ideological support, however, an examination of the major organizations involved in advancing accountability reveals that a relatively small group of foundations and business interests funded a handful of organizations in this effort, in which several of the same individuals, such as Kati Haycock, David Hornbeck, William Taylor, and Diane Piche', were key participants.

In addition to framing the larger debate about economic opportunity as solely a debate about education, the implementation of test-based accountability has been very lucrative. A 2014 report from the Software and Information Industry Association showed that sales for testing and assessment materials had increased 57 percent over a three-year period, reaching almost $2.5 billion by the 2012–2013 school year (Piehler 2014). A representative from the group emphasized the remarkable nature of the growth of the testing industry during a period of budgetary austerity: "We view the growth of the preK–12 testing and assessment market segment over the last several years as even more remarkable, given that it has occurred in difficult economic times during an overall preK–12 budget and spending decline" (Ibid.). By 2015, half of the $8 billion in global sales of one of the largest assessment companies, Pearson, came from the company's North American education division (Simon 2015). And after successfully lobbying the Gates Foundation to bankroll the campaign for the Common Core, David Coleman became CEO of the nonprofit College Board, and by 2019, he had earned over $1.4 million in reportable compensation plus an additional nearly $260,000 in other compensation (College Board 2019). The same year, the president of the nonprofit Educational Testing Service was paid over $1.3 million in reportable compensation plus nearly $42,000 in other compensation, while numerous individual board members were also compensated highly for their service to the nonprofit (Educational Testing Service 2019).

The movement for school choice paralleled the school accountability movement. Yet because of the historically limited support for choice policies, elites have also engaged in a continuous political campaign to shape public opinion in support of charter schools and school vouchers, the subject of Chapter 5.

5

Free Market Fantasy

The Politics of School Choice

The libertarians, God bless them, like to talk this way.
They like to talk about how the market is going to fix
everything. The unions were only too glad that they did
talk this way because they knew such views couldn't get
more than 30 percent of the vote. As long as your rhetoric
is exclusively on the free market and damn the regulation,
you're not going to win anything.

—JOHN E. COONS, *Annals of the American Academy of
Political and Social Science*

Introduction

In the years after *A Nation at Risk*, elites began a political campaign for
school choice. The two main school choice policies are publicly funded
school vouchers and privately run, publicly funded charter schools. Like
the movement for school accountability, supporters of vouchers and charters have advocated these policies as a means of providing economic opportunity to the disadvantaged on the assumption of a failing public school
system, a seemingly high-education, high-skill economy, and a perpetual skills gap. School choice policies are grounded in free market theory and therefore ask families to treat school selection in the same manner they would treat the purchase of any other product or service in the
marketplace. Business interests have been intertwined with the choice
movement, which posits a high-technology labor market and advocates
choice policies to sell technology products and services. Finally, the concept of data has been a critical part of choice campaigns, and foundations and corporations have funded several university-based institutes to
promote research in furtherance of their efforts.

But the public's ambivalence toward free market education policies
has created significant obstacles for the expansion of choice plans and
led to supporters' frequent use of misleading claims to advance their goals.

In 2000, law professor John E. Coons recognized the problem posed by free market messaging, arguing that the "rhetoric for vouchers has been largely captured since the 1970s by libertarian formulas. The libertarians, God bless them, like to talk this way. They like to talk about how the market is going to fix everything. The unions were only too glad that they did talk this way because they knew such views couldn't get more than 30 percent of the vote. As long as your rhetoric is exclusively on the free market and damn the regulation, you're not going to win anything" (Coons, Keegan, and Fair 2000, 109). Thus, after initial messaging focused on the benefits of free market competition in schooling, choice supporters began to downplay market language, including a retreat from the use of the word "voucher" as well as charter advocates' routine use of the term "public charter schools" and repeated insistence of their support for the public school system. And because the public has never been willing to embrace technology as a replacement for in-person instruction, I maintain that school choice backers have adopted a specialized vocabulary that obfuscates their technology advocacy. In recent years, the messaging of both free markets and technology has frequently been subsumed under a broader rubric of innovation, a term that connotes both free market and technology supremacy without explicit reference to either.

Finally, because the data of the school choice movement consists mainly of standardized test scores, which are closely watched, the creation of alternative data is simply not feasible. Therefore, as actors in a political campaign, funded researchers are compelled to frame *any* findings in school choice studies—many of which are strikingly negative—in a manner that consistently seeks to expand choice programs. I argue, then, that under no circumstances do advocates appear willing to reconsider the expansion of choice. Moreover, the long-term economic impacts of school choice programs on program participants appear to be implicitly off limits as this line of inquiry would necessarily draw attention to the predominantly low-wage, low-education labor market.

Yet despite a thirty-year effort supported by elites in both parties, numerous major foundations active in education, and many business groups and corporations, the expansion of charters and school vouchers has been limited mainly to urban areas with high concentrations of poverty. While 9/11 facilitated the passage of No Child Left Behind, tragic events like Hurricane Katrina and the Great Recession enabled the significant expansion of both charters and vouchers, neither of which has had the broad-based appeal to pass under normal political conditions. Moreover, vouchers have consistently been opposed by voters in a diverse group of states, only passing under unified Republican rule in state governments or in Congress.[1] Recognizing the limits of the expansion of choice programs, in recent years education reformers have refocused their efforts toward the sale of educational products and services, particularly online education.

Background

School choice originated with the work of economist Milton Friedman in 1955. His proposal depended on the distinction between publicly financed schools—which he supported—and publicly administered schools—which he opposed. Friedman sought a significant reduction in government and a larger private sector (M. Friedman 1955). While southern opponents of court-ordered school desegregation invoked Friedman's concept of school vouchers (MacLean 2017), the concept of school choice was confined to libertarian circles until the early 1970s, when the Nixon administration's Office of Economic Opportunity awarded grants to six school districts to study the feasibility of school voucher programs targeting low-income youth. However, only the Alum Rock district in San Jose, California, decided to implement a voucher program, which, because of state and local opposition, was eventually implemented as an open-enrollment public school program (Levinson 1976).

After the Nixon administration, the movement for school vouchers developed largely out of the spotlight but was advanced forcefully by President Reagan with the publication of *A Nation at Risk* in 1983. Subsequently, *Workforce 2000* decried the "public school monopoly" and argued that "educational vouchers could serve to stimulate experimentation and competition in local schools" (Johnston and Packer 1987, 108). The influential report even floated the possibility of the full privatization of the lowest-performing schools: "For the public educational system to succeed with the minorities, however, may require radical changes. In school districts with the most serious problems, not only vouchers but complete privatization of schools should be considered" (Ibid., 115). However, public sentiment would necessitate the abandonment of this type of language in the political campaign for school choice.

"Eighty Percent Lemons"?

While early voucher proponents framed their support in the blunt language of free markets, the original charter concept advocated by teachers' union leader Al Shanker was decidedly not articulated in free market terminology. Yet amid the constant drumbeat of the negative media coverage of the schools and the increasing power of the skills gap narrative as the primary cause of manufacturing-job loss and wage stagnation, Shanker implicitly adopted the assumptions of failing schools and an inadequate workforce in his original articulation of the charter school concept. Born and raised in New York City, Shanker taught math at a public school in East Harlem in the 1950s, went on to help found the United Federation of Teachers in 1960, and by the 1980s had become a significant figure in national education policy debate. In a March 1988 speech at the National Press Club, he identified a "radical and tiny movement" led by teachers in a handful of schools and districts (Shanker 1988, 10). Shanker called his proposal a "new type of school" in which a small group of teachers could work with parents to reach the students who were not being reached by traditional public schools (Ibid., 11). These new schools would experiment, teachers would team-teach and share ideas about successful strategies, and students would work collaboratively and at their own pace.

In Shanker's plan, proposals for a new charter school would be reviewed by panels that included union representatives, school board members, and outside citizens. Charter schools would necessarily be schools of choice, not based on traditional geographic attendance zones, and would be given a specified length of time—five to ten years—to demonstrate their effectiveness. However, Shanker maintained that the success of charter schools depended on two important factors: strong input from teachers and a commitment to racial and economic diversity. Yet Shanker's remarks implicitly accepted the dominant narrative of failing schools, and his proposal reflected the overwhelming power of the skills gap campaign. Although he offered pointed criticisms of standardized testing and top-down reforms, in the National Press Club speech he stated several times that the public schools were not reaching 80 percent of their students (Shanker 1988, 6, 9, 25). Shanker went on to state that "we have about the same results now in our schools as we had in 1940, as to the percentage of kids who are able to master certain intellectual tasks" (Ibid., 26). While conceding that "we are doing a lot better now because we're holding more of those who used to drop out," he still maintained that "we are not reaching that other point of educating the majority well" (Ibid.). Later in 1988, Shanker spoke at the Minnesota Foundation and repeated many of the same claims, going as far as to say that the public school system was a "lemon factory" that was producing "80 percent lemons" (Minnesota Public Radio Archive 1988).

Shanker's account of the purported failures of the public school system not only revealed the power of the skills gap campaign but also failed to grasp the magnitude of increases in literacy and educational attainment that had occurred since the middle twentieth century. By the most basic measures, America was a far better educated country in 1988 than in 1940. Also, longer term trends in the NAEP show modest increases in reading and math for all age groups dating from the early 1970s despite consistently high student poverty rates and ever-increasing racial and language diversity in public schools. Yet these significant increases in attainment were largely irrelevant in mitigating the wage stagnation and increasing economic inequality ushered in by neoliberalism. But because Shanker accepted the baseline assumption of failing public schools, business elites' policy preferences vis-à-vis the new charter school concept were given a tremendous boost. And when Minnesota's first charter school law was introduced in the state legislature, it included neither automatic collective bargaining rights for teachers nor universal teacher certification requirements (Kahlenberg and Potter 2014, 15). And in the years after the charter concept was introduced, the "new, more conservative charter vision" in which teachers had less influence "quickly swept the country" (Ibid.).

"Vouchers Are Not Even Necessary"

The first major work of funded research on school choice, *Politics, Markets, and America's Schools*, by John E. Chubb and Terry M. Moe, was published in 1990 by the Brookings Institution Press, where both Chubb and Moe were resident scholars. The book included the requisite data in the form of advanced statistics, yet as a work of political advocacy, it was written in straightforward prose with little jargon and became extremely influential. In fact, in 2011, Moe stated that the book "basically changed" his life (Esfahani Smith 2011). For the book, Chubb and Moe received funding from several sources, including Milwaukee's Lynde and Harry Bradley Foundation and the Olin Foundation. The Bradley Foundation is a strong proponent of free market principles and limited government (Lynde and Harry Bradley Foundation 2022). The Olin Foundation, founded in 1953 and dissolved in 2005, was transformed because of campus unrest in the late 1960s. Originally funding a variety of causes, John M. Olin, a multimillionaire alum and former trustee of Cornell University, was deeply troubled by events at his alma mater in April 1969 when roughly eighty Black students "marched in formation out of the student union, which they had seized, with their clenched fists held high in black-power salutes" (Mayer 2016). Olin did not like what he perceived as the antibusiness climate on campuses, and, according to Mayer, he "began to fund an ambitious offensive to reorient the political slant of American higher education to the right" (Ibid.), and Chubb and Moe's work fit squarely within this emphasis.

Chubb and Moe advocated a complete overhaul of the public school system but, I suggest, presented their proposal in a manner that attempted to downplay its sweeping impact. They argued that the democratic structure of public education was the root of the problem and stated that their "guiding principal in the design of a choice system is this: public authority must be put to use in creating a system that is almost entirely beyond the reach of public authority" (Chubb and Moe 1990, 218). For Chubb and Moe, the state would have the power to determine "what constitutes a 'public school,'" and these "criteria should be quite minimal" (Ibid., 219). They further suggested that "any group or organization that applies to the state and meets these minimal criteria must then be chartered as a public school and granted the right to accept students and receive public money" (Ibid.). However, they went to great lengths to distance their approach from the concept of school vouchers by using the word "voucher" a handful of times in a 230-page book and discussed Friedman's original proposal in an endnote (Ibid., 308–309). They went as far as to say that under their proposal, a "voucher system was not even necessary" (Ibid., 218) and even suggested that private schools "need not be" included in their school choice proposal (Ibid.), which was vastly more comprehensive than most traditional voucher plans.

School choice plans developed slowly in the early 1990s, yet elites were eager to study these new programs. In 1992, arguing that "the urgency of the topic is apparent," the Carnegie Foundation for the Advancement of Teaching was "impressed by the appeal of the supporting arguments" for school choice (Carnegie Foundation for the Advancement of Teaching 1992, xv). In one of the first-published overviews of the limited research on the topic, Carnegie acknowledged that choice did "not appear to be a panacea" (Ibid., xvi). Nonetheless, the organization advocated choice, arguing that "with proper planning and strong commitment, well-crafted 'choice' programs can, indeed, empower teachers, engage parents, and improve the academic performance of students" (Ibid.). The same report also surveyed the public, asking respondents which of two scenarios they agreed with regarding the best way to improve education: focusing on neighborhood schools and giving each school the "resources needed to achieve excellence" or letting "schools compete with each other for students," leading to the strengthening of successful schools and compelling weaker schools to improve or close. Eighty-two percent of respondents agreed with the former option, while 15 percent agreed with the latter (Ibid., 97). Clearly the public did not see schools within a free market framework.

Other contemporaneous national polls confirmed the lack of public support for school vouchers. In 1991, in the Gallup/Phi Delta Kappan (PDK) Education Poll, 68 percent of respondents opposed "allowing students and parents to choose a private school to attend at public expense" (Elam and Rose 1995, 46). By 1993, this number had increased to 74 percent, and it remained high at 65 percent in 1995 (Ibid.). The results of numerous state referenda on vouchers confirmed this lack of public support. Beginning in the late 1970s, private school voucher programs had been defeated by voters in an ideologically diverse group of states, including California, Colorado, Michigan, Oregon, Utah, and Washington, and in none of these states was public support for vouchers greater than 38 percent (Wermund 2016). Clearly school choice advocates had a major political challenge on their hands.

"This Attitude Has Caused Great Harm"

After the publication of Chubb and Moe's book, the Brookings Institution continued to play a major role in funding school choice advocacy. Brookings's Paul Hill, a political scientist, became the director of the newly created Center on Reinventing Public Education (CRPE), which was "founded in 1993 by the University of Washington's Daniel J. Evans School of Public Affairs" (Center on Reinventing Public Education 1999). Yet the research center's website—https://www.crpe.org—did not have the traditional university-affiliated domain of .edu. The new organization reiterated the emerging consensus of reformers, stating that the "ineffectiveness of big city public schools clouds the futures of millions of children" yet conceded that public education is "indispensable and talk of abandoning it is impractical" and that "market-based forms of service delivery must be constrained to preserve equality of access and respect for democratic institutions" (Ibid.).

However, the CRPE also maintained that it had a "definite point of view" and that "incremental efforts to improve urban public education without disturbing the school boards, unions, and central office administrators have failed, largely because roles, missions, and interests of those organizations are incompatible with effective schooling" (Center on Reinventing Public Education 1999). The CRPE promulgated the larger framing of the education reform movement by linking the economic opportunity of the disadvantaged to the education system: "If we are serious about using education to create opportunities for poor and minority children, as well as for middle class children, whose families depend on urban public schools, we must thoroughly re-think every element of our public education system" (Ibid.). Hill and his colleagues would therefore "openly contemplate methods of public oversight that do not include heavy regulation, constantly changing mandates, or civil service staffing of schools" (Ibid.). However, neither this type of messaging nor the extensive financial resources of school choice proponents helped the cause of charters in Washington State in the 1990s and early 2000s, when three statewide charter school initiatives failed.

In 1999, the Center for Research on Education Outcomes (CREDO) was founded under the direction of Margaret Raymond as part of the Wallis Institute on Political Economy at the University of Rochester (Center for Research on Education Outcomes 2001a). The institute was named after the university's former president and chancellor W. Allen Wallis, who was "known for his forceful defense of freedom," advised several Republican Presidents, and served as undersecretary of state of economic affairs in the Reagan administration (W. Allen Wallis Institute of Political Economy 2022). CREDO's rhetoric illustrated a new approach for choice advocates. By this time, with the ascendance of Education Trust, data had become a key part of the messaging of education reformers, who had now begun to suggest that research funded by proponents of school choice was totally objective, independent of ideology or policy preferences. Thus, CREDO offered its "support to districts and other agencies that want independent critiques of evaluation plans and results" (Center for Research on Education Outcomes 2001a). The organization also affirmed that it expected to "regularly distribute research and evaluation reports that can advance the development of good education policy" (Ibid.).

When it was created, CREDO stated that "two foundations" had committed "$1.25 million to fund a three-and one-half year initiative to address the current shortage of evaluation research in education policy matters" (Center for Research on Education Outcomes 2001a). The foundations were identified in a 1999 news article in the Rochester *Democrat and Chronicle* as the Packard Humanities Institute and the Smith Richardson Foundation (Wentzel 1999). The Smith Richardson Foundation was founded in 1935 by H. Smith Richardson, the son of the founder of the Vick Chemical Company, and his wife, Grace Jones Richardson. The foundation is a strong supporter of free markets, and their domestic public policy program emphasizes "more effective strategies to develop human capital and establishing an economic climate hospitable to entrepreneurship and growth" (Smith Richardson Foundation 2022). The Packard Humanities Institute was founded in 1987. David Packard, the cofounder and former CEO and chairman of the board of Hewlett-Pack-ard, was a prominent conservative. He served as deputy secretary of de-fense in the Nixon administration as well as on the boards of the Amer-ican Enterprise Institute, Stanford University's Hoover Institution, and the Herbert Hoover Foundation, and received the Presidential Medal of Freedom from President Reagan in 1988. According to the Packard Foun-dation's history, the Packard Humanities Institute was established in 1987 to "create tools for basic research in the Humanities and to foster pub-lic interest in the history, literature, and music of the past" (David and Lucile Packard Foundation 2022).

David Packard's public justification for the creation of CREDO was similar to the concern expressed by the participants of the 1993 *Educa-tion Week* roundtable on accountability—the lack of public understand-ing of the presumed poor quality of the nation's schools. At the time of CREDO's founding, Packard asserted: "Most people have some direct experience with the education system, and most people think that their own personal experiences are a reliable guide to policy." Yet he main-tained that "this attitude has caused great harm" (Wentzel 1999). Thus, public opinion had to be changed if major school reform policies like choice were to advance. Subsequently, CREDO relocated to the much higher profile Hoover Institution at Packard's alma mater Stanford Uni-versity (Center for Research on Education Outcomes 2001b). The Hoover Institution began as a library in 1919 and has become one of the pre-eminent free market research institutes in the country. A 2015 article in *Inside Philanthropy* outlined Hoover's largest funders, which include some of the most prominent free market foundations, such as the Sarah Scaife Foundation, the Walton Family Foundation, the Lynde and Harry Bradley Foundation, the William E. Simon Foundation, and the Howard Char-itable Foundation, among others (Adeniji 2015). Yet in recent years, CRE-DO has promoted itself as "unaffiliated with any of the ideological sides in the education debate" and as "independent, unbiased, and scientifi-cally based" (Center for Research on Education Outcomes 2022).

When one examines public opinion on school choice during this pe-riod, it becomes clear why elites established research centers like the CRPE and CREDO. In the early 2000s, school vouchers remained very unpopu-lar, public opinion polls also showed that support for charters was con-sistently below 50 percent despite their promotion by both political par-ties and by the philanthropic and corporate communities. Between 2000 and 2005, the PDK/Gallup Poll asked respondents various questions about charter schools several times. The first question included a general def-inition of charters and gauged respondents' support, and each year, public support was less than 50 percent. The second question asked respondents whether they believed that charter schools "should be accountable to the state in the way regular public schools should be accountable," and between 77 and 80 percent of respondents answered in the affirmative. Finally, when asked if they would favor charter schools in their community "if funding them meant reducing the amount of funds for the regular public schools," support dropped even more, to between 28 and 30 percent (L. Rose and Gallup 2005, 46). When the public was informed about the specific characteristics of charter schools, which, by definition, receive public funds yet are not accountable to citizens in the same manner that traditional public schools are, solid majorities remained opposed to the concept.

Despite the increased attention that elites gave to funded research, this work continued to show mixed results, as in a 2001 Rand study funded by the Gund, Spencer, and Annie E. Casey Foundations and the Carnegie Corporation and coauthored by former Columbia University Teachers College president J. Michael Timpane, as well as Karen E. Ross and Dominic J. Brewer (Gill et al. 2001, xxv). Despite framing their study within "today's context of widespread dissatisfaction with the public education system" (Ibid., xi), after an exhaustive review, the Rand researchers were left "without a crisp, bottom-line judgment of the wisdom of voucher and charter programs" (Ibid., 232) and maintained that "at the current scale of things, many important questions cannot be answered at all" (Ibid., 233). Consistent with its initial framing, the report concluded with a call for "better information on the performance of conventional public schools and alternative reform models" (Ibid.).

I argue that the emerging body of research showing that charters and vouchers were clearly falling short of the hopes of many school choice advocates necessitated a more aggressive data-research-based component of the campaign. And the journal *Education Matters*—published by Stanford's Hoover Institution with support from Harvard's Program on Education Policy and Governance, the Thomas B. Fordham Foundation, and the Manhattan Institute for Policy Research (*Education Next* 2001)— was created in 2001 to advance the research component of the education reform movement including school choice policies. By just its third quarterly issue, the new publication became *Education Next*, a title more consistent with the futuristic, technology-driven emphasis of education reformers. Unlike other reform-oriented publications, however, *Education Next* was peer reviewed, thereby adding a scholarly veneer to the school choice campaign. Despite relying on funders who advocated market-based school reforms and several prominent pro-school choice editors, including Moe, Chubb, Hill, Eric A. Hanushek, and Frederick Hess, however, *Education Next* adopted the assumption of failing schools while simultaneously declaring its ideological independence: "Bold change is needed in American K–12 education, but *Education Next* partakes of no program, campaign, or ideology. It goes where the evidence points" (Ibid.). This language reflected not only the all-encompassing power of neoliberalism—which is commonly understood as nonideological—but also the pervasiveness of the assumption of a failing education system upon which neoliberalism has been constructed.

In the first issue of the new journal was a piece entitled "The Private Can Be Public," by John Chubb (2001), who had become the chief education officer at Edison Schools, and the article was a pitch for the private management of schools. In the piece, Chubb promoted his own firm, Edison, and framed private management as most beneficial to low-income students: "Of all students, disadvantaged children could have the most to gain from the efficiencies of private management" (Ibid.). Writing as the debate about accountability was heating up in Washington, Chubb mused that "an injection of market forces" and "imposing rigorous standards of accountability" might "fall short of their desired effects" (Ibid.). Thus, he argued, "political pressures for more radical change will continue to mount," and he concluded: "For those who worry about the unpredictable consequences of vouchers, but who recognize the need to bring competition, choice, and change to public schools, private management offers a very attractive compromise. . . . In this sense, private management may be the best hope for keeping public education public" (Ibid.).

"Two Horses Pulling in the Same Direction"

By the early 2000s, the movement for school choice had an increasing presence in Washington, DC. In 2002, the Charter School Leadership Council was created as a "coalition of national school reform organizations, all of which supported charter schools," and it was incorporated as a nonprofit in 2004 (National Alliance for Public Charter Schools 2005a). In 2005, the group changed its name to the National Alliance for Public Charter Schools to "better reflect the organization's mission and role" (Ibid.). Funders included the Gates Foundation, Annie E. Casey Foundation, the Doris and Donald Fisher Fund, and the Walton Family Foundation (Philanthropy Roundtable 2014). Emphasizing the term "public charter schools" suggests that advocates were cognizant of the public's opposition toward privately controlled, publicly funded schools. In 2005, the National Alliance's language could be described as a kitchen-sink approach in its political campaign, which included mentioning the prospect of charter schools improving the traditional public school system: "Charter schools give parents greater say in the education of their children, offer educators freedom from burdensome rules and regulations, and ensure accountability for student learning. The Alliance believes strongly that the increased educational innovation, parental choice, and administrative freedom provided by charter schools will improve student academic achievement and generate much-needed reforms in the traditional public school system" (National Alliance for Public Charter Schools 2005b).

Another major development in the data and research component of the political campaign for school choice occurred in April 2005 when the University of Arkansas created the Department of Education Reform. The new endowed department was created with $20 million, including $10 million from an anonymous private foundation and the remaining $10 million from the university's matching gift program, "created by the Walton Family Charitable Support Foundation" (Arkansas Higher Education Coordinating Board 2005, 10). The total gift amounted to "one of the largest gifts ever received by any college of education in the country" (Ibid.). The anonymous donor was identified by local media as the Windgate Charitable Foundation of Siloam Springs, Arkansas (Smith 2005). Most of Windgate's assets were acquired through shares of Walmart stock (Ibid.; Windgate Foundation 2017). In 2022, the Department of Education Reform's website described its origins as made "possible through a $10 million private gift and an additional $10 million from the University's Matching Gift Program" (University of Arkansas, Department of Education Reform 2022).

Windgate's director in 2005, John Brown III, was a former state senator and president of John Brown University, a Christian university in Siloam Springs, Arkansas, founded in 1919 by Brown's grandfather, John Brown Sr. (*Arkansas Democrat and Gazette* 2019). Asked about his foundation's significant gift to establish the new department, Brown told the *Morning News* newspaper that while the two foundations (Windgate and Walton Family Charitable Support) may differ on the specifics of education reform, they were "two horses pulling in the same direction" (Smith 2005). He also reiterated reformers' increasing emphasis on independence and objectivity and the importance of university-based research: "That's why this is at a university. This is not a policy institute that has a specific perspective that they're trying to advocate" (Ibid.). The foundation wanted to "avoid any involvement so the university can maintain their credibility as neutral" (Ibid.). And Brown affirmed: "All of us have opinions and have things we advocate . . . but what you want is solid, credible research that shows what you're funding is important" (Ibid.). In the article, the dean of the university's College of Education also stated that the donors would not interfere with the new department, saying, "We don't have a situation where they are going to exercise any undue pressure on what we're going to do. There is and will be no unduly [*sic*] efforts on what we'll be doing" (Ibid.), suggesting an environment of no-holds-barred scholarly inquiry in the new department. However, the implicit emphasis on education as the source of economic opportunity—particularly for the disadvantaged—was not up for debate.

However, there was still little evidence that support for charters, or for school choice generally, was increasing, especially among the biggest target audience, African Americans. By this time, the accountability measures imposed by the No Child Left Behind law were widely unpopular, and a national backlash against standardized testing was underway. President George W. Bush, who signed a Republican-led law authorizing vouchers for two thousand low-income families in the predominantly Black Washington, DC, public schools, had barely increased his support among African American voters in his 2004 reelection. Recognizing the uphill battle school choice advocates faced, the University of Washington's Center on Reinventing Public Education also changed its original hard-hitting approach and now argued that "From its beginning, one question has dominated the Center's work: How can urban school systems provide strong, coherent schools that create equal opportunity for all children?" (Center on Reinventing Public Education 2005). Then on August 25, 2005, against a backdrop of an increasingly visible national campaign for school choice and charters, Hurricane Katrina devastated New Orleans and the Gulf Coast. As with 9/11, the nation watched the images coming out of the Gulf with horror and disbelief. Katrina left over 1,800 people dead and an estimated $151 billion in total damages (U.S. Census Bureau 2015). New Orleans's population was over 494,000 in July 2005 but dropped to just over 230,000 one year later (Ibid.), yet the public schools remained predominantly Black.

Like 9/11, the storm upended the normal state of political affairs, and education reformers saw the biggest natural disaster in modern American history as a rare opportunity in which their agenda could be implemented. On September 20, less than one month after the devastating storm hit the city, the CRPE's Paul Hill affirmed in *Education Week*: "In the case of post-hurricane New Orleans, American school planners will be as close as they have ever come to a green field opportunity: a large public education system will need to be built from scratch. It seems impossible to put the pre-existing New Orleans public school system together again. Even if that were possible, doing so would be misguided" (Hill 2005). In short order, reformers representing foundations and other non-profits initiated substantial changes in the New Orleans schools. This led to the firing of all 7,500 district employees, a majority of whom were Black teachers, administrators, and paraprofessionals, and their replacement with "young and predominantly White transplants from 'education reform' organizations like Teach for America (TFA), New Leaders for New Schools, and the New Teacher Project" (Dixson, Buras, and Jeffers 2015, 289). Louisiana passed a charter school law in 1995, but there were "only a handful of charters in New Orleans before the storm" (Jewson 2019). But by July 2019, the city had become "the first major American city without any traditional schools" (Ibid.). Further, the stage had been set for the creation of a statewide voucher program, and all of this was made possible only because of the tragedy of Katrina.

Innovation, Innovation, Innovation, and Equity

The widespread introduction of the internet in the early 2000s presented new opportunities for the choice movement, which had become more intertwined with technology interests. New products and services for education exploded, presenting untold opportunities for corporate interests in the education sector. Technology was given a significant boost by the 2005 publication of Tom Friedman's (2005) celebration of globalization *The World Is Flat*. Friedman reiterated many of the claims that education reformers had long made, including the STEM crisis myth, while also emphasizing the poor performance of American students on international assessments. For Friedman, this "quiet crisis involves the steady erosion of America's scientific and engineering base, which has long been the source of American innovation and our rising standard of living" (2005, 340). He also cited Marc Tucker of the NCEE approvingly, and Tucker subsequently referred to Friedman as "the legendary *New York Times* columnist" in the 2008 version of the NCEE's report *Tough Choices or Tough Times* (National Center on Education and the Economy 2008, xv). Friedman's book, a lengthy celebration of neoliberalism and modern technology, had an enormous influence on both popular debate and scholarly work on education.

But choice advocates had to face the fact that despite being advocated by major organizations such as the Carnegie Foundation and the Business Roundtable, technology as a major teaching tool never took off in the 1990s. Thus, I argue, the rhetoric of technology, like that of free markets, would eventually be incorporated under the banner of innovation, which was given a substantial boost with the 2005 publication of *Innovate America*, by the Council on Competitiveness. The business-led coalition argued that innovation will be the "single most important factor in determining America's success through the 21st century" and that "over the next quarter century, we must optimize our entire society for innovation" (Council on Competitiveness 2005, 7). The same year, another major coalition of fifteen major business-related organizations, including the Business Roundtable, the Council on Competitiveness, the National Association of Manufacturers, and the U.S. Chamber of Commerce, published *Tapping America's Potential: The Education for Innovation Initiative* (Education for Innovation Initiative 2005), reinforcing the link between innovation and education. In fact, the concept of innovation united the disparate segments of the education reform movement, from free market ideologues to neoliberal technology boosters and the myriad educational consultants selling an increasing number of products and services. In education policy discussion, innovation, like STEM, became impossible to question. The innovation-focused education reform agenda was advanced in a slew of popular and scholarly books published during the Great Recession under conditions of high unemployment and increasing economic insecurity. These works echoed the same claims articulated in *The Earth Is Flat* and reports such as the NCEE's *Tough Choices or Tough Times* and included Tony Wagner's *The Global Achievement Gap* (2008) and *Creating Innovators* (2012); Moe and Chubb's *Liberating Learning* (2009); *Surpassing Shanghai* (2011), edited by the NCEE's Marc Tucker; Moe's *Special Interest* (2011); and Darling-Hammond's *The Flat World and Education* (2010).

Darling-Hammond's book draws on research funded by the Ford, Rockefeller, Spencer, Wallace, Gates, Flora, and Morgan Family Foundations, as well as the Carnegie Corporation, Justice Matters, Atlantic Philanthropic Services, and the U.S. Department of Education (Darling-Hammond 2010, xiii, xiv), and was a work primarily intended for a higher education audience. While acknowledging the importance of out-of-school influences, Darling-Hammond also echoed the long-standing consensus of corporate education reformers that teaching was *the* most important variable in student outcomes: the book included a chapter entitled "Doing What Matters Most: Developing Competent Teaching."

To be sure, none of these works was solely about charters or vouchers, and some discussed school choice only occasionally. But the overall message in this literature was clear: the high-technology, global economy was continually producing new types of jobs for which the traditional public schools were not adequately preparing young people. The refrain that the public schools were built for an industrial era and therefore impeded innovation became conventional wisdom. Public schools obstructed economic opportunity for the poor. This had been the overarching message of reformers since the 1970s, from Armbruster to Columbia's IEE to Education Trust and many other education reformers since. Charter schools and private schools were, by definition, innovative, as was online education and *any* new educational product and service. By 2008, the National Alliance for Public Charter Schools connected several emerging themes of the choice movement by defining charters as "independent public schools that are free to be more innovative and are held accountable for improved student achievement" (National Alliance for Public Charter Schools 2008). Like accountability's promotion as a way of alleviating the achievement gap, school choice and online education were also increasingly promoted in terms of bringing greater equity to the system.

But the education reform movement has also long promoted technology as a measure that would reduce instructional costs. The National Center for Academic Transformation (NCAT) was "established in 1999 with funding from an $8.8 million grant from the Pew Charitable Trusts" at Rensselaer Polytechnic Institute in New York State (National Center for Academic Transformation, n.d.). The new center was "committed to providing the expertise necessary to help higher education institutions achieve their student access, success and retention goals while reducing their instructional costs" (Ibid.). And in 2009, Chubb again partnered with Moe in *Liberating Learning: Technology, Politics, and the Future of American Education* (Moe and Chubb 2009), which elaborated on the potential cost savings of a reduction in teachers resulting from online education while also advancing the theme of online education's ability to bring about more equity. The authors argued that online education could reduce the teaching force: "Fewer teachers will be necessary as students receive more instruction electronically" (Ibid., 97). The book also promoted Chubb's firm, EdisonLearning, which had partnered with "scores of cities and towns to operate or support highly innovative, technologically sophisticated public schools, often serving disadvantaged students," and had "recently become a major provider of online education with its acquisition of Provost Systems" (Ibid., vii). And to make the case for increased technology and online education, the authors recited the entire fantasy economy narrative of failing schools, including the more elaborate version of the skills gap, which advocated education reform to provide economic opportunity to the disadvantaged. In sum, American students lagged behind those of other nations and would continue to miss out on economic opportunity unless the school system was fundamentally changed (Ibid., 13–28).

But considering that the public very much appreciates in-person instruction, the cost savings associated with reduction in teaching staff has necessarily had limited popular appeal. Thus, Moe and Chubb also promoted online instruction as a way of creating "individualized curricula and approaches, heightened interest and participation, more efficient allocations of resources, a much broader array of choices, and a lot more" (Moe and Chubb 2009, 149–150). Technology allowed for students to have "more interaction with their teachers and with one another, including teachers and students who may be thousands of miles away or from different nations or cultures" (Ibid., 7). For Moe and Chubb, in an online education model, "learning will be liberated from the physical and institutional constraints that now hold it back—and it will be allowed to spread its wings" (Ibid., 98).

School choice was a key part of the larger effort to promote online instruction, and Moe and Chubb encouraged "entrepreneurs" to establish charter schools because state charter laws "give them many opportunities for setting up new cyberschools, and make their efforts much more difficult to block" (Moe and Chubb 2009, 121). For Moe and Chubb, "this is what innovation is all about: a new form of education was provided, students and parents were voluntarily choosing this new form in preference to the old, and the innovators—the school districts and their private partners—were benefitting from taking risks, making investments, and providing services that people value" (Ibid., 127). Yet "for the teachers' unions (and for many affected districts), innovation was a threat that needed to be stamped out" (Ibid.). Despite all these apparent innovations, school choice remained unpopular, and cyberschools never took off.

During this period, the public remained opposed to both vouchers and charters. In 2010, the pro–school choice *Education Next* poll included three similar questions about vouchers—which were labeled "other schooling opportunities"—all of which instructed respondents that government funds would pay for such a policy (*Education Next* 2010). And support for publicly subsidized vouchers ranged from 27 percent to 39 percent (Ibid.). While the 2010 PDK/Gallup Poll showed solid majority support for charters in three questions, respondents were not explicitly asked whether charters should be accountable like other public schools, nor were they informed that charters received public funding (Bushaw and Lopez 2010, 23). The same year, the *Education Next* poll randomly assigned respondents one of two questions gauging support for charter schools. One of these questions included the fact that charters are "publicly funded but are not managed by the local school board," while the other stated that charters "receive most of their funding from the government but they are privately managed," and in both cases, public support was 44 percent (*Education Next* 2010). Clearly neither charters nor vouchers had majority support.

Terry Moe continued his school choice advocacy in 2011 with *Special Interest: Teachers Unions and America's Public Schools*, also published by the Brookings Institution Press. Moe's analysis was also firmly rooted in the fantasy economy's narrative of failing schools and inadequate workforce. He restated the more politically savvy framing of the skills gap, which couched the issue in terms of the plight of racial minorities and the disadvantaged, yet implicitly held schools responsible for economic and social outcomes well beyond their control: "Without good schools, social inequity persists and festers, as children who are poor and minority are systematically denied the opportunities that only quality education can provide, and are at risk for being unemployed, getting involved in drugs and crime, going to prison, and even dying at an early age" (Moe 2011, 11). Moe used blunt, pro-technology rhetoric: because technology "has the capacity to transform the core components of schooling, it is disruptive to the jobs, routines, and resources that define the status quo" (Ibid., 375). Technology "can be substituted for labor in the learning process," which "translates into a reduction in jobs and money for the regular public schools and the people who work in them" (Ibid.). He repeated the common claims of corporate reformers revolving around customizing curricula and stressed the opposition of teachers' unions: "And as innovators push out the boundaries of what is possible, offering students and families a dazzling array of exciting new options in the cybersphere, the unions' tolerance of the information age evaporates" (Ibid.). He argued that teachers' unions were isolated on the left by citing the support for accountability of Education Trust and the Citizens Commission on Civil Rights, highlighting the political importance of both. And he attempted to bolster his position by characterizing two pro–school choice, pro-accountability, anti-union groups—Democrats for Education Reform and the Education Equality Project—as progressive organizations (Ibid., 347, 350, 488). And for Moe, "the old-line civil rights groups, particularly the N.A.A.C.P. . . . seem permanently stuck in the past and entirely without vision" (Ibid., 350).

Following the lead of CREDO and Arkansas's Department of Education Reform, by 2012, the University of Washington's Center on Reinventing Public Education also increasingly declared its independence. While it previously possessed a "point of view," it now stated that it "eschews ideological positions" (Center on Reinventing Public Education 2012). At the same time, the CRPE also boasted of its agenda-setting and framing roles, saying it "cultivates new ideas and fresh thinking" and "reframes the questions, redefines the problems" (Ibid.). The research center implicitly linked choice with innovation and sought to "design innovative and practical solutions for policymakers, elected officials, parents, educators, and community leaders" (Ibid.). It affirmed its commitment to public education while downplaying the use of the term "charter schools": "Public education is the goal. Particular institutions are only the means" (Ibid.). The CRPE also acknowledged their current and previous funders, a long list that included many of the most influential foundations active in education policy as well as the Business Roundtable (Ibid.). With this level of financial support, a third charter initiative in Washington State narrowly passed in 2012 with 50.69 percent of the total vote. Vouchers, however, remained very unpopular across a broad cross section of states. In 2012 and 2016, citizens in Florida and Oklahoma voted down efforts to repeal measures that prohibited the states from spending public funds on religious schools and thus limited their ability to fund private school voucher programs (Wermund 2016).

"If Charter Schools Are to Be Hotbeds of Educational Innovation"

By 2010, the body of research on school choice continued to show the mixed results of both charter and voucher programs. A study commissioned by the U.S. Department of Education found mixed overall effects of charter schools on academic achievement (Gleason et al. 2010). The Washington, DC, voucher program—strategically named the District of Columbia's Opportunity Scholarship Program—has also been the subject of several congressionally mandated evaluations by the U.S. Department of Education, which were led by Patrick Wolf of the University of Arkansas's Department of Education Reform. In the final report, Wolf and six colleagues found "no conclusive evidence that the O.S.P. affected student achievement," yet it increased recipients' likelihood of graduating high school by 12 percent (P. Wolf, Gutmann, et al. 2010, xv). The evaluation also found that the program "raised parents', but not students', ratings of school safety and satisfaction" (Ibid., xvi). Because all choice programs are voluntary, they necessarily consist of unrepresentative samples of students and families. Parents who enroll their children in choice programs are then, by definition, atypical, and so we should not be surprised if *any* sample of school choice students did not ultimately have at least somewhat higher attainment rates than a comparable group of students in public schools.

With research continuing to show mixed results, funded researchers increasingly relied on the theme of innovation in their reports. Beginning in 2008, the CRPE's National Charter School Research Project published several meta-analyses of charter school performance funded by numerous pro-charter foundations that consistently showed mixed results but also adopted the framing of charter schools as innovators. In the 2008 and 2011 reviews, the National Charter School Research Project acknowledged the same list of current and past funders, a list that included Anonymous, Achelis and Bodman Foundation, Annie E. Casey Foundation, Daniels Fund, Doris and Donald Fisher Fund, Thomas B. Fordham Foundation, Bill and Melinda Gates Foundation, the Heinz Endowments, Ewing Marion Kauffman Foundation, Rodel Charitable Foundation, the U.S. Department of Education, and the Walton Family Foundation (Betts and Tang 2008, 2011). The authors also acknowledged the support of the Walton Family and Ewing Marion Kaufman Foundations for the 2011 review (Betts and Tang 2011, 2) and the Walton Family Foundation for the 2014 review (Betts and Tang 2014).

In the 2008 review, economists Julian R. Betts and Y. Emily Tang stated that the "mission of charter schools is to offer innovative curricula and teaching methods" (2008, 26), which is certainly not the same as improving the academic achievement of charter students. They also characterized the mixed testing results of charter school students in terms of innovation: "The finding of considerable heterogeneity among charter schools probably reflects this spirit of innovation and experimentation" (Ibid.). The 2011 CRPE review explicitly linked charters with innovation: "Many view charter schools as a major innovation in the public school landscape because they have more freedom to experiment with alternative curricula and pedagogical methods and different ways of hiring and training teachers" (Betts and Tang 2011, 3). Again, the mixed results were described in terms of innovation within the context of the commonly utilized "what works" mantra of education reformers: "If charter schools are intended to be hotbeds of educational innovation, then successes should be identified, studied further, and the replicable parts of those models should be copied in other settings" (Ibid., 4). Their 2014 review again stressed the innovation theme, arguing that the "intent is that charter schools can provide students with alternative curricula, teaching methods, and teachers who may differ in educational background and training from teachers in traditional public schools. This freedom to experiment and innovate comes with the threat that the charter authorizer may shut down charter schools should they fail to meet academic standards or to maintain financial viability" (Betts and Tang 2014, 1). While all three reviews showed mixed results of charters on achievement, the expansion of charters did not appear up for debate, because, according to the 2014 review, charter schools represented "an increasingly important form of school choice in the United States" (Ibid.).

By 2012, the banner on CREDO's home page declared that the organization performed "Rigorous Research to Improve Public Education" (Center for Research on Education Outcomes 2012), and, over a period of several years, the center also published major national studies of charter schools. The press release for the 2009 CREDO charter school study, entitled "New Stanford Report Finds Serious Quality Challenge in National Charter School Sector," concluded that "there is a wide variance in the quality of the nation's several thousand charter schools with, in the aggregate, students in charter schools not faring as well as students in traditional public schools" (Center for Research on Education Outcomes 2009). But CREDO blamed state policies, such as caps on charter expansion and laws restricting charter authorizers, for inhibiting charter performance (Ibid.). The press release for the center's 2013 national study of charter schools was much more optimistic, stating, "Charter Schools Make Gains, According to 26-State Study," and it characterized the research as a "new, independent national study" (Center for Research on Education Outcomes 2013a). But the study's findings undermine this characterization. While the report found some gains in charter school achievement from the 2009 study, the detailed results for both reading and math achievement at each grade level were mixed. Still, CREDO concluded that the "charter sector was getting better on average, but not because existing schools are getting dramatically better; it is largely driven by the closure of bad schools" (Center for Research on Education Outcomes 2013b, 87). Steeped in the "what works" framing, the press release quoted the report's assertion that attention should be directed at "what plans, what models, what personnel attributes, and what internal systems provide the appropriate signals that lead to high-performing schools" (Center for Research on Education Outcomes 2013a).

CREDO characterized its 2015 urban charter school study in more unambiguously positive terms. Director Margaret Raymond stated, "This research shows that many urban charter schools are providing superior academic learning for their students, in many cases quite dramatically better. These findings offer important examples of school organization and operation that can serve as models to other schools, including both public charter schools and traditional public schools" (Center for Research on Education Outcomes 2015a). Yet when one examines the findings presented in the forty-five-page report, one finds a similar pattern of mixed results in both math and reading comparisons between charter students and those in public schools (Center for Research on Education Outcomes 2015b, vi). According to the report, urban charter schools "vary in quality" and "tend to reflect the strengths and weaknesses of the national charter sector" (Ibid., 37). The Gates Foundation echoed CREDO's framing of the 2015 charter school study, stating that "these urban public charter schools are providing particularly transformational experiences for disadvantaged students," and highlighted some positive findings (Gates Foundation 2016). For education reformers, charter schools were innovative approaches to educating the disadvantaged. Their continued expansion was not up for discussion, despite a growing body of research that consistently showed mixed results in terms of academic achievement.

"The U.S. Educational System Needs to Get Moving before the Jobs of the Twenty-First Century Do"

In 2014, Patrick Wolf coauthored a book about the Washington, DC, voucher program, *The School Choice Journey: School Vouchers and the Empowerment of Urban Families* (Stewart and Wolf 2014). Wolf's coauthor, Thomas Stewart, was president of Patten University, which was initially a nonprofit, evangelical institution that became a for-profit subsidiary of UniversityNow in 2012 (Western Association of Schools and Colleges 2012). The authors acknowledged receiving "a series of grants" from the Annie E. Casey Foundation (Stewart and Wolf 2014), and the book included a foreword from former Connecticut senator Joe Lieberman, an outspoken supporter of school choice programs. Like other pro–school choice works, *The School Choice Journey* is firmly grounded in the fantasy economy narrative of a failing school system and inadequate workforce. Stewart and Wolf claim that the "economy of the twenty-first century is information-based, with brains and service valued in place of the brawn and geographic location so important to the economy of the 20th century" (Ibid., 2). They further asserted that "globalization has metaphorically made the world 'flat'" (Ibid.). Thus, "capital and industry can 'vote with its feet,' moving to places around the world that possess a desirable mix of stable institutions, low costs of doing business, and, most importantly, a well-educated workforce. The U.S. educational system needs to get moving before the jobs of the twenty-first century do" (Ibid.).

As noted above, the final report of the Washington, DC, voucher program, led by Stewart, found "no conclusive evidence" that the program affected student achievement. Yet in *The School Choice Journey*, Stewart and Wolf argued that the "highly rigorous quantitative evaluation of the District of Columbia O.S.P. [Opportunity Scholarship Program] found that students tended to benefit educationally, clearly in terms of educational attainment and possibly also in terms of reading achievement" (Stewart and Wolf 2014, 37). And rather than reckon with the well-documented adverse effects of poverty on educational performance, they argued that the "program's ability to be fully effective in meeting the ultimate goal of improved student outcomes may have been hampered by resource limitations and the unanticipated demands associated with some families" (Ibid., 139). They further stated that "some participating schools . . . were by and large unprepared to cope with the academic and other needs of the O.S.P. students and the inability of many parents to meet school requirements for participation in their child's education" (Ibid.). Stewart and Wolf concluded that the "school choice journey might have been both longer and more rewarding if the tour guide had been better resourced and better prepared for the needs of the travelers" (Ibid.), an analysis that again seeks to keep the focus squarely on the schools and away from the proximate causes and effects of poverty and economic hardship.

Evaluations of the Louisiana voucher program funded by school choice advocates have also illustrated the tendency to present any findings in a manner that seeks to further voucher expansion. The University of Arkansas's Department of Education Reform's School Choice Demonstration Project, which is "devoted to the rigorous and unbiased evaluation of school choice programs and other school improvement efforts across the country" (School Choice Demonstration Project 2022), has participated in these evaluations, some of which have acknowledged the support of the Smith Richardson Foundation (Mills and Wolf 2016, 1; 2017, 1; 2019, 1). The 2016 and 2017 evaluations were also coproduced with Tulane University's Education Research Alliance for New Orleans, which is funded by the university's Murphy Institute (Education Research Alliance for New Orleans 2022), which was created with monies from the

Murphy family, the founders of the Murphy Oil Corporation (Murphy Institute 2022).

The first evaluation showed that after two years, program participants fared worse in both English Language Arts (ELA) and math but that only the math achievement data was statistically significant (Mills and Wolf 2016, 2). The report concluded by stating that the findings "indicate significant and substantial negative achievement impacts associated with using an LSP [Louisiana Scholarship Program] scholarship" (Ibid., 35). Yet the authors distanced themselves from their own methodology and findings: "At the same time, it is important to keep in mind that our analyses are based on a small subsample of LSP participants with performance data on the Louisiana state assessments. . . . Thus, in a real sense, this paper is not an evaluation of the entire program, but an evaluation of the experiences of students in grades three through seven at baseline, who participated in actual lotteries, with testing outcomes in Year 2. . . . Readers are encouraged not to draw firm conclusions from this initial analysis due to the severe threats to external validity posed by those limitations of the sample" (Ibid.).

The evaluation of the Louisiana program in the third year showed positive effects for achievement in ELA and negative effects for math, but neither was statistically significant (Mills and Wolf 2017, 2). Still, the authors stated that the "immediate effects of the Louisiana Scholarship Program on student test scores was negative but that the intermediate effects, after three years, are inconclusive and might reasonably be null or even positive given the high level of statistical uncertainty involved" (Ibid., 4), a characterization that also minimized the lack of improvement in achievement among voucher participants. The findings reported after four years were substantially negative, and Wolf and four colleagues from the Department of Education Reform stated that "participating in the LSP had a statistically significant negative impact on student English Language Arts (ELA) and math scores across most years of the evaluation, including the fourth year, and across most samples of students studied" (P. Wolf, Mills, et al. 2019, 2). Yet the paper emphasized previous positive results, while seeming to dismiss negative results by arguing that the program is a unique case: "Before considering what these impacts mean for private school choice, it is important to realize the Louisiana Scholarship Program's uniqueness," along with the "uniqueness" of the researchers' "analytical sample" (Ibid., 11, 12). They further define success partially in tautological terms by claiming that the means-tested program accomplished the goal of providing "private school options for disadvantaged families" (Ibid., 12).

The themes of school choice and online education as necessary innovations were also advanced in a 2016 report by Wolf and Anna J. Egalite entitled *Pursuing Innovation: How Can Educational Choice Transform K–12 Education in the U.S.?* (P. Wolf and Egalite 2016). The report was published by the Friedman Foundation for Educational Choice, which was founded in 1996 to promote "school choice as the most effective and equitable way to improve the quality of K–12 education in America" (Ibid.). Firmly grounded in neoclassical economics, Wolf and Egalite's analysis encouraged policy makers to adopt school choice legislation "flexible and thoughtful enough to facilitate new models of schooling that have not been widely implemented yet, especially those that rely on technology to leverage learning" (Ibid., 2). The authors argued that "pressure from charter schools and taxpayer-funded private school choice programs appears to be engineering the valuable process of creative destruction, as poor-performing public and private schools are closed and their enrollments absorbed by better-performing schools and school franchises" (Ibid., 32). Echoing long-standing libertarian themes, they maintained that school choice "certainly has the potential to reduce education spending and thereby increase school productivity" (Ibid., 23).

In a "Commitment to Methods and Transparency" found on the last page of *Pursuing Innovation*, the Friedman Foundation acknowledged that "many organizations (like our own) have specific missions or philosophical orientations" (P. Wolf and Egalite 2016, 42). However, the foundation maintained that "scientific methods, if used correctly and followed closely in well-designed studies, should neutralize these opinions and orientations. Research rules and methods minimize bias. We believe rigorous procedural rules of science prevent a researcher's motives, and an organization's particular orientation, from pre-determining results" (Ibid.). Yet the report is explicitly framed in the assumptions of free market economics, which are treated as a given. In this view, expanding school choice, reducing public spending, and increasing the use of technology with the goal of improving the "productivity" of schools are not questioned, and the larger discussion of economic opportunity must remain squarely on the education system and away from the free markets of neoliberalism, which have benefited relatively few.

After publishing *Pursuing Innovation*, the Friedman Foundation changed its name to EdChoice, and it recently stated that it was "funded by individuals and organizations who share our mission to make sure all K–12 students in the United States have the opportunity to access the schooling options that work for them, whether that's public, private, public charter, homeschooling or another type," while also affirming that it respects "the privacy of those who support" the organization's work "unless they tell us they want to be recognized for their generosity" (Ed-Choice 2022).

Conclusion

On December 10, 2014, CREDO's Margaret Raymond gave a talk to the City Club of Cleveland sponsored by the Thomas Fordham Institute (Strauss 2014), a leading free market think tank and sponsor of school choice research. In her remarks, Raymond declared CREDO's independence and nonpartisan research agenda: "For the past fifteen years, C.R.E.D.O. has made its mark by providing independent and nonpartisan and rigorous analysis of promising educational reform programs in American k–12 education" (City Club of Cleveland 2014). She stated: "We're not pro-charter, we're not anti-district, and we're not the reverse of those things. What we are is we're for great schools for all kids" (Ibid.). Raymond then outlined findings of CREDO's research on charter schools in Ohio that were decidedly mixed.

During the question-and-answer session, Raymond was asked what the findings of CREDO's research say about the policy environment in which charter schools operate. Her response, which was reported by the *Washington Post* (Strauss 2014), deviated from the traditional talking points of school choice advocates and indicated that free market theory does not actually describe the workings of education policy:

> This is one of the big insights for me. I actually am kind of a pro-market kind of girl. But it doesn't seem to work in a choice environment for education. I've studied competitive markets for much of my career. That's my academic focus for my work. And it's [education] the only industry/sector where the market mechanism just doesn't work. (City Club of Cleveland 2014)

Raymond's comments revealed the explicitly political nature of the school choice movement. Although she admitted that free market theory does not apply to education, the focus must remain on free market education policies because under neoliberalism, it is the education system's responsibility to provide economic opportunity.

The fantasy economy narrative rooted in failing schools and a perpetual skills gap has been central to the school choice movement. Because it is a political movement, shaping opinion is a major goal, and funded research has been a critical part of this strategy. And the language of reformers has evolved to accommodate consistent majority support for publicly funded, democratically controlled public schools. But, in the end, I argue that the data and research of school choice studies funded by advocates are largely irrelevant, as charters and vouchers, for education reformers, must necessarily be expanded, regardless of performance. This is the purpose of the "what works" framing—to keep the focus on reforming schools through policies such as choice. Because to expand the discussion of economic opportunity and mobility beyond the education system would necessarily lead to a much larger conversation about the nature of neoliberalism, and in the fantasy economy, such a conversation is necessarily out of bounds.

Over the last several years, sensing that school choice programs have reached their limits, the education reform movement has shifted its emphasis toward the promotion of online education and the sale of technology products and services, a subject I examine in the Epilogue.

Conclusion

Beyond the Fantasy and Back to Reality

It is extraordinary that an economic theory with "human"
in its title has so little to say about what makes us human
or about differences in human aspirations, motivations,
and identities.
—PHILLIP BROWN, HUGH LAUDER, AND SIN YI CHEUNG,
   The Death of Human Capital?

Introduction

In the conclusion, I briefly summarize the main findings, discuss the
growth of inequality and wage stagnation over the past several decades,
and offer several suggestions for transforming the larger discussion of
education and economic opportunity. Ultimately, we must see the fantasy economy for what it is—a misleading, political campaign in the interests of corporations and the wealthy. To get beyond the fantasy economy, then, it is necessary to begin from the assumption that policy makers
and business practices—not the education system—determine job opportunities and wage levels. This necessitates extracting education from
the suffocating confines of human capital theory and viewing both K–12
and higher education as vital institutions for human growth and the maintenance of democracy in an increasingly diverse, pluralistic society.

The Evolution of Education Reform:
From Human Capital Theory to
Advancing Neoliberalism

In the late 1950s and 1960s, human capital theory's rise to prominence
led to a new understanding of education's role in shaping individual economic outcomes. Yet labor unions remained strong, the social safety net

was expanding as Johnson's Great Society programs built on the New Deal, and, as a result, levels of income inequality were substantially lower than in previous periods. Relatively few citizens received bachelor's degrees, which were not necessary to obtain economic security and mobility. While the significant expansion of higher education in the 1960s created many new business opportunities, corporate elites also became increasingly concerned over the direction of both higher education and K–12 schooling. Schoolteachers went on strike in many cities, and college campuses became important sources of political protest movements, developments that led economic elites to believe that the trajectory of both K–12 and higher education needed to be changed. However, because foundation giving had always been understood as a reflection of the interests of corporations and the wealthy, it became politically necessary to reinvent foundations solely as public-spirited entities. And the creation of institutions such as *Change: The Magazine of Higher Learning* and the American Association for Higher Education, both of which advanced corporate elites' formulation of education reform, were key parts of this strategy.

The education reform movement symbolized by *Change* and the AAHE would eventually find common cause with the standards movement, which focused on the presumed failures of K–12 education, the essence of which was captured in 1977—a time of increasing deindustrialization—by the Hudson Institute's Frank Armbruster in *Our Children's Crippled Future*. Armbruster planted the seeds of the business-led skills gap campaign with a brief allusion to the coming high-education, high-skill labor market. But because his analysis was also rooted in the culture-of-poverty framing, which placed disproportionate emphasis on the attitudes and behavior of the poor, I argue that it could not engender widespread political support. Still, his advocacy of an accountability regime built on standardized testing would become a primary goal of education reformers many years later.

In the years after Armbruster's book, the contours of neoliberalism began to take shape, and Ronald Reagan's election in 1980 was a watershed moment in the creation of a new political economy, one that posited that unregulated market forces would enable all to proposer while an activist government would only cause the population economic hardship. However, most of the components of the neoliberal public policy agenda and new business culture were decidedly unpopular as they revolved around maximizing returns on capital income while minimizing the cost of labor. Ultimately, then, I argue that corporate elites needed a political strategy to advance neoliberalism. This led to the creation of a campaign I call the fantasy economy, which consisted of two overarching claims—the schools and the workforce were perpetually deficient. Conceptually, the campaign has emphasized three overarching themes— free markets, technology, and data.

As an interest group campaign, the fantasy economy produces its own data and research, including what I call alternative data. And the empirical support for its main tenets ranges from misleading to nonexistent. The evidence of a historically declining education system is, at best, distorted, and the main evidence cited in the skills gap campaign has consisted of interest group surveys and foundation- and corporate-funded research. Official data has shown that the education system's performance has been relatively consistent over time and that there have been more than enough qualified workers for available jobs, including in STEM fields. Rather than a skills gap, official data has shown consistently high numbers of underemployed workers in a labor market dominated by low-education, low-skill jobs. A few prominent early studies, including the National Center on Education and the Economy's first major report, *America's Choice*, and the Sandia Report, refuted the emerging narrative of an inadequate workforce. But these dissenting voices were drowned out by the political power of the skills gap campaign, much of which was directed at educators themselves. The skills gap was in the interests of business and elected officials who embraced neoliberal policies and business practices that led to stagnating wages, deindustrialization, the loss of labor unions, and the expansion of low-wage, low-education jobs.

The Reagan administration's *A Nation at Risk* and *Workforce 2000* were both foundational components of a larger political strategy of linking the declining economic opportunity faced by the majority of workers characteristic of neoliberalism to a purportedly failing education system and inadequate workforce. In addition to its many claims about the labor market and education reform, *Workforce 2000* also implicitly outlined the neoliberal policy agenda by questioning the relevance of major New Deal and Great Society programs, including Social Security, unemployment insurance, trade adjustment assistance, federal job training programs, and "many other federal programs" (Johnston and Packer 1987, viii), while also advocating welfare reform. In 1985, the Reagan administration's National Institute of Education funded the creation of the Institute on Education and the Economy within Columbia University's Teachers College as part of this larger strategy as well. In subsequent years, the IEE received funding from corporations and foundations, and in 1992 it succinctly stated that the overriding purpose of the education reform movement is to *"change the mission of K–12 schools to take educational responsibility for the economic futures of all students"* (Berryman and

Bailey 1992a, 7, emphasis in original). This was the essence of the emerging fantasy economy campaign and the ultimate expression of human capital theory: the education system would be held responsible for the economic livelihoods of the citizenry.

Much of reformers' activities during the late 1980s and early 1990s focused on school accountability and included foundation- and corporate-funded organizations such as California's Achievement Council, the American Association for Higher Education's schools-college partnership, and the Commission on Title I. And by the late 1980s, the skills gap campaign was so comprehensive that teachers' union leader Al Shanker lamented that the U.S. public schools were essentially failing a significant majority of their students in his original proposal for charter schools. In 1989, as manufacturing facilities continued to close and low-wage, nonunionized, service-sector jobs grew, business interests furthered the accountability campaign with the publication of the Business Roundtable's *Essential Components of a Successful Education System*. That year, President George H. W. Bush summoned governors to an Education Summit, and a lengthy front-page story in the *New York Times* described in considerable detail the difficulty corporate leaders experienced in finding qualified workers. But unlike the racism and cultural analysis of *Workforce 2000*, the new skills gap campaign framed young, low-income minority children as victims of a failing school system. In this analysis, the public schools were preventing children from escaping poverty, which would become a central theme of the education reform movement. During this period, the movement for charter schools and vouchers proceeded as well. Education reform advocates increasingly funded research in pursuit of their goals, including Chubb and Moe's *Politics, Markets, and America's Schools* and the creation of the Center on Reinventing Public Education in 1993 at the University of Washington under the direction of Brookings's Paul Hill.

But passing federal school accountability would constitute a major challenge, and in 1993, several prominent reformers, including Kati Haycock and David Hornbeck, talked in *Education Week* about the difficulty of overcoming public opposition to the corporate version of education reform, which consisted of an accountability system based on high-stakes, standardized tests. By this time, the Business Roundtable had created the "Keep the Promise" campaign focusing on major school reform, which included an advertisement featuring the rescue of Baby Jessica from a well in Texas in 1987. And the theme of saving children would become a key component of the strategy of accountability supporters. Yet as a political campaign, elites still needed to create a seemingly diverse coalition in support of accountability, and the schools-college collaboration at the AAHE evolved into Education Trust, which became pivotal for this purpose. Education Trust positioned itself as a civil rights organization, and its messaging replaced the culture of poverty with the racial achievement gap, which became central to the school accountability movement. The Citizens Commission on Civil Rights played a similar role. As a nonprofit established in the early 1980s to monitor civil rights in several different areas, in the years leading up to No Child Left Behind, the CCCR published reports that solely advocated school accountability that acknowledged the funding of foundations active in the accountability campaign.

In the political campaign for accountability, the achievement gap was caused by schools, teachers, and low standards. This analysis reflected traditionally conservative ideological assumptions that divorced educational performance from the realities of income and poverty and was most forcefully advanced by Education Trust. Critically, the group also acknowledged the existence of racism and elevated the concept of data in the education reform movement, thereby making the word "data" ultimately more important than data itself. Buttressed by the seeming objectivity of *any* data as well as the mere mention of racism, the political campaign for accountability seemed to have a winning formulation. As the accountability movement was advancing in Washington, charter school and voucher proponents made some inroads in the states. But because the public has never been supportive of diverting funds for traditional public schools to privately run schools, school choice plans tended to develop in high-poverty urban areas. To further the research and data components of the education reform campaign, in 1999 reformers created the Center for Research on Education Outcomes at the University of Rochester, which relocated to Stanford University's Hoover Institution shortly thereafter, and in 2001 created the publication *Education Matters*, the title of which was changed to *Education Next* by its third issue.

Running as a compassionate conservative and despite losing the popular vote, George W. Bush was elected president in 2000 and touted his state's school accountability program and the "Texas Miracle." Although scholarly research undermined the notion of any such miracle, school accountability, backed by major business interests, had momentum. The racial achievement gap in combination with the political power of the concept of data gave accountability bipartisan support in Washington. However, it would take the immense distraction and resulting patriotism of 9/11 to pass the No Child Left Behind law in 2002, which created a high-stakes, testing-and-accountability regime in public schools. As the law was implemented, several major yet foreseeable problems became readily apparent, leading to a public backlash against standardized testing and punitive accountability measures. School choice advocates also continued to face an uphill battle in public opinion and increasingly distanced themselves from free market terminology while affirming their independence and objectivity. As a result, voucher and charter proponents focused their campaigns on providing economic opportunity for the disadvantaged on the basis of an implicit assumption of a permanent skills gap, and in 2005, two foundations advocating market-based education policies funded the creation of the Department of Education Reform at the University of Arkansas with $20 million to produce school choice research. But the public remained largely opposed to diverting funding from public schools to either charter schools or voucher programs. Thus, a tragedy like Hurricane Katrina was necessary to significantly increase school choice programs.

Increasing technology's role has long been a goal of the corporate-led education reform movement, and some of the most well-known pro–school choice scholars, including Terry Moe and John Chubb, have also been among the biggest advocates of online education. Technology has been promoted as a potential cost savings measure to both K–12 and higher education, and online education was promoted in terms of the unlimited choices it provided students and faculty. But like television in the classroom in previous decades, online education clearly had limited market appeal. Ultimately, then, in lieu of using explicitly pro–free market or pro-technology language in their campaigns, reformers increasingly invoked the banner of innovation to advance their priorities. These developments occurred following a significant business-led campaign based on the concept of innovation, which also included an overwhelming push for increasing STEM education.

As implementation problems mounted with No Child Left Behind, elites mobilized and began to advocate for what would eventually become the Common Core, which the Gates Foundation was instrumental in advancing. And with little substantive public debate, in 2009, states were incentivized to adopt the Common Core as part of the Obama administration's Race to the Top initiative. With opposition to No Child Left Behind mounting, in 2015 Congress passed the Every Student Succeeds Act (ESSA). But the law left the same testing and accountability framework implemented through Title I funds in place while giving states more latitude in the creation of accountability systems. The standardized testing regime was here to stay, despite its many adverse consequences and inherent inability to reverse decades of growing economic inequality and stagnating wages, particularly for lower-earning workers.

By President George W. Bush's second term, corporations and foundations had begun to formulate a higher education reform agenda. And in 2008, with initial funding from the Gates, Lumina, and Ford Foundations, Anthony Carnevale founded the Center on Education and the Workforce at Georgetown University as a key part of these efforts. Data from the BLS continued to show a minority of total jobs typically requiring post–high school education, and research from the Federal Reserve consistently showed that one-third of all bachelor's degree holders were underemployed. But the CEW produced its own, alternative data that explicitly challenged BLS data by positing that a solid majority of all jobs required post–high school education, a narrative that was widely disseminated and uncritically accepted in the higher education policy ecosystem. And while the National Center for Education Statistics continued to project modestly fluctuating numbers of both high school graduates and higher education enrollments as far as its data went into the future, alternative data projecting a major decline in prospective college students in the distant future evolved into the dominant narrative of a demographic cliff. Together, the belief in a disproportionately high-education labor market and future demographic crisis facing higher education both reflected and reinforced higher education's politically weak status, enabling reformers to more easily advance an agenda rooted in austerity budgeting.

Throughout the 2010s, numerous studies on school choice programs—many of which were funded by school choice advocates—showed negative or mixed results of charter schools and voucher programs on academic achievement. But researchers funded by school choice advocates utilized the "what works" framing of their findings in an ongoing attempt to expand choice programs, which were also increasingly described as innovative. As evidenced by business interests' continual promotion of the notions of a perpetually underperforming education system and underqualified labor force, I maintain that economic elites could not, under any circumstances, back away from the larger narrative that individual economic opportunity was solely the responsibility of the education system. As a political campaign designed to protect the economic interests of corporations and the wealthy, the fantasy economy could not end.

Neoliberalism and the Growth of Economic Inequality

As Adam Kotsko has written, "increasing inequality appears to be the most consistent outcome of neoliberalism" (2018, 34). Growing inequal-

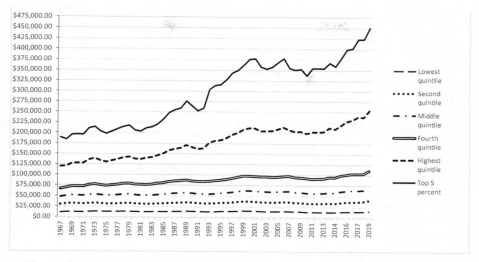

Figure C.1 Mean Household Income of Population, Quintiles and Top 5%, 1967–2019 (2019 Dollars) *(Source: U.S. Census Bureau 2020.)*

ity and stagnating wages for most workers have been characteristic of the economy over the last several decades. As shown in Figure C.1, since the late 1970s, inflation-adjusted incomes for most households have been largely flat, while those of a relatively small minority have grown considerably. In fact, the bottom 80 percent of households have received a steadily declining share of aggregate income, and this pattern has been most apparent among the lowest earners. For example, in 1980, the bottom 40 percent of households earned 14.4 percent of national income, but by 2018, they earned only 11.4 percent (U.S. Census Bureau 2019). During the same period, the share of household income going to the top 20 percent of households—those households earning over $130,000 in 2018—went from just over 44 percent to 52 percent (Ibid.). Inequality has become even more pronounced over the last two decades as the incomes of the highest earners pulled away further. Between 1999 and 2018, the median inflation-adjusted household income increased just 2.7 percent, while inflation-adjusted incomes at the ninety-fifth percentile of households increased nearly 16 percent (Ibid.). These wage trends contrast greatly with income changes during much of the twentieth century. To be sure, income inequality was high previously, but income disparities incrementally diminished. In the decades after the New Deal, poverty rates consistently decreased, median incomes increased, and inequality declined. And during this period, the annual income gains for the bottom 20 percent even outpaced those of the top 20 percent (Putnam 2015, 34), a significant contrast to income growth patterns of recent decades.

The growth of economic inequality ushered in by neoliberalism has become the subject of increasing scholarly and political debate. And an extensive body of research has documented the many proximate causes and effects of growing inequality and stagnating wages,[1] and many works by prominent social scientists have helped place inequality on the agenda of the media and policy makers. First published in 2013, Thomas Piketty's award-winning *Capital in the 21st Century* (2014) attracted considerable worldwide attention, was translated into numerous languages, and precipitated a larger debate in economics (Boushey, Delong, and Steinbaum 2017). The issue has also been addressed by many political scientists (Bartels 2016; J. Hacker and Pierson 2016, 2020; Putnam 2015) and has become a major focus of research in many other fields as well. Finally, the extreme inequality brought on by neoliberalism's transformed version of capitalism has also become the subject of a growing list of recent books by prominent nonfiction authors and journalists (K. Anderson 2020; Appelbaum 2019; Gelles 2022; Lemann 2019; Quart 2018).

Inequality has also become a central component of mainstream political debate. In 2016 and 2020, Democratic presidential candidate Senator Bernie Sanders emphasized stagnating wages and increasing income and wealth inequality and advocated several policies intended to address these problems, including Medicare for All, free public higher education, and increased taxes on the highest earners and corporations. Republican presidential candidate in 2016, Donald Trump tapped into public anxiety about declining economic opportunity and frequently discussed lost jobs and lower wages. But Trump linked these problems largely to immigrants and trade policies. Once in office, he largely abandoned any pretense of policies aimed at economically marginalized populations, however, by advocating an agenda of deregulation, tax cuts for corporations and the wealthy, the appointment of officials and judges opposed to organized labor, and the tightening of eligibility requirements for the Supplemental Nutrition Assistance Program (SNAP), while also adopting his party's steadfast opposition to the Affordable Care Act and minimum wage increases. Although Trump's appeal seemed inherently at odds with the benefits of formal education, his policy priorities were consistent with elites' seeming exclusive emphasis on formal education as the only means of achieving economic security and mobility.

But sentiment appears to be turning. The public and, increasingly, major media seem to understand that contemporary capitalism has been detrimental to most workers. Union organizing is increasing. Yet because educators have been primary targets of messaging claiming a failing education system and insufficient labor force, the institutional education system is on the outside looking in at these major developments. I maintain that the higher education establishment still implicitly accepts the proposition that it can fix inequality when it cannot. To become full participants in this critical debate, then, educators must first acknowledge the many empirical problems with human capital theory. This will allow for the emergence of a more comprehensive and humane view of both K–12 and higher education in which the education system is no longer held responsible for labor market outcomes well beyond its control.

Beyond Human Capital Theory: Reframing Opportunity and Reclaiming Education

Historically, education has been about much more than simply creating wage-earning workers, including the inculcation of citizenship, democratic values, and even democracy itself. Early in the twentieth century, John Dewey (1916) wrote at length about the mutually important relationship between democracy and education. While education was seen by many as a mechanism to bring individuals out of poverty (Groeger 2021), economic opportunity was understood as more than a function of individuals' formal education, and the importance of education's role in creating citizens and maintaining democracy was increasingly recognized. And at the dawn of the twenty-first century, Jennifer Hochschild and Nathan Scovronick insightfully described the multiple roles that the public expects the education system to perform: "Americans expect schools not only to help students reach their potential as individuals but also to make them good citizens who will maintain the nation's values and institutions, help them flourish, and pass them on to the next generation" (Hochschild and Scovronick 2003, 1, 2).

I argue that the public still expects the education system to perform these multiple roles, yet the dominance of human capital theory and the larger fantasy economy narrative have warped the many important purposes of education by erroneously linking it exclusively to individual labor market outcomes. I further maintain that successfully making K–12 and higher education solely responsible for the economic well-being of the citizenry—the founding assumption of the modern education reform movement—has allowed neoliberalism to take hold. Yet in the decades since *A Nation at Risk*, educational attainment levels have reached all-time highs, while wages have stagnated for most workers and economic inequality has increased significantly. And according to federal data, for at least the last several decades, those with post–high school education have substantially outnumbered jobs available for workers with that level of education, resulting in chronically high underemployment rates. Moreover, by narrowing education's role to a strictly economic one, human capital theory has minimized the inherent complexity of humanity. As economists Phillip Brown, Hugh Lauder, and Sin Yi Cheung have recently argued, "It is extraordinary that an economic theory with 'human' in its title has so little to say about what makes us human or about differences in human aspirations, motivations, and identities" (2020, 213). Further, like human capital theory generally, skill-biased technological change has often been assumed despite the absence of empirical support for its main assertions. The significant technological advances of recent decades have not led to substantially more jobs requiring higher education, leaving large numbers of highly educated persons underemployed.

The fallacies of skill-biased technological change become evident when we consider the fundamental nature of society and the world in which we live. While tech supremacy has been at the heart of the fantasy economy campaign and education reform movement, the notion that the economy or our society are primarily characterized by information, knowledge, or data is, quite simply, not an accurate reflection of reality. We live in a physical world, a world of objects. Knowledge and information exist in relation to the physical world and have not—and necessarily cannot—supplant it. Western economies are increasingly characterized by consumption, most of which involves the consumption of physical objects. The share of gross domestic product (GDP) in the United States consisting of personal consumption has been on an upward trajectory for decades, and recent data shows that nearly 70 percent of GDP consists of personal consumption (Federal Reserve Economic Data 2022). The consumer-driven society consists largely of objects that need to be grown, harvested, mined, manufactured, assembled, shipped, sold, used, worn, eaten, and then disposed of or recycled. Our digital lives are also driven by objects, as new versions of smartphones and other technology products are continually manufactured and sold to a world of eager consumers.

The world of objects is also evident in examinations of current labor market data that shows the abundance of jobs in fields such as retail sales, cashier work, food services, and warehouse work in comparison to the relatively small number of jobs in strictly technology- and information-related fields. Moreover, the two most common services, health care and education, revolve around human beings providing services—knowledge, treatments, and so forth—to other human beings in physical places made up of objects. And within the context of a growing population, our object-based economy is the foundation of the climate crisis. I argue that the information or knowledge economy is an artificial construct created by economic elites in substantial part to advance an unpopular neoliberal agenda, including the relocation of manufacturing overseas. While the interest group campaign I call the fantasy economy is rooted in knowledge (or data, or information), the real economy is rooted in the physical world in which we live, a world of objects.

The obvious empirical flaws of human capital theory combined with the reality that neoliberalism has adversely affected the economic well-being of most workers can help lay the groundwork for a reframing of economic opportunity. Neoliberalism has substantially eroded the dignity of work. This concept, which as the dignity of labor can be traced back centuries in various religious traditions, means, quite simply, that *all* work has dignity. But the forces of free market supremacy have transformed jobs that formerly provided something approximating a working- or middle-class income into jobs paying wages close to poverty. To provide one example, in 1985, hourly wages at the unionized Hormel meat-processing facility in Austin, Minnesota, were $10.69 in current dollars (Painter 2019), the equivalent of nearly $30 an hour in 2022 dollars, or an annual wage of roughly $60,000 (Bureau of Labor Statistics, n.d.). But according to the Bureau of Labor Statistics, the median hourly wage in 2021 for slaughterers and meat packers in the United States was $14.38, or just under $30,000 in annual wages (Bureau of Labor Statistics 2022c).

Similar patterns can be found in other service occupations requiring less formal education, as labor unions have been decimated and increases in the minimum wage exceedingly rare. And the fact that low-wage jobs are treated as undesirable also increases the political difficulty of raising the minimum wage and union organizing today, both of which continuously run up against the political and economic might of major business and trade groups. Education reformers have changed their messaging regarding the abundance of low-wage, service-sector jobs, and eventually, elites coalesced around the theme of linking individual labor market outcomes solely to formal education and training. And the success of these efforts has stigmatized millions of traditionally low-education jobs on which our consumption-driven economy depends, making it much easier to pay these workers low wages and keep labor unions out.

Because economic inequality is ultimately driven by wage inequality, the free market supremacy of neoliberalism in its entirety needs to be revisited. All work and workers need to be treated with dignity. The benefits of economic growth should be shared more equitably among all workers. Although it is a tall order, when we consider the simple fact that the education reform movement itself has increasingly shied away from free market language, the prospect of creating a more just economic order is not as politically difficult as it might appear. Although policies such as a universal basic income seem to have diverse ideological support, such approaches directly undermine the dignity of work by further incentivizing the many forces that have led to a predominantly low-wage economy and increasing inequality and should therefore be forcefully opposed. Public policy and business culture must facilitate the formation of labor unions, returning to the forceful guarantee of the right to collective bargaining, which has been gradually eroded since the middle twentieth century. The minimum wage should be increased regularly with inflation, and employers' ability to utilize noncompete agreements with employees should be curtailed. The tax code should explicitly encourage the creation of good jobs in the United States and discourage the movement of jobs out of the country. Tax avoidance by corporations and the wealthy should be meaningfully addressed by policy makers. Antitrust law should be utilized to maintain robust market competition in all sectors. In sum, public policy should facilitate all workers benefiting from economic growth.

Moreover, our historic moment compels us to reconsider the neoliberal paradigm that has led us to such extreme inequality and political instability. Pseudopopulism, racism, and authoritarianism thrive in a country in which elites routinely invoke a mythical skills gap in an economy dominated by low-education, low-wage jobs, and those with a high school degree are instructed that the only way to advance economically is if they obtain more formal education and training. Further, much of the corporate-led education reform agenda, which includes the instinctive erosion of the liberal arts and promotion of STEM and technical fields, must also be viewed within the context of the current fragile state of our democracy. Democratic stability is dependent on a population educated in liberal arts fields such as history, the social sciences, and the arts and humanities. These fields not only teach students about empirical reality and impart critical reading, thinking, research, and writing skills but also enable them to learn empathy and appreciate the complexities of the human experience. As this is being written in the summer of 2022, the future of American democracy is at stake. Maintaining broad-based liberal arts education for all students is more important now than at any point in modern American history.

Ultimately, then, to get beyond the fantasy economy, the multiple roles for education must be reestablished, which mandates removing education from the stultifying confines of human capital theory and reframing economic opportunity. I suggest that Hochschild and Scovronick's 2003 characterization of public opinion regarding the purposes of education remains accurate today. In fact, I argue that this is precisely why education reformers have engaged in a decades-long effort to change public opinion in a continuous attempt to implement unpopular and largely ineffective policies and priorities: Americans want a multifaceted, democratically run, well-funded, face-to-face, *public* education system. Citizens appreciate the human relationships between educators and their students that technology can never replace, learning about a wide range of fields, and developing diverse skills including social skills. The public well understands that educators help students in a multitude of ways beyond simple content delivery. Citizens clearly prefer a publicly funded, democratically run school system in which policy makers are accountable to voters, which is why public support for charter schools and vouchers has always been inherently limited. The public also strongly desires an affordable, publicly funded system of higher education, as evidenced by the growing push for free public higher education and student loan forgiveness in recent years.

Further, I maintain that Americans implicitly oppose a model of economic opportunity tied solely to formal education and training. Considering the widespread underemployment and low wages of millions of highly educated individuals, the public knows the realities of the labor market firsthand. And scholars have insightfully pointed out how the disappointing economic outcomes associated with higher education attainment for many have affected public policy. For example, Christopher Newfield has argued that "if even public colleges offer an economic and social benefit only to a minority, politicians will quite logically reduce their funding" (2016, 301). And Simon Marginson describes the politics of budget cutting in the University of California System as follows: "Successive state governments had learned that they could reduce public funding without a severe public backlash, but there was more likely to be public opposition if they sanctioned the tuition increases necessary for institutions to make up the shortfall" (2016, 137).

The public *does* allow legislators to punish education when it does not deliver the economic benefits promised. Hence education needs to stop promising benefits that it cannot deliver for large numbers of students and reclaim its multiple purposes within a new model of economic opportunity. The public would embrace a view of education revolving around human growth and the development of democratic citizenship as opposed to its current narrow function of developing job skills in what amounts to a game of education and economic lottery, especially for the disadvantaged. Moreover, students want to be able to pursue areas of study and careers that are of interest to them and not be limited to the ever-shrinking number of college majors that can facilitate earning middle-class wages in our highly unequal society. The public seems implicitly aware that the fantasy economy is a myth. It is a myth they accept only because it is all they have been offered. Citizens are eager for change, including a renewed view of the many purposes of education itself within a much different framing of economic opportunity and social mobility.

Toward this end, many scholars have raised critical questions regarding corporate influence on the education system and the gradual narrowing of education to skills training. Historical work documented the connections between corporate thinking and the development of higher education early in the twentieth century (Barrow 1990). More recent scholarship has chronicled the increasing corporate influence on both K–12 and higher education in neoliberalism. Diane Ravitch (2010, 2013, 2020) has been a pioneering voice for those concerned with the increasingly privatized world of K–12 education reform and has asked critical questions about the extraordinary influence of the nation's wealthiest individuals and institutions on the public education system. Marc Bousquet's (2008) influential work articulated how contemporary capitalism has affected the university and how the university has enabled contemporary capitalism as well. Other scholars have written about the decades-long decline in public support for higher education (Marginson 2016), including the relationship between this trend and growing inequality (Newfield 2008, 2016). Slaughter and Rhoades's (2004) work is loaded with insights and data about the significant and growing corporate influence on higher education.

We can build on the insights offered by these scholars as well as recent work on teaching and learning to begin to reclaim the many purposes of education and, in turn, create a new paradigm of economic opportunity. Education scholar Kevin Gannon (2020) has articulated an important perspective on contemporary higher education, and his analysis can be applied to K–12 education as well. Gannon is rightly skeptical of the market language and assumptions dominant in higher education today. He describes what he calls "classrooms of death" on our campuses, in which education has been reduced solely to skills training. Yet for Gannon, educators bear some of the responsibility for our predicament.

When challenged about abstract arguments regarding the purposes of education, educators "shift to a language we think will be taken more seriously by administrators, politicians, and cost-conscious parents: the language of marketable skills for the 'new economy,' and of terms like 'nimble' and 'agile' and 'multiple competencies'" (Gannon 2020, 17). Gannon is correct: we have adopted the language of what I call the fantasy economy because it is, effectively, the only language within the education establishment.

But, according to Gannon, when educators use this vocabulary, we "cede the terrain of the debate; we've implicitly declared higher education's real value is transactional and market oriented" (2020, 17). And when we further treat education as a series of binaries in which students have either "acquired the necessary skills and knowledge or they haven't, that they have either succeeded or failed, either gotten 'what they needed' or failed to do so," we dismiss "habits like self-examination, critical thinking, and questioning," and, ultimately, mistake "training for education" (Ibid.). Further, "higher education has let that happen in large part because we are afraid to embrace the full implications of how we ought to be talking about the ends we seek" (Ibid., 18).

I suggest that the faculty's reticence to discuss the proper ends of education is driven by the fact that the higher education establishment has reflexively accepted a paradigm of economic opportunity grounded in education itself. While this paradigm appears to validate the essential importance of education, it also sets educators up to fail because it assigns education a function that it cannot perform for many who receive it. I suggest, then, that the disconnect between the real economy and the fantasy economy has led to Gannon's classrooms of death. But an expanded view of schooling within a different framing of economic opportunity can help us transcend our classrooms of death and embrace what Gannon calls learning for life. A view of education based on human growth and democratic citizenship—learning for life—can free educators from the unattainable expectations associated with responsibility for individual economic outcomes far beyond their control. Learning for life can liberate and reinvigorate the teaching profession and refocus the discussion of economic opportunity where it belongs—on employers and policy makers—thereby placing education in its proper perspective.

Moreover, official labor market and education data as well as scholarly research support a reformed view that removes education from the impossible burden of providing economic opportunity and focuses on learning for life. The labor market is not becoming more specialized or technical in nature. There have been more than enough STEM workers for decades—including those with bachelor's and advanced degrees—and jobs in these fields consistently constitute a small portion of the total labor market. If the real economy possessed a huge supply of STEM and technical jobs, liberal arts majors would have disappeared at most colleges decades ago. Moreover, liberal arts fields prepare students for a wide assortment of jobs in both the business and nonprofit sectors, even if many of these jobs pay low wages, which, of course, cannot be attributed to the abilities of liberal arts faculty or the merits of these programs.

And as the Federal Reserve Bank of New York's long-term data set on labor market outcomes for college graduates clearly shows, the underemployment rates of bachelor's degree holders have remained remarkably durable for several decades, consistently hovering around one-third of all college graduates (Federal Reserve Bank of New York 2022a). But because of decades of wage stagnation, the wages of many jobs requiring bachelor's degrees have also stagnated, and these fields are disproportionately where liberal arts majors work. Thus, today liberal arts majors are increasingly seen as open only to economically more advantaged students because it is these students who can rely on family wealth to sustain them during and after their education. An expanded view of education based on the real economy and learning for life therefore means that all students should be free to pursue whatever field of study and career they are interested in, thereby allowing a much more representative group of students to study the liberal arts. Further, learning for life begins from the self-evident assumption that education—like life itself—is an in-person event. If online education had significant appeal, it would have replaced face-to-face instruction long before the COVID-19 pandemic. Ultimately, a reframed model of economic opportunity based on the real economy should enable the education establishment to easily make the case for an expanded view of education based on learning for life.

A revised formulation of the multiple purposes of education as learning for life would also have other important benefits. Higher education should be made as affordable and accessible as possible and will likely remain a path to employment for most who pursue it. But if we stipulate that it is not the education system's function to provide economic opportunity, expanding college access can properly be seen as providing a critical public service in a democracy—creating an educated citizenry. Such a shift would necessitate reversing the austerity paradigm ushered in by neoliberalism and funding public education—including higher education—in the same manner that other public services are funded. Public higher education should be made truly public again, and both K–12 and postsecondary education should be judged by their many important functions, such as promoting democratic citizenship in an increasingly diverse and pluralistic society, teaching critical thinking, and creating meaningful, fulfilled lives for graduates. Education in a democracy is about learning for life.

A new paradigm of education would also stipulate that many essential aspects of education are inherently nonquantifiable, which, I suggest, is also not as challenging as it might appear. The culture of quantification based on the deification of the word "data" has led to foreseeably negative consequences in classrooms and campuses every day, including the common practice of teaching to the test, the narrowing of curricular options, and the dehumanization of teaching and learning. The culture of quantification has directly shaped our classrooms of death, making them far too often evolve into places of anxiety and despair. Moreover, the supremacy of quantitative data in the education system has done nothing whatsoever to mitigate growing inequality, stagnating wages, and poverty. Yet many educators themselves, understandably, implicitly believe in quantitative data supremacy. But educators, like health professionals, should defend using their professional judgments and should be allowed to do so. Such judgments are based on empirical observations rooted in years of experience that are often nonquantifiable. As much of life is not quantifiable, much of learning for life is not quantifiable.

A reinvigorated view of education within an expanded model of economic opportunity cannot be accomplished without significant public engagement. For decades, corporate elites have correctly understood that shaping public opinion is the foundation of all politics and policy making. Scholars must also recognize this and direct some of their voluminous work to the public and policy makers. Scholars such as Jacob Hacker and Paul Pierson, Diane Ravitch, Andrew Hacker, Michael S. Teitelbaum, and Tressie McMillan Cottom—among a long list of others—provide powerful examples of what public intellectuals can accomplish.

And as officials with authority who are not subject to electoral pressures, educational administrators are also in a unique position to reframe a model of education based on learning for life within a renewed paradigm of economic opportunity. Over the last several decades, corporate interests have assiduously cultivated educational administrators, and these efforts have largely succeeded. Corporations and foundations are by far the dominant funding sources for the major higher education organizations, and, as a result, corporate language, assumptions, and interests dominate education politics and policy. In the language of interest groups, the higher education establishment has effectively been captured by corporate interests. But the perpetually weak political standing of higher education should be reason enough for higher education administration to question the corporate framing of economic opportunity that has made the crisis of inequality a crisis solely about education itself. Human capital theory solidified the operating assumption that in the current labor market, everyone needs higher education to have any economic stability and mobility. Although such education possesses an apparently essential service, however, the real labor market—grounded in the proximate causes of employment options and wage levels—dictates that higher education begins from a position of significant political weakness. The long-term disinvestment in public higher education would not have been possible if the promise of economic stability and mobility rang true for the great majority of college graduates. These larger forces reveal the inherent economic limitations of education and can provide the foundation for faculty and administrators to reframe the larger discussion of economic opportunity and reclaim education's many important purposes.

Today, however, higher education administrators too often reflexively reiterate the framing of education and individual economic opportunity created by corporate elites. This is understandable, given the fact that the corporate framing of economic opportunity is the dominant narrative within our neoliberal order. In higher education, this framing advances a series of specific priorities, all of which implicitly assume and advocate austerity budgeting, including the continuous reductions in faculty and staff, the elimination of liberal arts programs and expansion of programs assumed to have better job prospects, and the purchase of educational products and services ostensibly designed to fix enrollment-driven budget shortfalls rooted in a politically created tuition-driven system. And accountability and online education are always lurking in the background. But these priorities ultimately reflect the imposition of the preferences of the powerful on those with little or no power, including faculty, staff, and students. In the contemporary, austerity-driven university, classes get fewer and larger, and students end up suffering significantly. The interests of the legions of part-time faculty are especially hurt, as they are the first to be let go when budgets are cut for no reason other than the imposition of the political preferences of a small, economically privileged minority. And because of the power of the fantasy economy paradigm, the university is blamed for these deleterious developments.

Far from being immutable, state and federal taxing and spending policies are political choices. Austerity budgeting is a political decision rooted in interest group politics and must be seen as such. If the major elements of the current higher education reform agenda are fully implemented, the gulf between elite higher education and the majority of institutions will only widen. As the K–12 education reform movement has coincided with increasing economic inequality and stagnating wages, the current higher education reform agenda will likely increase economic inequality and, in turn, further destabilize democracy. Any redirection in either higher education or K–12, however, cannot happen by simply winning arguments. A new paradigm of economic opportunity and renewed purpose of education can only result from administration, faculty, and staff organizing to advocate for the interests of students and of the public. A well-funded, multipurpose education system is in the public interest and is in the interests of democracy.

Media have an indispensable role to play as well. In the never-ending attempt to shape opinion, business interests continually lobby the media to establish how basic economic issues are framed. Neoliberalism has reinforced a version of capitalism that encourages business interests to affirm that employers cannot find enough qualified workers because it is in their economic interests to do so. This framing shifts the entire debate about economic opportunity squarely onto the education system and workers themselves and has deflected attention away from the myriad factors that directly and indirectly shape jobs and wages. Official data has never supported the existence of a skills gap, yet the last several decades of education reform would not have been possible without seemingly constant media reports of a chronically inadequate workforce. Every claim of a skills gap or worker shortage appearing in press coverage should be accompanied by, at minimum, the wage rates offered for such jobs as well as the formal education and training levels required for them. The media and scholarly community should also consider the voluminous research and data produced by education reform organizations with the same level of scrutiny given to privately funded research in the sciences and health fields and to literature produced by traditional interest groups. As part of a political campaign, education reform organizations are interest groups.

In sum, this approach will require that faculty, educational administrators, and the media explicitly recognize what James Madison affirmed nearly two hundred forty years ago—that society is made of different groups that have different economic interests. And because of the imposition of neoliberalism, the economic interests of the wealthy and corporations have become paramount in all decision-making, which has created the extreme inequality characteristic of contemporary society. To ultimately get beyond the fantasy economy, then, the guiding assumptions and policies of neoliberalism that have placed the interests of owners and shareholders above all others need to be revisited. Only then can we create a truly humane political economy in which all work is valued, the multiple purposes of education in a democracy are restored, and all students can enjoy learning for life. The future of education, and of democracy itself, depends on it.

Epilogue

Parents and educators know that this bizarre concept of
"personalized learning" is a hoax because its stony heart
is defined by an interaction between a student and a
machine, not between humans. . . . Parents want their
children to have a human teacher who sees them, listens
to them, knows them, and cares about them. The students
will remember the teachers who inspired them for the rest
of their lives; they will not remember their Chromebook
and iPads.
—DIANE RAVITCH, *Slaying Goliath*

Introduction

The Epilogue discusses several recent events in both K–12 and higher education, including the effects of the COVID-19 pandemic on education policy and politics. The presidential campaign of 2016 and subsequent election of Donald Trump brought the issue of declining economic opportunity into the spotlight. And the pandemic presented an extraordinarily unique opportunity for reformers to attempt to expand online education at all levels. Mainstream analysts are increasingly grappling with the effects of neoliberalism on the production of economic inequality. But because of the dominance of corporate interests in the education reform movement, the overarching message heard by educators is that it is their job to provide economic opportunity and remedy inequality.

"Good Jobs"?

In 2016, Donald Trump's presidential campaign emphasized declining middle-class job opportunities in a deindustrialized America, which presented political problems for the business community. And in 2017, with funding from J. P. Morgan Chase, Georgetown's Center on Education and the Workforce launched the "Good Jobs" project to "investigate the impact structural economic change has had on workers at different education levels" (Center on Education and the Workforce, n.d.). The CEW staff used similar metrics in a 2018 report on educational adequacy for the Century Foundation, which also acknowledged the funding of the William T. Grant Foundation (Carnevale, Gulish, and Strohl 2018, 1). McKinsey's 2019 report, *The Future of Work in America*, also operationally defined salary levels associated with what it described as low-wage, middle-wage, and high-wage jobs.

The CEW defined "good jobs" as those with minimum annual earnings of $35,000 for workers under the age of forty-five and $45,000 and over for workers forty-five and over (Carnevale et al. 2017, 1). The Century Foundation report argued that in "order to be educationally adequate, a postsecondary program must provide its graduates with economic self-sufficiency" and proposed that "to be recognized as leading to such self-sufficiency, a program must leave its graduates earning more than $35,000 per year ten years after they have completed it" (Carnevale, Gulish, and Strohl 2018, 2). Regarding this wage level, in a report published in 2018, the authors concluded: "Importantly, the annual earnings figure of $35,000 is also the threshold into the middle class" (Ibid.). In terms of 2017 dollars, McKinsey defined "low-wage" jobs as those with annual wages of less than $27,500; "middle-wage" jobs as paying between $27,500 and $54,200; and "high-wage" jobs as paying over $54,200 (McKinsey Global Institute 2019, 4).

These reports are primarily written for business and media elites, and therefore a significant majority of the target audience is middle aged or elderly. And today, individuals in their fifties, sixties, or older likely recall a time when a job paying a wage of $35,000 annually *was* considered a good job and a $50,000 salary denoted solid middle-class status. But inflation—even at very low levels—erodes the value of money over time, and Table E.1 shows the value of McKinsey's wage definitions adjusted for inflation to 1990, as well as the inflation-adjusted equivalent in 2017 of these wage levels if paid in 1990 dollars, when a wage of $35,000 may have constituted a "good job."

I maintain that neither McKinsey's 2017 "middle-wage" (which is inclusive of both thresholds of the CEW's "good jobs" definition) nor its "high-wage" categories represent plausible definitions of these terms in the contemporary period, and this can be easily demonstrated by adjusting these wage levels for inflation. For example, no reasonable observer would have suggested an annual salary in the range of $15,000 to $20,000 earned in 1990 signified a middle wage, nor would, say, $30,000 have constituted anything close to a high wage at that time. Yet if McKinsey's 2017 definitions were paid in 1990 dollars and adjusted for inflation to 2017, they appear to be much more reasonable. Thus, a wage between

TABLE E.1 MCKINSEY'S 2017 DEFINITIONS OF "LOW-WAGE," "MIDDLE-WAGE," AND "HIGH-WAGE" JOBS IN INFLATION-ADJUSTED DOLLARS

Type of Job	2017 Wage-Level Definitions	1990 Value of 2017 Wage-Level Definitions	2017 Value of 1990 Wage-Level Definitions
Low Wage	Up to $27,500	Up to $14,427	Up to $52,418
Middle Wage	$27,500–$54,200	$14,427–$28,435	$54,418–$103,311
High Wage	Over $54,200	Over $28,435	Over $103,311

Source: McKinsey Global Institute 2019, 4. Bureau of Labor Statistics CPI Inflation Calculator used to adjust wages for inflation, which are based on January of each year.

roughly $54,000 and $103,000 in 2017 dollars would be at least closer to common understandings of a middle wage. And one could at least make the case that a salary over $103,000 constituted a high wage in 2017. Wage stagnation and increasing economic inequality happen one year at a time. And the operational definitions of the wages associated with "good," "middle-wage," and "high-wage" jobs offered in reports such as these are at least several decades out of date. Rather than illustrating a supposedly large number of "good jobs," when viewed within the context of the real value of wages, reports like these end up doing the opposite—illustrating and ultimately justifying a predominantly low-wage economy.

"A Mindset of Informed Self-Determination and Adaptability"

The realities of underemployment and low wages among college graduates have also led to some recent shifts in the rhetoric of elite higher education. In 2018, as part of its *Purposeful Work* initiative, Bates College of Maine partnered with Gallup, a pioneer in public opinion polling that has recently described itself as a "global analytics and advice firm that helps leaders and organizations solve their most pressing problems" (Gallup 2022). This partnership produced a national survey of college graduates and report entitled *Forging Pathways to Purposeful Work: The Role of Higher Education* (Gallup and Bates 2019). In the foreword of the report, Bates College president A. Clayton Spencer used many of the more common talking points of the fantasy economy, including references to the world's "complexity, uncertainty, and volatility," while affirming that "the rate of change continues to accelerate" (Ibid., 1). With regard to higher education, Spencer maintained: "For higher education, the accelerating rate of change means that it is no longer sufficient or even plausible to prepare our students for lives based on a notion of 'career' as a stable and well-defined pathway through working life" (Ibid.). She also utilized an extremely common line among higher education reformers when she asserted: "Rather, the average college graduate can expect to have more than 11 distinct jobs before the age of 50, many of which do not yet exist" (Ibid.).

But rather than simply reiterating the importance of higher education, Spencer took a different approach, conveying a message of informed resignation: "If reliable career paths are no longer to be defined externally, the ability to sustain work over a lifetime will increasingly depend on individual agency. Thus, colleges and universities must help students develop not only the content knowledge and cognitive and interpersonal skills required for employment, but also a mindset of informed self-determination and adaptability" (Gallup and Bates 2019, 1). *Forging Pathways* appeared to foreshadow a new, seemingly darker rhetorical strategy in the literature of the fantasy economy: higher education, while necessary, is no longer sufficient for one seeking a decent standard of living and any measure of employment stability. The political and economic arrangements of neoliberalism, which have benefited a small minority yet have created wage stagnation, unstable work, and widespread underemployment for so many—including graduates of elite institutions, to say nothing of those with less formal education—are here to stay. Rather than questioning the extreme inequality brought on by neoliberalism and speculating about alternative arrangements, then, higher education must help students develop a "mindset of informed self-determination and adaptability."

The Grand Prize: Higher Education Accountability

Over the last several years, foundations, business interests, and education reformers have increasingly argued in favor of higher education accountability, which, at its core, seeks to hold colleges and universities responsible for graduates' job and wage outcomes well beyond the control of higher education. Higher education accountability has also been uncritically accepted by higher education scholars, whose work is firmly grounded in human capital theory and a misleading account of the labor market (Arum and Roska 2011; Kelchen 2018). Arum and Roska's universally acclaimed *Academically Adrift*, which was promoted by the authors in an article in *Change* magazine (Roska and Arum 2011), acknowledged the financial support of the Lumina, Ford, and Teagle Foundations and the Carnegie Corporation of New York, as well as a "Fulbright New Century Scholar 'Higher Education in the 21st Century: Access and Equity' award" (Arum and Roska 2011, ix). The book implicitly accepts the assumption of a chronically underqualified workforce, yet the authors do not consider long-term data on educational attainment rates, nor do they engage in any sustained discussion of the real labor market. Rather, their primary evidence of the lack of qualifications of the college-educated workforce are two employer surveys, one of which was done on behalf of the corporate- and foundation-funded Association of American Colleges and Universities by Washington-based consultant Hart Research, while the other was produced by a business coalition consisting of the Conference Board, Corporate Voices for Working Families, the Partnership for 21st Century Skills, and the Society of Human Resource Management (Ibid., 143, 236).

With this body of evidence, then, it is not surprising that Arum and Roska conclude that the "dissatisfaction of corporate leaders in the private sector with the quality of U.S. undergraduate education has, however, become palpable as they claim that 'the current state of affairs is unacceptable' and that 'many of the skills and abilities they seek can— and should—be taught on campus'" (Arum and Roska 2011, 143). The authors characterize their findings as a "mandate for reform" and advance several specific proposals, including an extended discussion of higher education accountability (Ibid., 121–142). Because their influential book fails to consider the jobs and wage rates of the real labor market, however, ultimately Arum and Roska endorse neoliberalism's ability to expand access to higher education among the disadvantaged. They argue that "neoliberal policymakers who have advocated for increased privatization and market-based educational reforms have produced a system that has expanded opportunity for all" (Ibid., 137), a claim that simply cannot be substantiated when we consider the decades of wage stagnation faced by most workers, including many who are college educated. Robert Kelchen's work on higher education accountability begins by citing the "ambitious goals for college attainment rates" of the Gates and Lumina Foundations, as well as the data of the Center on Education and the Workforce (2018, 1, 2). His analysis, which also includes little discussion of the real labor market, leads him to uncritically embrace the misguided notion that increasing college attainment rates is a viable solution to economic inequality.

The erroneous assumption of a high-education, high-skill labor market also impedes attempts to view the larger economic context within which higher education exists. Students and their families experience underemployment and low wages firsthand and therefore correctly see higher education as the crapshoot that it is for many, especially those without the social and family networks that can facilitate obtaining good jobs. This economic anxiety hangs over every aspect of the student experience and undoubtedly affects educational performance, the focus of Arum and Roska's extraordinarily influential book. And because the interest group–driven claims of a knowledge economy and an insufficiently skilled college-educated workforce are rarely questioned, higher education is politically powerless to fend off major reform proposals—all of which are rooted in budgetary austerity—including higher education accountability.

In 2019, the Gates Foundation created the Postsecondary Value Commission (PVC), which was managed by the Institute for Higher Education Policy (Institute for Higher Education Policy 2022b). The PVC was yet another education reform entity labeled a "commission" despite lacking official status. The organization's website listed several organizations as resources for its work, many of which are Gates Foundation–funded organizations, including the Brookings Institution (Brookings Institution 2020), the New America Foundation (New America 2019), Opportunity Insights (Opportunity Insights 2019), and *Washington Monthly's* College Guide and Rankings (*Washington Monthly* 2020), as well as the Center on Education and the Workforce itself, which the PVC called a "nationally recognized research and policy institute focusing on the link between education, career qualifications and workforce demands" (Postsecondary Value Commission 2019). Other commission resources listed included the U.S. Department of Education's College Scorecard, the College Board, *The Economist*, the U.S. Chamber of Commerce Foundation's Launch My Career, the *New York Times College Access Index*, and Third Way (Ibid.).

In 2020, as part of the higher education reform campaign, the CEW's authors produced the shrewdly entitled book *The Merit Myth: How Our Colleges Favor the Rich and Divide America* (Carnevale, Schmidt, and Strohl 2020). Written within the context of increasing calls for free public higher education, the book contains scant labor market data, however. Rather, *The Merit Myth* is heavily dependent on the reports produced by the CEW itself and includes a blurb on the jacket by Lumina's Merisotis, in which he praises the book for its "unassailable data, compelling stories, and smart reasoning" and asserts that "the best path to upward mobility is through high quality postsecondary learning" (Ibid.). Like a long line of educational reformers, the authors of *The Merit Myth* frame their book in concern for the disadvantaged: "The unskilled labor pool—which predominantly consists of people who are racial and ethnic minorities or from low-income backgrounds—has been increasingly left behind" (Ibid., 77), a statement that assumes the wages paid to the tens of millions of individuals working in lower-skilled occupations are pre-ordained. Yet at the same time, their analysis approaches the traditional culture-of-poverty framing that education reformers have worked diligently to distance themselves from, as they argue that the "knowledge economy not only requires more formal education, but also emphasizes skills, such as the ability to interact easily with coworkers and customers, most associated with the cultural capital possessed by people who are middle class and above" (Ibid.).

In terms of curricular changes, *The Merit Myth* takes issue with the reform movement ushered in by *A Nation at Risk* for being "fixated" on improving STEM education while occupations in these fields "currently account for about 5 percent of the workforce but are seen as crucial for global economic domination" (Carnevale, Schmidt, and Strohl 2020, 17). The authors stipulate the numerous significant benefits of a liberal arts education, including "encouraging republican values and discouraging intolerance and authoritarianism," as well as developing several critical skills. Yet they still suggest a desire to scale back liberal arts majors: "Courses in such fields [humanities and liberal arts] should remain a major part of general education, and students should remain free to place one foot in them through a double major, or to major solely in them if they're confident they'll pursue graduate education" (Ibid., 213). According to Carnevale and his coauthors, "students should be made aware that they will likely do better in the labor market if they combine what they learn in general education courses with study in specific fields designed toward labor market outcomes" (Ibid.). But the authors do not discuss in detail which fields these are, particularly for the millions of disadvantaged students who rely the most on the economic promise of higher education.

The title of the concluding chapter of *The Merit Myth*—"College for All"—succinctly captures one of the major goals of the corporate- and foundation-led education reform movement. The chapter offers several proposals, some of which have long been advocated by progressives, including the reduction of college entrance exams, elimination of legacy admissions, and continued use of both race- and class-based admissions policies. Calling the current system of accreditation "demonstrably flawed," the authors also propose "Measuring Outcomes Rather Than Inputs" (Carnevale, Schmidt, and Strohl 2020, 211), implicitly adopting the framing of continued austerity and a definition of accountability that holds higher education responsible for labor market outcomes well beyond its control. And as a work of interest group advocacy, *The Merit Myth* creates what it calls a "political argument"—"14 is the new 12" (Ibid., 217)—to advance the goal of increasing postsecondary attainment. Widespread underemployment among the highly educated and the dominance of low-education, low-wage jobs in the labor market are not part of the story of *The Merit Myth*, which is yet another in a long line of works advocating the misguided assumption that increasing higher education attainment will reverse decades of wage stagnation and growing inequality.

In May 2021, the Postsecondary Value Commission published *Equitable Value: Promoting Economic Mobility and Social Justice through Postsecondary Education*. Presumably writing for an audience of higher education administrators, media, and policy makers, the authors maintained that their work was "backed by quality data, rigorous research, and diverse perspectives" (Postsecondary Value Commission 2021, 23). Yet *Equitable Value* relies heavily on Gates-funded organizations, most notably the CEW. The report also relies on the "expertise" of another corporate- and foundation-funded organization that has received Gates Foundation funding, Jobs for the Future, to argue that there are "multiple skills gaps depending on cause, occupation, industry, and region, with each requiring its own solution" (Ibid., 93). Jobs for the Future has also received funding from corporations including Google and Walmart (Jobs for the Future 2022). And rather than present straightforward and readily accessible official data on labor markets, educational attainment by race, and the cost of higher education, the report relies on high-level statistics well beyond the understanding of most educated readers, including a "set of disaggregated thresholds and a set of indices—the Economic Value Index (EVI) and the Economic Value Contribution (EVC)" (Ibid., 29).

Like *The Merit Myth*, *Equitable Value* is framed largely in terms of racial justice. The foreword begins with a quote from Martin Luther King Jr., and the first sentence of chapter 1 states: "While structural racism has been part of the United States since before even its founding, continued racial and gender violence alongside the coronavirus pandemic have catalyzed nationwide activism and led to renewed conversations about who has true access to opportunity in this country" (Postsecondary Value Commission 2021, 1, 8). Crucially, the report implicitly assumes an adequate supply of high-education, high-skill jobs for college graduates. And despite citing the work of the CEW's "Good Jobs" project, the PVC did not include the wage levels specified in the CEW's original definition of this key concept. Rather, *Equitable Value* stated that "more than half (56 percent) of 'good jobs'—defined by the Georgetown University Center on Education and the Workforce (CEW) as those that pay a family-sustaining wage—require at least a bachelor's degree" (Ibid., 9). But because the term "family sustaining" is not self-defining, this definition obfuscates the realities of a predominantly low-wage labor market. Finally, at the very end of the report, in an appendix, is a table outlining annual median earnings for graduates of associate's and bachelor's degree programs disaggregated by race and type of institution attended on the basis of an analysis of 2015–2016 federal data (Ibid., 114). And nearly all these wage levels are below—and some well below—the lower thresholds of the CEW's original operational definition of "Good Jobs" as those paying at least $35,000 per year for workers under forty-five and at least $45,000 per year for workers forty-five and over (Carnevale, Strohl, Cheah, and Ridley 2017, 1).

"Charter Schools' Goal of Educational Improvement Is Unevenly Met"

In recent years, much of the research on school choice has continued to show disappointing results. Two federally mandated studies of the Washington, DC, voucher program concluded that it had negative or neutral effects on participants' academic outcomes in both reading and math test scores (Dynarski et al. 2017, 2018). Faced with these results, funded scholars have increasingly argued that future research should take into consideration variables other than test scores. A 2018 paper on the Indiana Choice Scholarship Program (ICSP), by R. Joseph Waddington and Mark Berends, is an example of this approach. The authors acknowledged funding from the University of Notre Dame's Center for Research on Educational Opportunity (CREO)—which is part of the university's Institute of Educational Initiatives—as well as from the Walton Family and Spencer Foundations (Waddington and Berends 2018, 805). The authors conceded that their findings "do not provide robust support that the I.C.S.P. has been successful to date at improving student achievement for low-income students who use a voucher to switch from a public to a private school" (Ibid., 804). However, Waddington and Berends then went on to argue for analysis of indicators other than academic achievement: "Although academic achievement outcomes are important for researchers, policy makers, and practitioners to consider, parents make schooling decisions for their children based on a multitude of factors, including academics, location, safety, and religion. Therefore, researchers need to examine outcomes beyond test scores (e.g., educational attainment, engagement, social and emotional learning, character, civic participation, and other nonacademic outcomes)" (Ibid., 804). Despite more negative findings regarding student achievement in choice programs, for researchers funded by school choice advocates, expanding market-based education policies was not up for discussion.

In the years since Margaret Raymond's 2014 public admission that free market theory does not apply to education policy, CREDO has also continued to implicitly reaffirm its unwillingness to reconsider the expansion of charter schools despite largely negative research findings. The research center's 2019 evaluation of South Carolina's charter schools showed largely negative or neutral results in terms of academic achievement, with "remarkably weaker growth in both reading and math" results for online charter schools (Center for Research on Education Outcomes 2019). Yet in the press release, Raymond fell back on the "what works" framing funded school choice researchers have long relied on. Raymond affirmed that "charter schools' goal of educational improvement is unevenly met" yet went on to state: "However, we do see shares of schools showing high growth and high achievement, particularly in reading. Those schools present an opportunity to serve as valuable models for all South Carolina schools to emulate" (Ibid.). The expansion of charters, regardless of performance, was not up for debate.

School choice advocates have also continued to echo the core claims of the fantasy economy campaign. In 2019, Diane Tavenner, the CEO of the Summit chain of charter schools, published the book *Prepared: What Kids Need for a Fulfilled Life*. Like other charter advocates, Summit has often avoided the charter school label, typically referring to itself as "Summit Public Schools" (Summit Public Schools 2022; Tavenner 2019). In *Prepared*, Tavenner stated that a "majority of the founding Summit parents were professionals and employers. They had a first-hand view of the skills they looked for in hiring and had a hard time finding in employees" (Tavenner 2019, 133). Like so much of the literature of education reformers, the skills gap was a given.

"The Lens Must Shift from Schools to Students"

Despite elites' continuous campaign for school choice, however, signs of slowing growth in choice programs had been building for several years. In 2016, the NAACP called for a moratorium on charter schools, and citizens in Massachusetts voted heavily against charter school expansion (Ravitch 2020, 269). These were not encouraging developments for school choice advocates, and in 2018, the Center on Reinventing Public Education expressed concern over the trajectory of charter schools, conceding that "many early successes are plateauing" (Lake 2018, 17). These trends, I suggest, prompted reformers to revise their language in their advocacy. In 2021, the CRPE stressed its ostensive support for public education, stating that it envisions "a public education system that truly prepares every student for the challenges of the future" (Center on Reinventing Public Education 2021). The same year, "Rigorous Research to Improve Public Education" was the main banner on CREDO's home page (Center for Research on Education Outcomes 2021). But I argue that a much more significant effect of the slowing expansion of school choice programs has been a shift in emphasis among reformers toward online education and technology products and services. This is the major theme of the CRPE's 2018 report commemorating its twenty-fifth anniversary, *Thinking Forward: New Ideas for a New Era of Public Education* (Lake 2018), which acknowledged the funding of the Carnegie Corporation and Walton Family Foundation and argued that the "lens must shift from schools to students" (Ibid., 6), in language that encapsulated the new emphasis on technology products and services.

Thinking Forward is a case study of the language and claims of the fantasy economy. For instance, the authors claimed, "Automation is not the future; it is now. New technologies are already replacing lower-wage jobs in apple orchards and factories, and may soon make redundant what have been bedrock middle-class jobs as well" (Lake 2018, 8). Contributor Ashley Jochim asserted "a growing skills gap" (Jochim 2018, 56). And echoing decades-old talking points of corporate education reformers, *Thinking Forward* maintained that the current K–12 education system "still focuses on preparing students for an older, simpler, more predictable world. . . . Designed more than 100 years ago, America's public education system is not preparing students for today's realities of civic and global competitiveness, much less tomorrow's" (Lake 2018, 3, 15). But, according to *Thinking Forward*, "we cannot successfully face an age of agility and customization if our education system remains moribund through rigidity and sameness" (Ibid., 17). Ultimately, the "need to reinvent public education is more urgent than ever—and yet the roadmap is unclear" (Ibid.).

The problem, however, according to *Thinking Forward*, is that "educators, students, and families who want something better are thwarted by an outdated delivery model" (Lake 2018, 16). Hence, the CRPE declared that its "mission" was to "reinvent the education delivery model, in partnership with education leaders, to prepare all American students to solve tomorrow's challenges" (Ibid.). But because of the nagging unpopularity of online education, the authors utilized a vocabulary that, I suggest, is designed to obfuscate this goal. Thus, the CRPE seeks to create an "agile," "nimble," "customized," "radically personalized," "individualized," "curated," "unbundled," and "permeable" education system for students, and this terminology appears throughout the ninety-five-page report. In addition, many specific technology-related products and services are referenced, including CommunityShare, ReSchool, Remake Learning, and KnowledgeWorks (Ibid.).

In the essay entitled "Funding a Nimble System," Travis Pillow and CRPE founder Paul Hill acknowledged that a "personalized education system, including all the learning opportunities and community assets described in the other essays in this collection, will almost certainly cost more than the current one, even for students who are of normal school age" (Pillow and Hill 2018, 82). But they were clear about their preference for public funding for an increasingly online public K–12 education system and argued that it is "possible to describe a feasible alternative public funding system that could support a great deal of personalization. It would combine the money traditionally available for K–12 education with funds from other sources" (Ibid., 83). Specifically, they suggested that for younger students, funds could be shifted away from "existing public programs dedicated to social and youth services" from the "departments of Labor, Health and Human Services, Justice, Agriculture, Education and Housing and Urban Development" (Ibid.). Older students could, according to Pillow and Hill, "receive funds from existing job training programs and state support for postsecondary education," while parents of low-income students could "reserve their share of federal Head Start funding for this purpose" (Ibid.). This austerity-driven agenda led *Thinking Forward* to support public funding for an increasingly online education system, but not necessarily for democratically run, public schools: "We view public education as a shared objective, not a particular institution" (Ibid., 89).

"Will the Inevitable Restructuring and Reorganization [of Higher Education] Intentionally Prioritize Quality, Equity, and Inclusion?"

While the school choice movement had already begun to reorient its focus toward an emphasis on expanding online education, in late 2019 a novel coronavirus was first identified in Wuhan, China. On March 11, 2020, the World Health Organization declared COVID-19 a global pandemic, and states and cities across the United States began to shut schools down shortly thereafter. Online education quickly became one of the largest experiments in the history of American public policy, and corporate elites immediately sought to define the moment as one that would forever change both K–12 and higher education. Just a month into the pandemic, the *Chronicle of Higher Education*'s cover story of April 17 affirmed: "The Coronavirus Will Change Everything" (*Chronicle of Higher Education* 2020). Shortly thereafter, higher education was inundated with calls for a permanent change to more online education, reflecting reformers' larger shift toward technology products and services.

By early May, elites had also initiated an extensive campaign to permanently increase online instruction in K–12 education, and the Gates Foundation partnered with New York State to "reimagine education" (Blad 2020). At a press conference on May 5, New York governor Andrew Cuomo announced his state's partnership with the foundation, stating: "The old model of everybody goes and sits in a classroom and the teacher is in front of that classroom and teaches that class, and you do that all across the city, all across the state, all these buildings, all these physical classrooms. Why, with all the technology you have?" (Ibid.). Cuomo's comments also included a slide that reflected the long-standing corporate framing of technology's ability to increase educational equity: "How can we use technology to provide more opportunities to students no matter where they are?" and "How can technology reduce educational inequality, including English as a new language students?" and "How can technology break down barriers to K–12 and colleges and universities to provide greater access to high quality education no matter where the student lives?" (Ibid.).

But after months of online instruction, parents, students, and educators across the country increasingly pressured schools to open for a return to face-to-face teaching. In fact, the belief in the superiority of in-person instruction is one of the few things that unites Americans of different demographic and partisan backgrounds. Online instruction simply cannot replicate in-person instruction, and, as Diane Ravitch has argued: "Parents and educators know that this bizarre concept of 'personalized learning' is a hoax because its stony heart is defined by an interaction between a student and a machine, not between humans. . . . Parents want their children to have a human teacher who sees them, listens to them, knows them, and cares about them. The students will remember the teachers who inspired them for the rest of their lives; they will not remember their Chromebooks and iPads" (Ravitch 2020, 270).

As the pandemic wore on, even as the value of face-to-face teaching became increasingly apparent to the nation, the push for more online instruction at the postsecondary level intensified, based on the assumption of continued budgetary austerity, which is also a goal of the higher education reform movement. But because of the lack of popular appeal of either online education or further austerity, this campaign was built on the theme of expanding equity through increased college access. For example, the January 2021 conference of the corporate- and foundation-funded American Association of Colleges and Universities (Association of American Colleges and Universities 2019), entitled "Revolutionizing Higher Education after Covid-19," asked: "Will the inevitable restructuring and reorganization [of higher education] intentionally prioritize quality, equity, and inclusion?" (Association of American Colleges and Universities 2021). Conference attendees would be sharing "effective educational practices and exploring new financial models," and "campus leaders at all levels and from institutions of all types will together begin to work out what undergraduate education will look like in a post-pandemic future" (Ibid.). The magnitude of the pandemic eclipsed events like 9/11 and Katrina, and corporate interests were determined to take advantage of this unprecedented historical moment to impose a major overhaul of higher education. Beginning in middle 2020, the "post-COVID" framing was seemingly everywhere in the literature of higher education.

Perhaps the most elaborate statement of elites' political strategy to remake higher education, however, was a report produced by Georgetown University's Graduate Program in Learning, Design, and Technology in January 2021 entitled *Openings: Higher Education's Challenge to Change in the Face of the Pandemic, Inequity and Racism* (Graduate Program in Learning, Design, and Technology 2021). The report acknowledged the support of the Baker Trust for Transformational Learning (Ibid.), which aims "to create a new paradigm of learning in which the development of the mindsets and capacities to navigate the 21st century are at the heart of every student's education" (Baker Center 2019). The mythical high-education, high-wage labor market and concomitant skills gap are the implicit assumptions of the report, which, like most of the work produced by education reformers, frames the issue largely as a matter of racial justice.

Openings contains jargon aimed squarely at faculty and administrators and calls for "a critical studies approach to higher education," "a vision of learning that is transformative and wholistic, equitable and inclusive," and advocates "decolonizing the curriculum" (Graduate Program in Learning, Design, and Technology 2021, 10, 10, 44). Yet I argue that the report's most striking characteristic is its seeming refusal to argue in favor of online instruction on the merits. And because austerity budgeting is the underlying assumption, the authors did not feel it necessary to argue in favor of potentially reduced costs associated with online education. Rather, according to the report, the discussion simply occurred "in the context of new financial constraints" (Ibid., 43). Like the Association of American Colleges and Universities, *Openings* assumed that fundamentally changing higher education after the pandemic was a given: "The question is, 'Is higher education adaptable and resilient when drastic change is required'" (Ibid., 22).

The report's linkage of systemic inequality to the higher education system is apparent from the outset. In the foreword, Eddie Maloney, the founding director of the Learning, Design, and Technology program, argues that the transition to online instruction "required a shift in emphasis that put the pedagogical relationship between the students and the faculty front and center. In doing so, it necessitated a new attention on how we teach and on the central role of learning in higher ed" (Graduate Program in Learning, Design, and Technology 2021, 8). But then, like so many education reformers, Maloney directed his analysis at higher education's role in shaping racial inequality: "Almost simultaneously, the increased attention on racial injustice in the United States has highlighted the role that higher education has played in structural racism throughout the history of this country. Challenges of equity, access, and inclusion are fundamental to a future of higher education that seeks to fulfill its promise of serving the common good" (Ibid.).

Without question, colleges and universities have played a significant role in perpetrating racism and inequalities. Further, as Tressie McMillan Cottom (2017) has forcefully argued, for-profit higher education has exploited racial and economic inequalities to advance its economic interests while frequently leaving graduates saddled with debt and poor job prospects. And given decades of disinvestment by state governments, public higher education is incentivized primarily to maximize enrollment, which necessarily precludes any honest discussion of labor market outcomes for graduates, including those for racial minorities and low-income students. But during a historical moment characterized by structural racial and economic inequalities precipitated by events in law enforcement and a global pandemic, education reformers sought to attach systemic inequality to higher education in a campaign to further austerity budgeting and advance online instruction.

The fact that the professoriate has historically done far more than most other major institutions in American society to educate the citizenry about the origins, effects, and ongoing patterns of racism and inequality was clearly not a primary interest to the authors of *Openings*, which, like the achievement gap campaign decades earlier, attempted to paint the education system as a primary barrier to expanding economic opportunity. And austerity itself—which is necessarily a political choice imposed through sheer power—is treated as a given in the report. Ultimately, *Openings* succinctly captured the essence of the political argument advanced by corporations and the wealthy since the advent of neoliberalism—it is the job of the education system to provide economic opportunity. And presumably increasing online education in higher education on a grand scale would contribute to a lessening of systemic inequalities. Considering the decades of defunding of public higher education that have led to a student loan crisis, consistently high levels of underemployment among the college educated, and wage stagnation for many working in jobs commensurate with their high education levels, such an analysis borders on the absurd.

Meanwhile, Back in the Real Economy

In 2022, the BLS also published updated projections of the educational requirements of the labor market, which showed that nearly 61 percent of all jobs still typically required only a high school education or less, with little change in educational requirements projected by 2030 (Bureau of Labor Statistics 2022d). The educational requirements of the labor market had changed little since the predictions of the coming high-education, high-skill economy began to proliferate numerous decades ago. Also in 2022, the Census Bureau released new data showing that the educational attainment of the population continued to reach all-time highs. The high school completion rate of those twenty-five and over topped 91 percent, and over 63 percent of the population had at least some education beyond high school (U.S. Census Bureau 2022). Remarkably, in a country in which few received even bachelor's degrees just decades ago, over 14 percent of all adults reported receiving an advanced degree (Ibid.). Once again, the real economy stood in stark contrast with the fantasy economy.

Notes

INTRODUCTION

1. In 2022, the CRPE relocated to the Mary Lou Fulton Teachers College at Arizona State University.

2. The authors of *The Jobs Revolution* were Steve Gunderson, Robert Jones, and Kathryn Scanland. Gunderson, a former member of Congress, was president and CEO of the Association of Career Education Colleges and Universities and was also formerly the CEO of the Council on Foundations (Career Education Colleges and Universities 2020). As of 2022, Jones worked for the U.S. Chamber of Commerce Foundation as president of Education Workforce Policy. His biography stated that, among other positions, he was a "Co-Director of the Lumina funded Credential Transparency Initiative," served in two Republican presidential administrations, had "senior positions in two major U.S. corporations," and "played a lead role in the [Reagan administration's] landmark research project and report, Workforce 2000: Work and Workers for the 21st Century" (U.S. Chamber of Commerce Foundation 2022). In 2022, Scanland's biography at Greystone Global stated that she was "an avid student of strategy and leadership and has focused on helping others strategize, plan, learn, and lead mission-driven organizations for more than 25 years" (Greystone Global 2022).

3. I owe the analogy between support for STEM and support for the troops to one of my former students and a 2012 political science graduate of UWRF, Richard Simones.

CHAPTER 2

1. For reviews of the research on racial achievement gaps, see National Center for Education Statistics 2015; Kotok 2017; and Rothstein 2004. For reviews of the literature on the relationship between income and educational achievement, see Dun-

can and Brooks-Gunn 1997; Duncan and Murnane 2011; Hanushek et al. 2020; Michelmore and Dynarski 2016; and K. White 1982a.

2. The twelfth-grade assessment for mathematics was changed significantly in 2005, and therefore results from earlier years cannot be compared with results since 2005 (National Center for Education Statistics 2020c).

3. The BLS uses numerous sources to assign occupations to educational attainment and training categories, including the "Census Bureau's American Community Survey (ACS); data on education, work experience, and on-the-job training requirements from the Occupational Information Network (O*NET); and data on postsecondary program completions from the National Center for Education Statistics." BLS economists also utilize "qualitative information obtained from educators, employers, workers in the occupation, training experts, and representatives of professional and trade associations and unions" (Bureau of Labor Statistics 2021a).

4. The complete list of funders in the Community College Research Center's 2018–2019 *Biennial Report* is as follows: Achieving the Dream, American Association of Community Colleges, Andrew W. Mellon Foundation, Arnold Ventures, Ascendium Education Group, Bill and Melinda Gates Foundation, Capitol One Foundation, Carrol and Milton Petrie Foundation, Charles A. Dana Center (University of Texas at Austin), ECMC Foundation, Education Commission of the States, Foundation for California Community Colleges, Institute for Evidence-Based Change, Jobs for the Future, Joyce Foundation, J-Pal North America, J. P. Morgan Chase Foundation, Kresge Foundation, Leona M. and Harry B. Helmsley Charitable Trust, Lumina Foundation, MDRC, National Science Foundation, Office of Community College Research and Leadership (University of Illinois at Urbana-Champaign), Ralph C. Wilson Foundation, Schmidt Futures, Strong Start to Finish, U.S. Department of Education (Institute of Education Sciences), Walton Family Foundation, William T. Grant Foundation, and Anonymous (Community College Research Center 2019, 12).

CHAPTER 3

1. For a sampling of the research in medicine and health sciences documenting the impact of funding sources on research outcomes, see Bekelman, Li, and Gross 2003; Lexchin et al. 2003; Nejstgaard et al. 2020; Nestle 2013, 2018; and Yaphe et al. 2001. For a summary of the *New York Times*' extensive coverage of this issue, see *New York Times* 2018. For a review of the research on the many ways that medical professionals' behavior is affected by several implicit biases, see Sah and Fugh-Berman 2013. For a review of several common methods of corporate influence of research across many industries, see J. White and Bero 2010. For a discussion of the development of key opinion leaders, see Sismondo 2013. For an excellent overview of the literature on conflicts of interest in the academy, see Lessig 2018, chapter 4.

2. This analysis is based on an examination of twenty different copies of *Workforce 2000*, all of which are in the author's possession. In addition, I have three digital versions—two partially declassified versions and one from the Department of Education's Education Resources Information Center (ERIC) database.

3. The 2010 Technical Summary also criticizes the BLS because its "estimates do not explicitly incorporate 'skill-biased technological change,' a dynamic which is prominent in other trend data" (Carnevale, Smith, and Strohl 2010b, 10).

CHAPTER 4

1. In 1999, ten contributors of $5,000 or more were identified, including several corporations and foundations as well as one anonymous donor of $1 million (Achieve 1999). In 2000, seven donors of $5,000 or more were identified, with Pew listed as providing $633,000 in cash and a pledge of $867,000 (Achieve 2000).

2. The literature on the many negative consequences of No Child Left Behind is voluminous, a sampling of which includes Meier and Woods 2004; Owens 2015; Ravitch 2010; Jack Schneider 2017; and Jack Schneider and Berkshire 2020.

CHAPTER 5

1. According to the National Alliance for Public Charter Schools, over 58 percent of charter schools are located in central cities (National Alliance for Public Charter Schools 2022). Approximately 60 percent of all charter school students are either Black or Hispanic, with roughly thirty percent white (National Center for Education Statistics 2022d). Today, charter school students represent roughly 7 percent of all total public school enrollment (Ibid.). The growth of school vouchers has been much slower. As of 2017, 14 states and Washington D.C. had some sort of voucher program in place (National Center for Education Statistics 2017b).

CONCLUSION

1. The literature on the many causes of wage stagnation and growing inequality is voluminous. For example, on the decline of labor unions, see Belman and Heywood 1990; Bureau of Labor Statistics 2019c; and Western and Rosenfeld 2011. For the decline in manufacturing employment, see Bluestone and Harrison 1984; Judd and Swanstrom 2014; and Kraus 2000. For analyses of the minimum wage, see Bartels 2016; Card and Krueger 1995; and Bureau of Labor Statistics 2019a. For the wage effects of increasing monopolization of the labor market, see Appelbaum 2019; Barkai 2020; and Naidu, Posner, and Weyl 2018. For the effects of the offshoring of employment on wages, including the increase in "domestic offshoring," see Autor et al. 2020. For the impact of the significant growth in employers' use of noncompete agreements on wages, see Dougherty 2017; Starr, Frake, and Agarwal 2019; and U.S. Department of the Treasury 2016. For the history of CEO compensation patterns, see Edmans, Gabaix, and Jenter 2017; Kaplan and Rauh 2013; and Piketty and Saez 2003. For austerity's impact on the wages of public-sector and nonprofit workers, see Cohen and Gebeloff 2018. For the impact of increases in health-care costs, see Catlin and Cowan 2015. For the erosion of retirement security, see J. Hacker 2006; and the Bureau of Labor Statistics 2019e. For the politics of economic inequality, see Bartels 2016; J. Hacker and Pierson 2010, 2016, 2020; and Putnam 2015. For the role that capitalism has played in creating inequality, see Piketty 2014. For the negative health effects of growing inequality, see Braveman et al. 2010; Chetty et al. 2016; Cutler, Deaton, and Lleras-Muney 2006; Duggan, Gillingham, and Greenlees 2008; Kitagawa and Hauser 1973; Marmot 2005; Waldron 2013; and B. Wolf, Evans, and Seeman 2012. For the impact of growing inequality on social mobility, see Ermisch, Jantti, and Smeeding 2012; and Song et al. 2020. For the increasing racial and class segregation that has accompanied growing income inequality, see Dreier, Mollenkopf, and Swanstrom 2014; Massey and Denton 1993; and Sampson 2012.

References

Abamu, Jenny. 2017. "Researchers Push Back as Betsy DeVos, ALEC Advance Virtual School Expansion." *EdSurge*, 18 July. Available at https://www.edsurge.com/news/2017-07-18-researchers-push-back-as-betsy-devos-alec-advance-virtual-school-expansion.

Abbott, Frank C. N.d. *A History of the Western Interstate Commission on Higher Education: The First Forty Years.* N.p.: Western Interstate Commission for Higher Education, publication no. 2A348B. Available at https://www.wiche.edu/wp-content/uploads/2018/resources/First40Years.pdf.

Abel, Jaison R., Richard Deitz, and Yaqin Su. 2014. "Are Recent College Graduates Finding Good Jobs?" *Current Issues in Economics and Finance* 20 (1): 1–8. Federal Reserve Bank of New York.

Achieve. 1998. *Form 990-PF for Tax Year Beginning July 1, 1998, and Ending June 30, 1999.* Cambridge, MA: Achieve.

———. 1999. *Form 990-PF for Tax Year Beginning July 1, 1999, and Ending June 30, 2000.* Cambridge, MA: Achieve.

———. 2000. *Form 990-PF for Tax Year Beginning July 1, 2000, and Ending June 30, 2001.* Cambridge, MA: Achieve.

———. 2008. *Out of Many, One: Toward Rigorous Common Core Standards from the Ground Up.* Cambridge, MA: Achieve. Available at https://www.achieve.org/files/OutofManyOne.pdf.

———. 2017. *Twenty Years of Driving Student Success.* Cambridge, MA: Achieve. Available at https://www.achieve.org/publications/twenty-years-driving-student-success.

Achieve and National Governors Association. 2005. *National Summit on High Schools.* Cambridge, MA: Achieve. Available at https://files.eric.ed.gov/fulltext/ED496277.pdf.

ACT. 2022. "ACT WorkKeys for Workforce and Economic Developers." Iowa City, IA: ACT. Available at https://www.act.org/content/act/en/products-and-services/workkeys-for-workforce-developers.html.

Adeniji, Ade. 2015. "How the Hoover Institution Vacuums up Big Conservative Bucks." *Inside Philanthropy*, 21 April.

Akers, Joshua. 2011. "Separate and Unequal: The Consumption of Public Education in Post-Katrina New Orleans." *International Journal of Urban and Regional Research* 36 (1): 29–48.

American Association for Higher Education. 1969. *Articles of Incorporation*, 27 February. Washington, DC: American Association for Higher Education.

———. 1997. "What Are A.A.H.E.'s Technology Projects?" Washington, DC: American Association for Higher Education. Internet Archive, 2 July. Available at https://web.archive.org/web/19970412134652fw_/http://www.aahe.org/tltr.htm.

American Association for Higher Education and Accreditation. "American Association for Higher Education." Grandview, MO: American Association for Higher Education and Accreditation. Available at https://www.aahea.org/index.php.

American Chemical Society. 1955. "Esso Education Foundation." *Chemical and Engineering News* 33 (42): 4398.

American Diploma Project. 2004. *Ready or Not: Creating a High School Diploma That Counts*. Cambridge, MA: Achieve. Internet Archive, 23 May 2021. Available at https://web.archive.org/web/20120523015741/https://www.achieve.org/files/ReadyorNot.pdf.

American Presidency Project. 1979. "Department of Transportation Nomination of William B. Johnston to Be Assistant Secretary." Santa Barbara, CA: American Presidency Project. Available at https://www.presidency.ucsb.edu/documents/department-transportation-nomination-william-b-johnston-be-assistant-secretary.

Anderson, Gary L. 2007. "Media's Impact on Educational Policies and Practices: Political Spectacle and Social Control." *Peabody Journal of Education* 82 (1): 103–120.

Anderson, Kurt. 2020. *Evil Geniuses: The Unmaking of America; A Recent History*. New York: Random House.

Appelbaum, Binyamin. 2019. *The Economists' Hour: False Prophets, Free Markets, and the Fracture of Society*. New York: Little Brown.

Applied Population Laboratory, University of Wisconsin, Madison. 2019. *Projecting Public School Enrollment in Wisconsin, 2019*. Madison: University of Wisconsin, Madison. Available at https://cdn.apl.wisc.edu/publications/Proj_Public_School_Enroll_2019.pdf.

Arkansas Democrat and Gazette. 2019. "High Profile: John Elward Brown III Found His Own Way While Following in His Grandfather's Footsteps." 6 October. Available at https://www.arkansasonline.com/news/2019/oct/06/john-elward-brown-iii-20191006/.

Arkansas Higher Education Coordinating Board Meeting. 2005. *Academic Program Proposals*, 29 April. Little Rock, AR: Arkansas Division of Higher Education. Available at https://static.ark.org/eeuploads/adhe/Web_page_summaries_of_academic_proposals_April_2005.pdf.

Armbruster, Frank E. 1972. *The Forgotten Americans: A Survey of Values, Beliefs, and Concerns of the Majority*. With contributions by Doris Yokelson. New Rochelle, NY: Arlington House.

———. 1977. *Our Children's Crippled Future: How American Education Has Failed*. With Paul Bracken. New York: Quadrangle/New York Times Book.

Arum, Richard, and Josipa Roska. 2011. *Academically Adrift: Limited Learning on College Campuses.* Chicago: University of Chicago Press.

Association of American Colleges and Universities. 2019. "Donors to A.A.C. and U." Washington, DC: Association of American Colleges and Universities. Internet Archive, 24 February. Available at https://web.archive.org/web/201902 24022446/https://www.aacu.org/about/donors.

———. 2021. *A.A.C. and U. News: News and Events.* Washington, DC: Association of American Colleges and Universities. Internet Archive, 4 December. Available at https://web.archive.org/web/20211214184038/https://www.aacu .org/aacu-news/newsletter/meetings-projects-and-publications-30.

Autor, David, David Dorn, Lawrence F. Katz, Christina Patterson, and John Van Reenen. 2020. "The Fall of the Labor Share and the Rise of Superstar Firms." *Quarterly Journal of Economics* 135, no. 2 (May): 645–709.

Baker Center, Georgetown University. 2019. "The Baker Center." Washington, DC: Georgetown University, Baker Center. Internet Archive, 17 October. Available at https://web.archive.org/web/20191017031829/https://futures.georgetown.edu /baker-center/.

Ballotpedia. N.d. "National Alliance for Public Charter Schools." 2023. Ballotpedia. Available at https://ballotpedia.org/National_Alliance_for_Public_Char ter_Schools.

Barkai, Simcha. 2020. "Declining Labor and Capital Shares." *Journal of Finance* 75 (5): 2421–2463.

Barrow, Clyde W. 1990. *Universities and the Capitalist State: Corporate Liberalism and the Reconstruction of American Higher Education, 1894–1928.* Madison: University of Wisconsin Press.

Bartels, Larry M. 2016. *Unequal Democracy: The Political Economy of the New Gilded Age,* second edition. New York: Russel Sage Foundation.

Bartlett, Tom. 2005. "American Association for Higher Education Will Shut Down." *Chronicle of Higher Education,* 25 March.

Bassok, Daphna, Scott Latham, and Anna Rorem. 2016. "Is Kindergarten the New First Grade?" *AERA Open* 2 (1): January–March.

Bauman, Kurt J., and Nikki Graf. 2003. *Educational Attainment 2000: Census 2000 Brief.* Washington, DC: U.S. Census Bureau.

Becker, Gary S. 1964. *Human Capital: A Theoretical and Empirical Analysis, with Special Reference to Education.* Chicago: University of Chicago Press.

———. 2011. "Bad and Good Inequality." *Becker-Posner Blog,* 30 January. Available at https://www.becker-posner-blog.com/2011/01/bad-and-good-inequality -becker.html.

Bekelman, Justin E., Yan Li, and Cary Gross. 2003. "Scope and Impact of Financial Conflicts of Interest in Biomedical Research." *Journal of the American Medical Association* 289 (4): 454–465.

Bell, Daniel. 1973. *The Coming of Post-industrial Society.* New York: Basic Books.

Belman, Dale, and John S. Heywood. 1990. "Union Membership, Union Organization and the Dispersion of Wages." *Review of Economics and Statistics* 72, no. 1 (February): 148–153.

Berliner, David C. 2011. "The Context for Interpreting PISA Results in the USA: Negativism, Chauvinism, Misunderstanding, and the Potential to Distort the Educational Systems of Nations." In *PISA under Examination: Changing Knowl-*

edge, Changing Tests, and Changing Schools, edited by Miguel A. Pereyra, Hans-Georg Kotthoff, and Robert Cowen, 77–96. Rotterdam: Sense.

Berliner, David C., and Bruce J. Biddle. 1995. *The Manufactured Crisis: Myths, Fraud, and the Attack on America's Public Schools*. New York: Basic.

Berry, Jeffrey M., and Clyde Wilcox. 2018. *The Interest Group Society*, sixth edition. New York: Routledge.

Berryman, Sue E., and Thomas R. Bailey. 1992a. *The Double Helix of Education and the Economy*, executive summary. New York: Institute on Education and the Economy, Teachers College, Columbia University.

———. 1992b. *The Double Helix of Education and the Economy*. New York: Institute on Education and the Economy, Teachers College, Columbia University.

Betts, Julian R., and Y. Emily Tang. 2008. *Value-Added and Experimental Studies of the Effect of Charter Schools on Student Achievement: A Literature Review*. Seattle, WA: National Charter School Research Project, Center on Reinventing Public Education, University of Washington Bothell. Available at https://crpe.org/wp-content/uploads/pub_ncsrp_bettstang_dec08_0.pdf.

———. 2011. *The Effect of Charter Schools on Student Achievement: A Meta-analysis of the Literature*. Seattle, WA: National Charter School Research Project, Center on Reinventing Public Education, University of Washington Bothell. Available at https://files.eric.ed.gov/fulltext/ED526353.pdf.

———. 2014. *A Meta-analysis of the Literature on the Effect of Charter Schools on Student Achievement*. Seattle, WA: National Charter School Research Project, Center on Reinventing Public Education, University of Washington Bothell. Available at https://crpe.org/wp-content/uploads/CRPE_meta-analysis_charter-schools-effect-student-achievement_workingpaper.pdf.

Bishop, John H., and Shani Carter. 1990. "The Worsening Shortage of College Graduate Workers." Center for Advanced Human Resource Studies Working Paper 90-15. Ithaca, NY: Cornell University, School of Industrial and Labor Relations, Center for Advanced Human Resource Studies. Available at http://digitalcommons.ilr.cornell.edu/cahrswp/380.

———. 1991. "How Accurate Are Recent BLS Occupational Projections?" *Monthly Labor Review* 114 (10): 37–43.

Blad, Evie. 2020. "New York State Teams with Gates Foundation to 'Reimagine Education' amid Pandemic." *Education Week*, 5 May.

Bluestone, Barry, and Bennett Harrison. 1984. *The Deindustrialization of America: Plant Closings, Community Abandonment, and the Dismantling of Basic Industry*. New York: Basic.

Blumenstyk, Goldie. 2020. "By 2020, They Said, 2 out of 3 Jobs Would Need More Than a High-School Diploma. Were They Right?" *Chronicle of Higher Education*, 22 January.

Boe, Erling E., and Sujie Shin. 2005. "Is the United States Really Losing the International Horse Race in Academic Achievement?" *Phi Delta Kappan* 86 (9): 688–695.

Bonham, George W. 1972. "Inside Academe." In *Inside Academe: Culture in Crisis*, from the editors of *Change*, 9–11. New Rochelle, NY: Change Magazine.

Boushey, Heather, J. Bradford DeLong, and Marshall Steinbaum, eds. 2017. *After Piketty: The Agenda for Economics and Inequality*. Cambridge, MA: Harvard University Press.

Bousquet, Marc. 2008. *How the University Works: Higher Education and the Low-Wage Nation*. New York: New York University Press.

Bowen, William G., Mathew M. Chingos, and Michael S. McPherson. 2009. *Crossing the Finish Line: Completing College at America's Public Universities*. Princeton, NJ: Princeton University Press.

Bowen, William G., and Julie Ann Sosa. 1989. *Prospects for Faculty in the Arts and Sciences: A Study of Factors Affecting Demand and Supply, 1987–2012*. Princeton, NJ: Princeton University Press.

Boyer, Ernest L. 1983. *High School: A Report on Secondary Education in America*. New York: Carnegie Foundation for the Advancement of Teaching.

———. 1991. *Ready to Learn: A Mandate for the Nation*. Princeton, NJ: Carnegie Foundation for the Advancement of Teaching.

Braveman, Paula A, Catherine Cubbin, Susan Egerter, David R. Williams, and Elsie Pamuk. 2010. "Socioeconomic Disparities in Health in the United States: What the Patterns Tell Us." *American Journal of Public Health*, 100 (suppl. 1): S186–S196.

Brookings Institution. 2020. "The Brookings Institution's Contributors List." Washington, DC: Brookings Institution. Available at https://www.brookings.edu/wp-content/uploads/2020/04/The-Brookings-Institutions-Contributors-List-Fiscal-Year-2020.pdf.

Brown, Phillip, Hugh Lauder, and Sin Yi Cheung. 2020. *The Death of Human Capital? Its Failed Promise and How to Renew It in an Age of Disruption*. New York: Oxford University Press.

Brundage, Vernon, Jr. 2017. "Profile of the Labor Force by Educational Attainment." *Spotlight on Statistics*, Bureau of Labor Statistics, August. Washington, DC: U.S. Department of Labor. Available at https://www.bls.gov/spotlight/2017/educational-attainment-of-the-labor-force/home.htm.

Bureau of Labor Statistics. 2009. *Employment Projections: 2008–18 News Release*, 10 December. Washington, DC: U.S. Department of Labor. Available at https://www.bls.gov/news.release/archives/ecopro_12102009.htm.

———. 2012. "Table 9 Employment and Total Job Openings by Education, Work Experience, and On-the-Job Training Category, 2010 and Projected 2020." *Employment Projections—2010–2020 News Release*. Washington, DC: U.S. Department of Labor.

———. 2019a. "Characteristics of Minimum Wage Workers, 2018." *BLS Reports*, March. Washington, DC: U.S. Department of Labor. Available at https://www.bls.gov/opub/reports/minimum-wage/2018/home.htm.

———. 2019b. *Employment Projections: Employment, Wages, and Projected Change in Employment by Typical Entry Level Education, 2016–2026*. Washington, DC: U.S. Department of Labor. Internet Archive, 12 July. Available at https://web.archive.org/web/20190712112634/https://www.bls.gov/emp/tables/education-summary.htm.

———. 2019c. *Glossary*. Washington, DC: U.S. Department of Labor. Internet Archive, 29 April. Available at https://web.archive.org/web/20190429031022/https://www.bls.gov/bls/glossary.htm#S.

———. 2019d. "Union Membership Rate 10.5 Percent in 2018, Down from 20.1 Percent in 1983." *TED: The Economics Daily*, 25 January. Washington, DC: U.S. Department of Labor. Available at https://www.bls.gov/opub/ted/2019/union

-membership-rate-10-point-5-percent-in-2018-down-from-20-point-1-percent-in-1983.htm?view_full.

———. 2019e. "Union Workers More Likely Than Nonunion Workers to Have Retirement Benefits in 2019." *Economics Daily*, 25 October. Washington, DC: U.S. Department of Labor. Available at https://www.bls.gov/opub/ted/2019/union-workers-more-likely-than-nonunion-workers-to-have-retirement-benefits-in-2019.htm.

———. 2020. *Household Data: Annual Averages. 7. Employment Status of the Civilian Noninstitutional Population 25 Years and Over by Educational Attainment, Sex, Race, and Hispanic or Latino Ethnicity*. Washington, DC: U.S. Department of Labor. Internet Archive, 5 February. Available at https://web.archive.org/web/20200205150953/https://www.bls.gov/cps/cpsaat07.pdf.

———. 2021a. "Employment Projections: Measures of Education and Training." Washington, DC: U.S. Department of Labor. Available at https://www.bls.gov/emp/documentation/education/tech.htm.

———. 2021b. *Employment Projections: Table 5.2 Employment, Wages, and Projected Change in Employment by Typical Entry Level Education*. Published 12 April. Internet Archive 18 August. Available at https://web.archive.org/web/20210818112017/https://www.bls.gov/emp/tables/education-summary.htm.

———. 2021c. "Occupational Employment Statistics: Charts of the Largest Occupations in Each Area." Washington, DC: U.S. Department of Labor. Available at https://www.bls.gov/oes/current/area_emp_chart/area_emp_chart.htm.

———. 2021d. *Occupational Requirements Survey: Credentials*. Washington, DC: U.S. Department of Labor. Available at https://www.bls.gov/ors/factsheet/credentials.htm.

———. 2022a. *Employment Projections: Employment in S.T.E.M. Occupations: Table 1.11 Employment in S.T.E.M. Occupations, 2020 and Projected 2030*. 19 April. Washington, DC: U.S. Department of Labor. Available at https://www.bls.gov/emp/tables/stem-employment.htm.

———. 2022b. "Employment Projections: Table 5.2 Employment, Wages, and Projected Change in Employment by Typical Entry-Level Education." Washington, DC: U.S. Department of Labor. Available at https://www.bls.gov/emp/tables/education-summary.htm.

———. 2022c. "Occupational Employment and Wages, May 2021: 51–3023 Slaughterers and Meat Packers." Washington, DC: U.S. Department of Labor. Available at https://www.bls.gov/oes/current/oes513023.htm.

———. 2022d. *Occupational Outlook Handbook*. Washington, DC: U.S. Department of Labor. Available at https://www.bls.gov/ooh/.

———. N.d. "CPI Inflation Calculator." Washington, DC: U.S. Department of Labor. Available at https://www.bls.gov/data/inflation_calculator.htm.

Bushaw, William J., and Shane J. Lopez. 2010. "A Time for Change: The 42nd Annual Phi Delta Kappa/Gallup Poll of the Public's Attitudes toward the Public Schools." *Phi Delta Kappan* 92 (1): 9–26.

Business Roundtable. 1989. *Essential Components of a Successful Education System: The Business Roundtable Education Public Policy Agenda*. New York: Business Roundtable.

———. N.d. "Education and the Workforce: The Skills Gap, Explained." Washington, DC: Business Roundtable. Available at https://www.businessroundtable

.org/policy-perspectives/building-americas-tomorrow-ready-workforce/closing
-the-skills-gap/the-skills-gap-explained.

California Employment Development Department. 2021. "Employment Projections: 2018–2028." *Occupations with the Most Job Openings.* Available at https://www.labormarketinfo.edd.ca.gov/data/employment-projections.html.

Callahan, David. 2017. *The Givers: Wealth, Power, and Philanthropy in a New Gilded Age.* New York: Vintage.

Campbell, Donald T. 1979. "Assessing the Impact of Planned Social Change." *Evaluation and Program Planning* 2 (1): 67–90.

Card, David, and Alan B. Krueger. 1995. *Myth and Measurement: The New Economics of the Minimum Wage.* Princeton, NJ: Princeton University Press.

Career Education Colleges and Universities. 2020. "Steve Gunderson, President & CEO." Arlington, VA: Career Education Colleges and Universities. Internet Archive, 14 June. Available at https://web.archive.org/web/20200614153850/https://www.career.org/stevegundersonbio.html.

Carlson, Scott. 2017. *The Future of Work: How Colleges Can Prepare Students for the Jobs Ahead.* Washington, DC: Chronicle of Higher Education.

Carnegie, Andrew. 1901. *The Gospel of Wealth, and Other Timely Essays.* New York: Century.

Carnegie Foundation for the Advancement of Teaching. 1992. *School Choice: A Special Report.* Princeton, NJ: Carnegie Foundation for the Advancement of Teaching.

Carnevale, Anthony P. 2007. "A World of Opportunity." *Community College Journal* 78 (3): 24–27.

———. 2008. "College for All?" *Change: The Magazine of Higher Learning* 40 (1): 22–31.

———. 2020a. *CEW Quarterly,* Winter. Available at https://mailchi.mp/georgetown/cew-winter-newsletter-1276365?e=885a7e473a.

———. 2020b. "Ignore the Hype. College Is Worth it." *Inside Higher Ed,* 13 February. Available at https://www.insidehighered.com/views/2020/02/13/why-one
-should-ignore-reports-and-commentary-question-value-college-degree-opinion.

———. 2021. Personal communication with author, 30 July.

Carnevale, Anthony P., Artem Gulish, and Jeff Strohl. 2018. *Educational Adequacy in the Twenty-First Century.* Washington, DC: Century Foundation. Available at https://tcf.org/content/report/educational-adequacy-twenty-first-century/?agreed=1.

Carnevale, Anthony P., and Steven J. Rose. 2011. *The Undereducated American.* Washington, DC: Georgetown University, Center on Education and the Workforce. Available at https://1gyhoq479ufd3yna29x7ubjn-wpengine.netdna-ssl.com/wp-content/uploads/2014/11/undereducatedamerican.pdf.

———. 2012. "The Convergence of Postsecondary Education and the Labor Market." In *Universities and Colleges as Economic Drivers,* edited by Jason E. Lane and D. Bruce Johnston, 163–190. Albany: State University of New York Press.

Carnevale, Anthony P., Peter Schmidt, and Jeff Strohl. 2020. *The Merit Myth: How Our Colleges Favor the Rich and Divide America.* New York: New Press.

Carnevale, Anthony P., and Nicole Smith. 2016a. "The Economic Value of Diversity." In *Our Compelling Interests: The Value of Diversity for Democracy and a Prosperous Society,* edited by Earl Lewis and Nancy Cantor, 106–157. Princeton, NJ: Princeton University Press.

———. 2016b. "Preparing Today's Youth for Tomorrow's Jobs." In *Shared Prosperity in America's Communities*, edited by Susan M Wachtler and Lei Ding, 118–128. Philadelphia: University of Pennsylvania Press.

Carnevale, Anthony P., Nicole Smith, and Jeff Strohl. 2010a. *Help Wanted: Projections of Jobs and Education Requirements through 2018*. Washington, DC: Center on Education and the Workforce, Georgetown University. Available at https://1gyhoq479ufd3yna29x7ubjn-wpengine.netdna-ssl.com/wp-content/uploads/2014/12/fullreport.pdf.

———. 2010b. *Help Wanted: Projections of Jobs and Education Requirements through 2018*, Technical Summary. With Avinash Bhati. Washington, DC: Center for Education and the Workforce, Georgetown University. Available at https://cew.georgetown.edu/wp-content/uploads/Help_Wanted_Technical_Appendix.pdf.

———. 2013a. "Postsecondary Education and Economic Opportunity." In *Preparing Today's Students for Tomorrow's Jobs in Metropolitan America*, edited by Laura W. Perna, 93–120. Philadelphia: University of Pennsylvania Press.

———. 2013b. *Recovery: Job Growth and Education Requirements through 2020*, Executive Summary. Washington, DC: Georgetown University, Center on Education and the Workforce. Available at https://1gyhoq479ufd3yna29x7ubjn-wpengine.netdna-ssl.com/wp-content/uploads/2014/11/Recovery2020.ES_.Web_.pdf.

Carnevale, Anthony P., Jeff Strohl, Ban Cheah, and Neil Ridley. 2017. *Good Jobs That Pay without a B.A.* Washington, DC: Georgetown Center for Education and the Workforce. Available at https://goodjobsdata.org/wp-content/uploads/Good-Jobs-wo-BA.pdf.

Catlin, Aaron C., and Cathy A. Cowan. 2015. *History of Health Spending in the United States, 1960–2013*. Washington, DC: Center for Medicare and Medicaid Services.

CBS News. 2019. "Full 60 Minutes Interview with Fed Chair Jerome Powell." 10 March. Available at https://www.cbsnews.com/news/full-transcript-60-minutes-interview-with-fed-chair-jerome-powell/.

Center for Research on Education Outcomes. 2001a. "Project Overview." Rochester, NY: University of Rochester. Internet Archive, 22 May. Available at https://web.archive.org/web/20010522041908/http://www.rochester.edu/CREDO/overview.html.

———. 2001b. "Project Overview." Stanford, CA: Center for Research on Education Outcomes, Stanford University. Internet Archive, 5 August. Available at https://web.archive.org/web/20010805203007/http://credo.stanford.edu/overview.htm.

———. 2009. "New Stanford Report Finds Serious Quality Challenge in National Charter School Sector." Stanford, CA: Center for Research on Education Outcomes, Stanford University. Internet Archive, 2 April 2010. Available at https://web.archive.org/web/20100402023552/http://credo.stanford.edu/reports/National_Release.pdf.

———. 2012. "Home Page." Stanford, CA: Center for Research on Education Outcomes. Internet Archive, 21 April. Available at https://web.archive.org/web/20120421004403/http://credo.stanford.edu:80/.

———. 2013a. "Charter Schools Make Gains, According to 26-State Study." Stanford, CA: Center for Research on Education Outcomes, Stanford University. Internet Archive, 12 October. Available at https://web.archive.org/web/201310

12013447/http://credo.stanford.edu/documents/UNEMBARGOED%20Na tional%20Charter%20Study%20Press%20Release.pdf.

——. 2013b. *National Charter School Study*. Stanford, CA: Center for Research on Education Outcomes, Stanford University. Internet Archive, 24 December. Available at https://web.archive.org/web/20131224082928/http://credo.stan ford.edu/documents/NCSS%202013%20Final%20Draft.pdf.

——. 2015a. "C.R.E.D.O. Study Finds Urban Charter Schools Outperform Traditional School Peers." 18 March. Stanford, CA: Center for Research on Education Outcomes, Stanford University. Available at http://urbancharters.stan ford.edu/news.php.

——. 2015b. *Urban Charter School Study Report on 41 Regions*. Stanford, CA: Center for Research on Education Outcomes, Stanford University. Available at http://urbancharters.stanford.edu/download/Urban%20Charter%20School%20 Study%20Report%20on%2041%20Regions.pdf.

——. 2019. "C.R.E.D.O. at Stanford University Releases First In-Depth Examination of Charter School Impacts in South Carolina." 19 November. Stanford, CA: Center for Research on Education Outcomes, Stanford University. Available at https://credo.stanford.edu/wp-content/uploads/2021/08/south_carolina _press_release_.pdf.

——. 2021. "Home Page." Stanford, CA: Stanford University. Internet Archive, 24 January. Available at https://web.archive.org/web/20210124142316/https:// credo.stanford.edu/.

——. 2022. "Our Approach." Stanford, CA: Center for Research on Education Outcomes, Stanford University. Available at https://credo.stanford.edu/our-ap proach/.

Center on Education and the Workforce. 2009. "Mission Statement." Washington, DC: Georgetown University, Center on Education and the Workforce. Internet Archive, 13 June. Available at http://web.archive.org/web/20090613023059 /http://cew.georgetown.edu/mission.html.

——. 2010. "New Report on the Economic Value of 171 College Majors Links College Majors to Earnings." Press release, 15 June. Washington, DC: Georgetown University, Center on Education and the Workforce. Available at https:// cew.georgetown.edu/wp-content/uploads/HelpWanted_Press-Release-Final _MC.pdf.

——. 2022a. "Anthony P. Carnevale: Director and Research Professor." Washington, DC: Georgetown University, Center on Education and the Workforce. Available at https://cew.georgetown.edu/about-us/staff/anthony-p-carnevale/.

——. 2022b. "FAQs." Washington, DC: Georgetown University, Center on Education and the Workforce. Available at https://cew.georgetown.edu/about-us/faqs/.

——. N.d. "Good Jobs Project." Washington, DC: Georgetown University, Center on Education and the Workforce. Available at https://cew.georgetown.edu /good-jobs-project/.

Center on Reinventing Public Education. 1999. "Home: Overview." Seattle: University of Washington. Internet Archive, 5 November. Available at https://web .archive.org/web/19991105154119/http://www.crpe.org/AboutCRPE/overview .html.

——. 2005. "About C.R.P.E." Seattle: University of Washington. Internet Archive, 8 February. Available at https://web.archive.org/web/20050208012931 /http://www.crpe.org/about.shtml.

———. 2012. "About C.R.P.E." Seattle: University of Washington. Internet Archive, 6 January. Available at https://web.archive.org/web/20120106191312/http://www.crpe.org/cs/crpe/print/csr_docs/aboutus.htm.

———. 2021. "About the Center for Reinventing Public Education." Seattle, WA: University of Washington. Internet Archive, 12 February. Available at https://web.archive.org/web/20210212005203/https://www.crpe.org/about-us/crpe.

Central Intelligence Agency Library. 2012. *Workforce 2000: Work and Workers for the 21st Century*. Declassified in part, sanitized copy approved for release 10 October. Langley, VA: Central Intelligence Agency Library. Internet Archive, 23 January 2017. Available at https://web.archive.org/web/20170123140247/https://www.cia.gov/library/readingroom/docs/CIA-RDP90-00530R000300600001-7.pdf.

———. 2013. *Workforce 2000: Work and Workers for the 21st Century*. Declassified in part, sanitized copy approved for release 15 April. Langley, VA: Central Intelligence Agency. Available at https://www.cia.gov/readingroom/docs/CIA-RDP90-00530R000802050001-1.pdf.

Chen, Grace. 2020. "Nation's Public School Personnel Embroiled in Cheating Scandals." *Public School Review*, 30 December. Available at https://www.publicschoolreview.com/blog/nations-public-school-personnel-embroiled-in-cheating-scandals.

Chenoweth, Karin. 1998. "In Education We Trust." *Black Issues in Higher Education* 15 (2): 14.

———. 2007. *"It's Being Done": Academic Success in Unexpected Schools*. Cambridge, MA: Harvard Education Press.

———. 2009. *How It's Being Done: Urgent Lessons from Unexpected Schools*. Cambridge, MA: Harvard Education Press.

———. 2017. *Schools That Succeed: How Educators Marshal the Power of Systems for Improvement*. Cambridge, MA: Harvard Education Press.

———. N.d. "Biography." Available at https://www.karinchenoweth.com/bio.htm.

Chenoweth, Karin, and Christina Theokas. 2011. *Getting It Done: Leading Academic Success in Unexpected Schools*. Cambridge, MA: Harvard Education Press.

Chetty, Raj, Michael Stepner, Sarah Abraham, Shelby Lin, Benjamin Scuderi, Nicholas Turner, Augustin Bergeron, and David Cutler. 2016. "The Association between Income and Life Expectancy in the United States, 2001–2014." *Journal of the American Medical Association* 315 (16): 1750–1766.

Children's Defense Fund. 1991. *The State of America's Children: 1991*. Washington, DC: Children's Defense Fund.

Childress, Herb. 2019. *The Adjunct Underclass: How America's Colleges Betrayed Their Faculty, Their Students, and Their Mission*. Chicago: University of Chicago Press.

Christenson, Jerome. 2011. "Ramaley Coined STEM Term Now Used Nationwide." *Winona Daily News*, 13 November.

Chronicle of Higher Education. 1997. "American Assn. for Higher Education to Get First Female Leader." 4 April.

———. 2019. *The Looming Enrollment Crisis: How Colleges Are Responding to Shifting Demographics and New Student Needs*. Washington, DC: Chronicle of Higher Education.

———. 2020. "The Coronavirus Will Change Everything." 17 April.

Chubb, John E. 2001. "The Private Can Be Public." *Education Matters* 1 (1): 6–15. Internet Archive, 23 December. Available at https://web.archive.org/web/2001 1223085130/http://www.educationnext.org/2001sp/6chubb.html.

Chubb, John E., and Terry M. Moe. 1990. *Politics, Markets, and America's Schools. Politics, Markets, and America's Schools.* Washington, DC: Brookings Institution Press.

Cialdini, Robert B. 2007. *Influence: The Psychology of Persuasion*, revised edition. New York: Collins.

Citizens Commission on Civil Rights. 1982. *Articles of Incorporation*, 2 December 1982 Washington, DC: Citizens Commission on Civil Rights.

———. 2001. *Closing the Deal: A Preliminary Report on State Compliance with Final Assessment and Accountability Requirements under the Improving America's Schools Act of 1994.* Washington, DC: Citizens Commission on Civil Rights.

———. 2007. *Form 990 for Tax Year Beginning September 1, 2007, and Ending on August 31, 2008.* Washington, DC: Citizens Commission on Civil Rights.

City Club of Cleveland. 2014. "Are Ohio Charter Schools Improving?" 10 December. Cleveland, OH: City Club of Cleveland. Available at https://www.cityclub .org/inc/audio-player.php?event_id=360.

Cobet, Aaron E., and Gregory A. Wilson. 2002. "Comparing 50 Years of Labor Productivity in U.S. and Foreign Manufacturing." *Monthly Labor Review*, June, 51–65. Washington, DC: U.S. Department of Labor, Bureau of Labor Statistics.

Cody, Anthony. 2014. *The Educator and the Oligarch: A Teacher Challenges the Gates Foundation.* New York: Garn.

Cohen, Patricia, and Robert Gebeloff. 2018. "Public Servants Are Losing Their Foothold in the Middle Class." *New York Times*, 22 April.

College Board. 2019. *Form 990: For the 2019 Calendar Year.* New York: College Board.

Columbia University Record. 1985. "Grant to TC Funds Research Institute." 13 December, 11, 16.

Columbo, Hayleigh. 2017. "USA Funds' New Tack: Bet Millions on Education Startups." *Indianapolis Business Journal*, 13 July.

Commission on Chapter 1. 1992a. *Interim Report.* Baltimore: Commission on Chapter 1.

———. 1992b. *Making Schools Work for Children in Poverty: A New Framework.* Washington, DC: American Association for Higher Education and Council of Chief State School Officers.

Community College Journal. 2007. "Lumina Foundation Taps New CEO." Vol. 78, no. 3 (December): 8.

Community College Research Center. 2019. *Biennial Report, 2018–2020.* New York: Teachers College, Columbia University, Community College Research Center. Available at https://ccrc.tc.columbia.edu/images/easyblog_articles/177/ccrc -2018-2020-biennial-report.pdf.

Coons, John E., Lisa Graham Keegan, and T. Willard Fair. 2000. "The Pro-voucher Left and the Pro-equity Right." *Annals of the American Academy of Political and Social Science* 572:98–114.

Cooper, Kerris, and Kitty Stewart. 2017. "Does Money Affect Children's Outcomes? An Update." Center for Analysis of Social Exclusion Paper 203. London: London School of Economics and Political Science. Available at http://sticerd.lse.ac .uk/dps/case/cp/casepaper203.pdf.

Cottom, Tressie McMillan. 2017. *Lower Ed: The Troubling Rise of For-Profit Colleges in the New Economy.* New York: New Press.

Council on Competitiveness. 2005. *Innovate America: National Innovation Initiative Summit and Report.* Washington, DC: Council on Competitiveness. Internet Archive, 7 March 2022. Available at https://web.archive.org/web/202203 07201503/https://www.compete.org/storage/images/uploads/File/PDF%20Files /NII_Innovate_America.pdf.

Cumming, Tammie, and Peter Ewell. 2017. "Introduction: History and Conceptual Basis of Assessment in Higher Education." In *Enhancing Assessment in Higher Education: Putting Psychometrics to Work,* edited by Tammie Cumming and M. David Miller. New York: City University of New York (CUNY), CUNY Academic Works. Available at https://academicworks.cuny.edu/cgi/viewcontent.cgi ?article=1236&context=ny_pubs.

Cutler, David M., Angus S. Deaton, and Adriana Lleras-Muney. 2006. "The Determinants of Mortality." *Journal of Economic Perspectives* 20 (3): 97–120.

D'Amico, Carol. 1997. "Back to the Future: A Current View of Workforce 2000 and Projections for 2020." *Employment Relations Today,* Autumn, 1–11.

Darling-Hammond, Linda. 2010. *The Flat World and Education: How America's Commitment to Equity Will Determine Our Future.* New York: Teachers College Press.

Darling-Hammond, Linda, and Robert Rothman, eds. 2015. *Teaching in a Flat World: Learning from High-Performing Systems.* New York: Teachers College Press.

David and Lucile Packard Foundation. 2022. *Fifty Years of Lasting Change.* Los Altos, CA: David and Lucile Packard Foundation. Available at https://timeline .packard.org/#page0.Davidson, Cathy N. 2017. *The New Education: How to Revolutionize the University to Prepare Students for a World in Flux.* New York: Basic Books.

Deloitte. 2011. *Boiling Point? The Skills Gap in U.S. Manufacturing.* New York: Deloitte and Manufacturing Institute. Internet Archive, 28 October. Available at https://web.archive.org/web/20111028060653/https://www.themanufactur inginstitute.org/~/media/A07730B2A798437D98501E798C2E13AA.ashx/.

———. 2018. *The Jobs Are Here, but Where Are the People? Key Findings from the 2018Deloitte and the Manufacturing Institute Skills Gap and Future of Work Study.* New York: Deloitte and Manufacturing Institute. Available at https:// www.themanufacturinginstitute.org/wp-content/uploads/2020/03/MI-DI-The -jobs-are-here-where-are-the-people.pdf.

DePass, Dee. 2019. "Manufacturing Advocates Warn of Looming Labor Crisis at Twin Cities Event." *Minneapolis Star Tribune,* 25 February.

Dewey, John. 1916. *Democracy and Education: An Introduction to the Philosophy of Education.* New York: Macmillan.

Diamond, David. 1981. "The Subtle Control of a Vast Fortune." *New York Times,* 25 October.

Diamond, Sara. 1995. *Roads to Dominion: Right-Wing Movements and Political Power in the United States.* New York: Guilford.

Dixson, Adrienne D., Kristin L. Buras, and Elisabeth K. Jeffers. 2015. "The Color of Reform: Race, Education Reform, and Charter Schools in Post-Katrina New Orleans." *Qualitative Inquiry* 21 (3): 288–299.

Dougherty, Conor. 2017. "How Noncompete Clauses Keep Workers Locked In." *New York Times*, 13 May.

Dreier, Peter, John Mollenkopf, and Todd Swanstrom. 2014. *Place Matters: Metropolitics for the 21st Century*, third edition, revised. Lawrence: University Press of Kansas.

Duggan, James E., Robert Gillingham, and John S. Greenlees. 2008. "Mortality and Lifetime Income: Evidence from U.S. Social Security Records." *IMF Staff Papers 55* (4): 566–594.

Duncan, Greg J., and Jeanne Brooks-Gunn. 1997. *Consequences of Growing Up Poor*. New York: Russell Sage.

Duncan, Greg J., Katherine Magnuson, Ariel Kalil, and Kathleen Ziol-Guest. 2011. "The Importance of Early Childhood Poverty." *Social Indicators Research* 108 (1): 87–98.

Duncan, Greg J., and Richard J. Murnane, eds. 2011. *Whither Opportunity? Rising Inequality, Schools, and Children's Life Chances*. New York: Russell Sage.

Dynarski, Mark, Ning Rui, Ann Webber, and Babette Gutmann. 2017. *Evaluation of the DC Opportunity Scholarship Program: Impacts after One Year* (NCEE 2017–4022). Washington, DC: National Center for Education Evaluation and Regional Assistance, Institute of Education Sciences, U.S. Department of Education.

———. 2018. *Evaluation of the DC Opportunity Scholarship Program: Impacts Two Years after Students Applied* (NCEE 2018–4010). Washington, DC: National Center for Education Evaluation and Regional Assistance, Institute of Education Sciences, U.S. Department of Education.

EdBuild. 2019a. "EdBuild Impact." Jersey City, NJ: EdBuild. Internet Archive, 31 March. Available at https://web.archive.org/web/20190331044603/https://edbuild.org/impact.

———. 2019b. "Home Page." Jersey City, NJ: EdBuild. Internet Archive, 21 April. Available at https://web.archive.org/web/20190421055111/https://edbuild.org/.

———. 2022. "Home Page." Jersey City, NJ: EdBuild. Available at https://edbuild.org/.

EdChoice. 2022. "Who Funds EdChoice?" Indianapolis, IN: EdChoice. Available at https://www.edchoice.org/school-choice/faqs/who-funds-edchoice/.

Edmans, Alex, Xavier Gabaix, and Dirk Jenter. 2017. "Executive Compensation: A Survey of Theory and Evidence." NBER Working Paper Series 23596. Cambridge, MA: National Bureau of Economic Research.

Educational Testing Service. 2019. *Form 990: For the Tax Year Beginning October 1, 2018, and Ending September 30, 2019*. Princeton, NJ: Educational Testing Service.

Education for Innovation Initiative. 2005. *Tapping America's Potential*. Washington, DC: Business Roundtable. Available at https://files.eric.ed.gov/fulltext/ED485768.pdf.

Education Next. 2001. "About Education Next." Cambridge, MA: Education Next. Internet Archive, 30 October. Available at https://web.archive.org/web/20011030181757/http://www.educationnext.org/about.html.

———. 2010. *PEPG Survey—2010*. Cambridge, MA: Education Next. Available at https://www.educationnext.org/wp-content/uploads/2020/07/EN-PEPG_Complete_Polling_Results_2010.pdf.

Education Research Alliance for New Orleans. 2022. "About." New Orleans, LA: Tulane University. Available at https://educationresearchalliancenola.org/about.

Education Resources Information Center. 1987. *Document Resume: Workforce 2000; Work and Workers for the 21st Century.* Washington, DC: U.S. Department of Education.

———. 2021. Personal communication with author, 5 April.

Education Resources Institute and Institute for Higher Education Policy. 1995. *College Debt and the American Family.* Boston: Education Resources Institute and Institute for Higher Education Policy. Available at https://www.ihep.org/wp-content/uploads/2014/05/uploads_docs_pubs_collegedebt.pdf.

———. 1996. *Life After Forty: A New Portrait of Today's—and Tomorrow's—Postsecondary Students.* Washington, DC: The Education Resources Institute and The Institute for Higher Education Policy. Available at https://www.ihep.org/wp-content/uploads/2014/05/uploads_docs_pubs_lifeafterforty.pdf.

———. 1997a. *Now What? Life After College for Recent College Graduates.* Washington, DC: The Education Resources Institute and The Institute for Higher Education Policy. Available at https://www.ihep.org/wp-content/uploads/2014/05/uploads_docs_pubs_nowwhat.pdf.

———. 1997b. *Taxing Matters: College Aid, Tax Policy and Equal Opportunity.* Boston: The Education Resources Institute and The Institute for Higher Education Policy. Available at https://www.ihep.org/wp-content/uploads/2014/05/uploads_docs_pubs_taxingmatters.pdf.

———. N.d. *Graduating into Debt: The Burdens of Borrowing for Graduate and Professional Students.* Boston: The Education Resources Institute and The Institute for Higher Education Policy. Available at https://www.ihep.org/wp-content/uploads/2014/05/uploads_docs_pubs_graduatingintodebt.pdf.

Education Trust. 1996a. *Articles of Incorporation*, 9 February. Washington, DC: Education Trust.

———. 1996b. *Education Watch: The 1996 Education Trust State and National Data Book.* Washington, DC: Education Trust.

———. 1997a. "Home Page." Washington, DC: Education Trust. Internet Archive, 30 March. Available at https://web.archive.org/web/19970330010225/http://www.edtrust.org/.

———. 1997b. *Form 990: 1997.* Washington, DC: Education Trust.

———. 1998a. "Education Trust Press Conference: Remarks by Kati Haycock." Washington, DC: Education Trust. Internet Archive, 29 January 1999. Available at https://web.archive.org/web/19990129014454/http://www.edtrust.org/Statement.htm.

———. 1998b. *Form 990: 1998.* Washington, DC: Education Trust.

———. 1999. *Form 990: 1999.* Washington, DC: Education Trust.

———. 2000. *Form 990: 2000.* Washington, DC: Education Trust.

———. 2001. *Form 990: 2001.* Washington, DC: Education Trust.

———. 2002. *Form 990: 2002.* Washington, DC: Education Trust.

———. 2003a. *ESEA: Myths versus Realities.* Washington, DC: Education Trust. Internet Archive, 1 April. Available at https://web.archive.org/web/20030401133103/http://www.edtrust.org/main/main/index.asp.

———. 2003b. *Form 990: 2003.* Washington, DC: Education Trust.

———. 2004. *Form 990: 2004.* Washington, DC: Education Trust.

———. 2005. *Form 990: 2005.* Washington, DC: Education Trust.

———. 2006. *Form 990: 2006.* Washington, DC: Education Trust.

———. 2007. *Form 990: 2007.* Washington, DC: Education Trust.

———. 2008. *Form 990: 2008.* Washington, DC: Education Trust.

———. 2009. *Form 990: 2009.* Washington, DC: Education Trust.

———. 2010. *Form 990: 2010.* Washington, DC: Education Trust.

———. 2011. *Form 990: 2011.* Washington, DC: Education Trust.

———. 2012. *Form 990: 2012.* Washington, DC: Education Trust.

———. 2013. *Form 990: 2013.* Washington, DC: Education Trust.

———. 2022a. "Supporters." Washington, DC: Education Trust.

———. 2022b. "Who We Are." Washington, DC: Education Trust. Available at https://edtrust.org/who-we-are/.

Education Week. 1993a. "The Roundtable: Introduction." 21 April, *Education Week.*

———. 1993b. "The Roundtable: 'Raising Public Awareness.'" 21 April, *Education Week.*

Elam, Stanley M., and Lowell C. Rose. 1995. "The 27th Annual Phi Delta Kappa/Gallup Poll of the Public's Attitudes toward the Public Schools." *Phi Delta Kappan* 77, no. 1 (September): 41–56.

Emmons, William R., Ana H. Kent, and Lowell R. Ricketts. 2019. "Is College Still Worth It? The New Calculus of Falling Returns." *Federal Reserve Bank of St. Louis Review*, Fourth Quarter, 297–330.

Ermisch, John, Markus Jantti, and Timothy M. Smeeding, eds. 2012. *From Parents to Children: The Intergenerational Transmission of Advantage.* New York: Russell Sage Foundation.

Esfahani Smith, Emily. 2011. "Profile in School Reform: Terry Moe." *Defining Ideas: A Hoover Institution Journal*, 15 April. Available at https://www.hoover.org/research/profile-school-reform-terry-moe.

Evangelauf, Jean. 1991. "Study Predicts Dramatic Shifts in Enrollments." *Chronicle of Higher Education*, 18 September, A40.

Every Learner Everywhere. 2022. "About Us." Boulder, CO: WICHE. Cooperative for Educational Technologies and Western Interstate Commission on Higher Education. Available at https://www.everylearnereverywhere.org/about-us/.

Federal Reserve Bank of New York. 2022a. "The Labor Market for Recent College Graduates: Labor Market Outcomes of College Graduates by Major." New York: Federal Reserve Bank of New York. Available at https://www.newyorkfed.org/research/college-labor-market/index.html#/outcomes-by-major.

———. 2022b. "The Labor Market for Recent College Graduates: Underemployment." New York: Federal Reserve Bank of New York. Available at https://www.newyorkfed.org/research/college-labor-market/index.html#/underemployment.

Federal Reserve Economic Data. 2022. "Shares of Gross Domestic Product: Personal Consumption Expenditures." St. Louis, MO: Federal Reserve Economic Data. Available at https://fred.stlouisfed.org/series/DPCERE1Q156NBEA.

Ferguson, Karen. 2013. *Top Down: The Ford Foundation, Black Power, and the Reinvention of Racial Liberalism.* Philadelphia: University of Pennsylvania Press.

Fischer, Karin. 2018. "Can a Huge Online College Solve California's Work-Force Problems?" *Chronicle of Higher Education*, 29 July.

Fiske, Edward B. 1989a. "Education; Lessons." *New York Times*, 13 September.

———. 1989b. "Impending U.S. Jobs 'Disaster': Work Force Unqualified to Work." *New York Times*, 25 September.

Ford Foundation. 2007. "Beyond Current Program Structure." *Ford Foundation Grants Data Base.* New York: Ford Foundation. Available at https://www.ford foundation.org/work/our-grants/awarded-grants/awarded-grant/to-conduct-re search-and-policy-analysis-on-changing-educational-and-training-requirements -for-the-la/104378.

Frank, Thomas. 2016. *Listen, Liberal: Or, Whatever Happened to the Party of the People?* New York: Metropolitan.

Freeman, Richard B. 1976. *The Overeducated American.* New York: Academic Press.

Frey, Carl Benedict. 2019. "About." Personal website. Available at https://www .carlbenediktfrey.com/about.

Frey, Carl Benedict, and Michael A. Osborne. 2017. "The Future of Employment: How Susceptible Are Jobs to Computerisation?" *Technological Forecasting and Social Change* 114 (January): 254–280.

Friedman, Milton. 1955. "The Role of Government in Education." In *Economics and the Public Interest,* edited by Robert A. Solo, 123–144. New Brunswick, NJ: Rutgers University Press.

Friedman, Thomas L. 2005. *The World Is Flat: A Brief History of the Twenty-First Century.* New York: Picador.

Gallup. 2022. "Who We Are." Washington, DC: Gallup. Available at https://www .gallup.com/corporate/212381/who-we-are.aspx.

———. 2023. *Presidential Approval Ratings: George W. Bush.* Washington, DC: Gallup. Available at https://news.gallup.com/poll/116500/presidential-approval -ratings-george-bush.aspx.

Gallup and Bates. 2019. *Forging Pathways to Purposeful Work: The Role of Higher Education.* Washington, DC: Gallup. Available at https://www.bates.edu /purpose/files/2019/05/Bates_PurposefulWork_FINAL_REPORT.pdf.

Gannon, Kevin M. 2020. *Radical Hope: A Teaching Manifesto.* Morgantown: West Virginia University Press.

Gardner, Lee. 2019. *Preparing for Tough Conversations: How to Set the Stage for Major Change on Your Campus.* Washington, DC: Chronicle of Higher Education.

Gates, Bill. 2005. "National Education Summit on High Schools, Prepared Remarks." 26 February. Seattle, WA: Gates Foundation. Available at https://www .gatesfoundation.org/media-center/speeches/2005/02/bill-gates-2005-national -education-summit.

———. 2008. "Testimony before the Committee on Science and Technology, U.S. House of Representatives." 12 March. Seattle: Microsoft. Available at https:// news.microsoft.com/2008/03/12/bill-gates-testimony-before-the-committee-on -science-and-technology-u-s-house-of-representatives/.

———. 2017. "Remarks at the Council of Great City Schools." *Gates Notes: The Blog of Bill Gates,* 19 October. Available at https://www.gatesnotes.com/Edu cation/Council-of-Great-City-Schools.

Gates Foundation. 2008a. "Grant to Georgetown University to Support a Project Aligning Education and Training Systems with Career Requirements to Increase Opportunity for Low and Moderate Income Youth." Seattle, WA: Gates Foundation. Available at https://www.gatesfoundation.org/about/committed-grants /2008/05/opp50576.

———. 2008b. "New Initiative to Double the Number of Low-Income Students in the U.S. Who Earn a Postsecondary Degree—Bill and Melinda Gates Foundation." Seattle, WA: Gates Foundation. Available at https://www.gatesfoundation.org/Media-Center/Press-Releases/2008/12/New-Initiative-to-Double-the-Number-of-LowIncome-Students-in-the-US-Who-Earn-a-Postsecondary-Degree.

———. 2016. "CREDO Study: Urban Charter Schools Making Significant Positive Impact." 27 May. Seattle, WA: Gates Foundation. Available at https://usprogram.gatesfoundation.org/news-and-insights/articles/credo-study-urban-charter-schools-making-significant-positive-impact.

———. 2022. "Postsecondary Success." Seattle, WA: Gates Foundation. Available at https://www.gatesfoundation.org/our-work/programs/us-program/postsecondary-success.

Gelles, David. 2021. "After Riot, Business Leaders Reckon with Their Support for Trump." *New York Times*, 7 January.

———. 2022. *The Man Who Broke Capitalism: How Jack Welch Gutted the Heartland and Crushed the Soul of Corporate America—and How to Undo His Legacy*. New York: Simon and Schuster.

Gerstner, Louis V. 1994. *Reinventing Education: Entrepreneurship in America's Public Schools*. With Roger D. Semerad, Denis Philip Doyle, and William B. Johnston. New York: Plume.

Gill, Brian, P. Mike Timpane, Karen E. Ross, and Dominic J. Brewer. 2001. *Rhetoric versus Reality: What We Know and What We Need to Know about Vouchers and Charter Schools*. Santa Monica, CA: Rand.

Giridharadas, Anand. 2018. *Winners Take All: The Elite Charade of Changing the World*. New York: Knopf.

Gleason, Philip, Melissa Clark, Christina Clark Tuttle, and Emily Dwoyer. 2010. *The Evaluation of Charter School Impacts, Final Report*. Washington, DC: U.S. Department of Education, National Center for Education Evaluation and Regional Assistance, Institute of Education Sciences.

Golann, Joanne, and Mira Debs. 2019. "The Harsh Discipline of No-Excuses Charter Schools: Is It Worth the Promise?" *Education Week*, 9 June.

Goldin, Claudia, and Lawrence F. Katz. 2008. *The Race between Education and Technology*. Cambridge, MA: Belknap.

Goldstein, Dana. 2014. *The Teacher Wars: A History of America's Most Embattled Profession*. New York: Doubleday.

Governing. 2018. "Education Spending per Student by State." Folsom, CA: eRepublic. Available at https://www.governing.com/gov-data/education-data/state-education-spending-per-pupil-data.html.

Graduate Program in Learning, Design, and Technology. 2021. *Openings: Higher Education's Challenge to Change in the Face of the Pandemic, Inequity, and Racism*. Washington, DC: Georgetown University. Available at https://ldt.georgetown.edu/wp-content/uploads/Openings_FINAL-1.pdf.

Grawe, Nathan D. 2018. *Demographics and the Demand for Higher Education*. Baltimore: Johns Hopkins University Press.

———. 2021a. *The Agile College: How Institutions Successfully Navigate Demographic Changes*. Baltimore: Johns Hopkins University Press.

———. 2021b. "How to Survive the Enrollment Bust." *Chronicle of Higher Education*, 22 January.

Greeley, Andrew M. 1972. "Malice in Wonderland." In *Inside Academe: Culture in Crisis*, from the editors of *Change*, 95–110. New Rochelle, NY: Change Magazine.

Greystone Global. 2022. "Dr. Kathryn Scanland." Chicago: Greystone Global. Available at https://greystoneglobal.com/dr-kathryn-scanland-2/.

Groeger, Cristina Viviana. 2021. *The Education Trap: Schools and the Remaking of Inequality in Boston*. Cambridge, MA: Harvard University Press.

Grubb, W. Norton, and Marvin Lazerson. 2004. *The Education Gospel: The Economic Power of Schooling*. Cambridge, MA: Harvard University Press.

Gunderson, Steve, Robert Jones, and Kathryn Scanland. 2004. *The Jobs Revolution: Changing How America Works*. Chicago: Copywriters.

Hacker, Andrew. 2016. *The Math Myth: And Other STEM Delusions*. New York: New Press.

Hacker, Jacob S. 2006. *The Great Risk Shift: The New Economic Insecurity and the Decline of the American Dream*, revised and expanded edition. New York: Oxford University Press.

Hacker, Jacob S., and Paul Pierson. 2010. *Winner-Take-All Politics: How Washington Made the Rich Richer—and Turned Its Back on the Middle Class*. New York: Simon and Schuster.

———. 2016. *American Amnesia: How the War on Government Led Us to Forget What Made America Prosper*. New York: Simon and Schuster.

———. 2020. *Let Them Eat Tweets: How the Right Rules in an Age of Extreme Inequality*. New York: Liveright.

Handel, Michael J. 2003. "Skills Mismatch in the Labor Market." *Annual Review of Sociology* 29:135–165.

Haney, Walt. 2000. "The Myth of the Texas Miracle in Education." *Education Policy Analysis Archives* 8, no. 41 (August). Available at https://epaa.asu.edu/index.php/epaa/article/view/432/828.

Hannon, Simona M., Kevin B. Moore, Irina Stefanescu, and Max Schmeiser. 2016. "Saving for College and Section 529 Plans." *FEDS Notes*, 3 February. Washington, DC: Board of Governors of the Federal Reserve System.

Hanushek, Eric A., Paul E. Peterson, Laura M. Talpey, and Ludger Woessmann. 2020. "Long-Run Trends in the U.S. SES-Achievement Gap." National Bureau of Economic Research Working Paper 26764. Cambridge, MA: National Bureau of Economic Research.

Harris, Katelynn, and Michael D. McCall. 2019. "The Relative Weakness in Earnings of Production Workers in Manufacturing, 1990–2018." *Monthly Labor Review*, U.S. Bureau of Labor Statistics, December. Washington, DC: U.S. Department of Labor. Available at https://www.bls.gov/opub/mlr/2019/article/earnings-of-production-workers-in-manufacturing-1990-2018.htm.

Harvey, David. 2005. *A Brief History of Neoliberalism*. New York: Oxford University Press.

Haycock, Kati. 1993. "Why We Care about Chapter 1." *American Association for Higher Education Bulletin* 45, no. 7 (March): 6.

———. 2001. "Dear Friends and Colleagues." 21 September. Washington, DC: Education Trust. Internet Archive. Available at https://web.archive.org/web/20011025035049if_/http://www.edtrust.org/conf_teach2001nov/conf7.asp.

———. 2003. Testimony, Subcommittee on 21st Century Competitiveness of the Committee on Education and the Workforce, U.S. House of Representatives, 20 May.

Haycock, Kati, and David Hornbeck. 1995. "Making Schools Work for Children in Poverty." In *National Issues in Education: Elementary and Secondary Education Act*, edited by John F. Jennings, 77–89. Bloomington, IN: Phi Delta Kappa International.

Haycock, Kati, and Susana M. Navarro. 1988. *Unfinished Business: Fulfilling Our Children's Promise*. Oakland, CA: Achievement Council.

Hess, Frederick M., ed. 2005. *With the Best of Intentions: How Philanthropy Is Reshaping K–12 Education*. Cambridge, MA: Harvard Education Press.

———. 2019. Curriculum vitae. Washington, DC: American Enterprise Institute. Available at https://www.aei.org/wp-content/uploads/2014/06/hess_cv_2019 March.pdf.

Hess, Frederick M., and Max Eden. 2017. Introduction to *The Every Student Succeeds Act: What It Means for Schools, Systems, and States*, edited by Frederick M. Hess and Max Eden 1–11. Cambridge, MA: Harvard Education Press.

Hess, Frederick M., and Jeffrey R. Henig, eds. 2015. *The New Education Philanthropy: Politics, Policy, and Reform*. Cambridge, MA: Harvard Education Press.

Hill, Paul T. 2005. "Re-creating Public Education in New Orleans." *Education Week*, 20 September.

Hira, Ron. 2018. "Bridge to Permanent Immigration or Temporary Labor? The H-1B Visa Program Is a Source of Both." In *U.S. Engineering in a Global Economy*, edited by Richard B. Freeman and Hal Salzman, 263–283. Chicago: University of Chicago Press.

Hochschild, Jennifer L., and Nathan Scovronick. 2003. *The American Dream and the Public Schools*. New York: Oxford University Press.

Hornbeck, David W. 1991. "New Paradigms for Action." In *Human Capital and America's Future: An Economic Strategy for the '90s*, edited by David W. Hornbeck and Lester M. Salamon, 360–389. Baltimore: Johns Hopkins University Press.

Hornbeck, David W., and Lester M. Salamon, eds. 1991. *Human Capital and America's Future: An Economic Strategy for the '90s*. Baltimore: Johns Hopkins University Press.

Huelskamp, Robert M. 1993. "Perspectives on Education in America." *Phi Delta Kappan* 74, no. 9 (May): 718–721.

Institute for Higher Education Policy. 2022a. "Home Page." Washington, DC: Institute for Higher Education Policy. Available at https://www.ihep.org/.

———. 2022b. Personal communication with author, 12 April.

Institute on Education and the Economy. 1995. *Using What We Must to Get the Schools We Need: A Productivity Focus for American Education*. New York: Columbia University, Institute on Education and the Economy.

———. N.d. "About IEE." New York: Columbia University, Teachers College. 2023. Available at https://www.tc.columbia.edu/centers/iee/About.htm.

Jaffe, Matthew P. 1987. *Workforce 2000: Forecast of Occupational Change, Technical Appendix*. Indianapolis, IN: Hudson Institute.

Jewson, Marta. 2019. "New Orleans Becomes First Major American City without Traditional Schools." *The Lens*, 1 July. Available at https://thelensnola.org/20 19/07/01/new-orleans-becomes-first-major-american-city-without-traditional -schools/.

Jobs for the Future. 2022. "Who We Are: Our Partners." Washington, DC: Jobs for the Future. Available at https://www.jff.org/about/.

Jochim, Ashley. 2018. "Educational Equality in the Future: Risks and Opportunity." In *Thinking Forward: New Ideas for a New Era of Public Education*, edited by Robin J. Lake, 54–64. Seattle: University of Washington, Center on Reinventing Public Education. Available at https://www.crpe.org/sites/default/files/crpe-thinking-forward-new-ideas-new-era-public-education.pdf.

Johnston, William B., Jane Newitt, and David Reed. 1987. *Michigan beyond 2000*. Lanham, MD: University Press of America and Hudson Institute.

Johnston, William B., and Arnold H. Packer. 1987. *Workforce 2000: Work and Workers for the 21st Century*. Indianapolis, IN: Hudson Institute.

Judd, Dennis R., and Todd Swanstrom. 2014. *City Politics*, ninth edition. New York: Pearson.

Judy, Richard W., and Carol D'Amico. 1997. *Workforce 2020: Work and Workers in the 21st Century*. Indianapolis, IN: Hudson Institute.

Kahlenberg, Richard D., and Halley Potter. 2014. *A Smarter Charter: Finding What Works for Charter Schools and Public Education*. New York: Teachers College Press.

Kamola, Isaac A. 2019. *Making the World Global: U.S. Universities and the Production of the Global Imaginary*. Durham, NC: Duke University Press.

Kaplan, Steven N., and Joshua Rauh. 2013. "It's the Market: The Broad-Based Rise in the Return to Top Talent." *Journal of Economic Perspectives* 27, no. 3 (Summer): 35–56.

Kelchen, Robert. 2018. *Higher Education Accountability*. Baltimore: Johns Hopkins University Press.

Kelly, Andrew P., and Kevin J. James. 2015. "Philanthropy Goes to College." In *The New Education Philanthropy: Politics, Policy, and Reform*, edited by Frederick M. Hess and Jeffrey R. Henig, 79–104. Cambridge, MA: Harvard Education Press.

Kiley, Kevin. 2013. "The Pupil Cliff." *Inside Higher Ed*, 11 January. Available at https://www.insidehighered.com/news/2013/01/11/wiche-report-highlights-decline-high-school-graduates-and-growing-diversity.

Kitagawa, Evelyn M., and Philip Hauser. 1973. *Differential Mortality in the United States: A Study in Socioeconomic Epidemiology*. Cambridge, MA: Harvard University Press.

Klein, Alyson. 2015. "No Child Left Behind: An Overview." *Education Week*, 10 April.

Klein, Stephen P., Laura S. Hamilton, Daniel F. McCaffrey, and Brian M. Stecher. 2000. "What Do Test Scores in Texas Tell Us?" Issue Paper 202, *Rand Education*. Santa Monica, CA: Rand.

Kotok, Stephen. 2017. "Unfulfilled Potential: High-Achieving Minority Students and the High School Achievement Gap in Math." *High School Journal* 100, no. 3 (Spring): 183–202.

Kotsko, Adam. 2018. *Neoliberalism's Demons: On the Political Theology of Late Capital*. Stanford, CA: Stanford University Press.

Kovacs, Philip E., ed. 2011. *The Gates Foundation and the Future of U.S. 'Public' Schools*. New York: Taylor and Francis.

Kovacs, Philip E., and H. K. Christie. 2011. "The Gates' Foundation and the Future of U.S. Public Education: A Call for Scholars to Counter Misinformation Campaigns." In *The Gates Foundation and the Future of U.S. 'Public' Schools*, edited by Philip E. Kovacs, 145–167. New York: Taylor and Francis.

Kraus, Neil. 2000. *Race, Neighborhoods, and Community Power: Buffalo Politics, 1934–1997*. Albany: State University of New York Press.

———. 2008. "Concentrated Poverty and Urban School Reform: 'The Choice Is Yours' in Minneapolis." *Equity and Excellence in Education* 41 (2): 262–274.

———. 2013. *Majoritarian Cities: Policy Making and Inequality in Urban Politics*. Ann Arbor: University of Michigan Press.

Kuehn, Daniel, and Hal Salzman. 2018. "The Engineering Labor Market: An Overview of Recent Trends." In *U.S. Engineering in a Global Economy*, edited by Richard B. Freeman and Hal Salzman, 11–46. Chicago: University of Chicago Press and National Bureau of Economic Research.

Lake, Robin J., ed. 2018. *Thinking Forward: New Ideas for a New Era of Public Education*. Seattle: University of Washington, Center on Reinventing Public Education. Available at https://crpe.org/wp-content/uploads/crpe-thinking-forward-new-ideas-new-era-public-education.pdf.

Layton, Lindsey. 2014a. "Full Interview with Bill Gates on the Common Core." *Washington Post*, 7 July. Available at https://www.youtube.com/watch?v=VfRJx6x764U.

———. 2014b. "How Bill Gates Pulled Off the Swift Common Core Revolution." *Washington Post*, 7 July.

Learning Policy Institute. 2022. "About the Institute." Palo Alto, CA: Learning Policy Institute. Available at https://learningpolicyinstitute.org/about.

Lemann, Nicholas. 2019. *Transaction Man: The Rise of the Deal and the Decline of the American Dream*. New York: Farrar, Straus, and Giroux.

Lessig, Lawrence. 2018. *America, Compromised*. Chicago: University of Chicago Press.

Levinson, Elliot. 1976. *The Alum Rock Voucher Demonstration: Three Years of Implementation*. Santa Monica, CA: Rand.

Lexchin, Joel, Lisa A. Bero, Benjamin Djulbegovic, and Otavio Clark. 2003. "Pharmaceutical Industry Sponsorship and Research Outcome and Quality: Systematic Review." *British Medical Journal* 326 (29 May): 1167–1170.

Loveless, Tom. 2013. "PISA's China Problem." Brookings Institution, Brown Center Chalkboard Series Archive. Washington, DC: Brookings Institution. Available at https://www.brookings.edu/research/pisas-china-problem/.

Lowell, B. Lindsay, and Hal Salzman. 2007. "Into the Eye of the Storm: Assessing the Evidence on Science and Engineering Education, Quality, and Workforce Demand." Washington, DC: Urban Institute.

Lumina Foundation. 2007. Grant 5217, Georgetown University, October 1, 2007, through October 1, 2009. Indianapolis, IN: Lumina Foundation. Available at https://www.luminafoundation.org/grant/5217/.

———. 2009. Grant 6006, Georgetown University, July 1, 2009, through November 1, 2013. Indianapolis, IN: Lumina Foundation. Available at https://www.luminafoundation.org/grant/6006/.

———. 2019. "Jamie Merisotis with Tony Carnevale Part 1: A Decade of New Insights on College, Training, Jobs." Indianapolis, IN: Lumina Foundation. Available at https://www.youtube.com/watch?v=i7ix7HgP-zg.

———. 2022a. "Home Page: The Nation's Progress." Indianapolis, IN: Lumina Foundation. Available at https://www.luminafoundation.org/.

———. 2022b. "President and CEO: Jamie Merisotis." Indianapolis, IN: Lumina Foundation. Available at https://www.luminafoundation.org/person/jamie-mer isotis/.

Lumina Foundation for Education. 2007. *From the Ground Up: An Early History of the Lumina Foundation*. Indianapolis, IN: Lumina Foundation for Education.

Lynde and Harry Bradley Foundation. 2022. "Guiding Principles." Milwaukee, WI: Lynde and Harry Bradley Foundation. Available at https://www.bradleyfdn .org/about/guiding-principles.

Lynn, Leonard, Hal Salzman, and Daniel Kuehn. 2018. "Dynamics of Engineering Labor Markets: Petroleum Engineering Demand and Responsive Supply." In *U.S. Engineering in a Global Economy*, edited by Richard B. Freeman and Hal Salzman, 243–262. Chicago: University of Chicago Press and National Bureau of Economic Research.

MacLean, Nancy. 2017. *Democracy in Chains: The Deep History of the Radical Right's Stealth Plan for America*. New York: Penguin.

Marchese, Ted, and Margaret A. Miller. 2018. "The History of *Change* Magazine." *Change* 50, no. 3/4 (May–August): 18–21.

Marginson, Simon. 2016. *The Dream Is Over: The Crisis of Clark Kerr's California Idea of Higher Education*. Oakland: University of California Press.

Marmot, Michael. 2005. "Social Determinants of Health Inequalities." *Lancet* 365 (9464): 1099–1104.

Maryland Manual On-Line. N.d. "Former Superintendent: David Hornbeck, Ph.D." State Department of Education. Annapolis, MD. Available at https://msa.mary land.gov/msa/mdmanual/13sdoe/former/html/msa15113.html.

Massey, Douglas S., and Nancy A. Denton. 1993. *American Apartheid: Segregation and the Making of the Underclass*. Cambridge, MA: Harvard University Press.

Maxarth. 2022. "Home Page." Potomac, MD: Maxarth. Available at https://max arth.com/.

Mayer, Jane. 2016. "How Right-Wing Billionaires Infiltrated Higher Education." *Chronicle of Higher Education*, 12 February.

McGuinn, Patrick J. 2006. *No Child Left Behind and the Transformation of Federal Education Policy, 1965–2005*. Lawrence: University Press of Kansas.

———. 2013. "The Federal Role in Educational Equity: The Two Narratives of School Reform in the Debate over Accountability." In *Education, Justice, and Democracy*, edited by Danielle Allen and Rob Reich, 221–242. Chicago: University of Chicago Press.

McKinsey Global Institute. 2019. *The Future of Work in America: People and Places, Today and Tomorrow*. New York: McKinsey.

Meier, Deborah, and George Wood, eds. 2004. *Many Children Left Behind: How the No Child Left Behind Act Is Damaging Our Children and Our Schools*. Boston: Beacon.

Merisotis, Jamie. 2015. *America Needs Talent: Attracting, Educating, and Deploying the 21st-Century Workforce*. New York: Rosetta Books.

———. 2020. *Human Work in the Age of Smart Machines*. New York: Rosetta Books.

Michelmore, Katherine, and Susan Dynarski. 2016. "The Gap within the Gap: Using Longitudinal Data to Understand Income Differences in Student Achievement." National Bureau of Economic Research, Working Paper 22474. Cambridge, MA: National Bureau of Economic Research.

Microsoft. 2012. *A National Talent Strategy: Ideas for Securing U.S. Competitiveness and Economic Growth*. Seattle, WA: Microsoft. Available at https://news.microsoft.com/download/presskits/citizenship/MSNTS.pdf.

Miller, Julie A. 1991. "Report Questioning 'Crisis' in Education Triggers an Uproar." *Education Week*, 9 October.

Mills, Jonathan N., and Patrick J. Wolf. 2016. *The Effects of the Louisiana Scholarship Program on Student Achievement after Two Years*. Fayetteville: University of Arkansas, School Choice Demonstration Project; New Orleans, LA: Tulane University, Education Research Alliance. Available at http://www.uaedreform.org/downloads/2016/02/report-1-the-effects-of-the-louisiana-scholarship-program-on-student-achievement-after-two-years.pdf.

———. 2017. *The Effects of the Louisiana Scholarship Program on Student Achievement after Three Years*. Fayetteville: University of Arkansas, School Choice Demonstration Project; New Orleans, LA: Tulane University, Education Research Alliance. Available at http://www.uaedreform.org/downloads/2017/06/the-effects-of-the-louisiana-scholarship-program-on-student-achievement-after-three-years.pdf.

———. 2019. "The Effects of the Louisiana Scholarship Program on Student Achievement after Four Years." EDRE Working Paper 2019-10. Fayetteville: University of Arkansas, Department of Education Reform. Available at https://cpb-us-e1.wpmucdn.com/wordpressua.uark.edu/dist/9/544/files/2019/04/Mills-Wolf-LSP-Achievement-After-4-Years-final-ut3mor.pdf.

Minnesota Public Radio Archive. 1988. "Itasca Seminar: Albert Shanker—Balancing Educational Excellence and Equity in the Public Schools." Saint Paul: Minnesota Public Radio. Available at https://archive.mpr.org/stories/1988/12/12/itasca-seminar-albert-shanker-balancing-educational-excellence-and-equity-in-the-public.

Mishel, Lawrence, and Richard Rothstein. 2007. "Improper Diagnosis, Reckless Treatment." *Phi Delta Kappan* 89, no. 1 (September): 31–32, 49–51.

Mishel, Lawrence, and Ruy A. Teixeira. 1991. *The Myth of the Coming Labor Shortage: Jobs, Skills, and Incomes of America's Workforce 2000*. Washington, DC: Economic Policy Institute.

Moe, Terry M. 2011. *Special Interest: Teachers Unions and America's Public Schools*. Washington, DC: Brookings Institution Press.

Moe, Terry M., and John E. Chubb. 2009. *Liberating Learning: Technology, Politics, and the Future of American Education*. New York: Jossey-Bass.

Muller, Jerry Z. 2018. *The Tyranny of Metrics*. Princeton, NJ: Princeton University Press.

Muro, Mark, Robert Maxim, and Jacob Whiton. 2019. *Automation and Artificial Intelligence: How Machines Are Affecting People and Places*. With Ian Hathaway. Washington, DC: Brookings Institution.

Murphy Institute. 2022. "About." New Orleans, LA: Tulane University. Available at https://murphy.tulane.edu/about.

Naidu, Suresh, Eric A. Posner, and E. Glen Weyl. 2018. "Antitrust Remedies for Labor Market Power." *Harvard Law Review* 132:536–601.

National Academy of Sciences. 1984. *High Schools and the Changing Workplace: The Employers' View*. Washington, DC: National Academy Press.

National Academy of Sciences, National Academy of Engineering, and Institute of Medicine. 2007. *Rising above the Gathering Storm: Energizing and Employing America for a Brighter Economic Future.* Washington, DC: National Academies Press.

National Alliance for Public Charter Schools. 2005a. "About Us: History." Washington, DC: National Alliance for Public Charter Schools. Internet Archive, 12 December. Available at https://web.archive.org/web/20051212160244/http://www.publiccharters.org/aboutus.asp?c=1.

———. 2005b. "About Us." Washington, DC: National Alliance for Public Charter Schools. Internet Archive, 12 December. Available at https://web.archive.org/web/20051212160323/http://www.publiccharters.org/aboutus.asp.

———. 2008. "Home Page." Washington, DC: National Alliance for Public Charter Schools. Internet Archive, 15 July. Available at https://web.archive.org/web/20080715064823/http://publiccharters.org/.

———. 2022. "Where Are Charter Schools Located?" Washington, DC: National Alliance for Public Charter Schools. Available at https://data.publiccharters.org/digest/charter-school-data-digest/where-are-charter-schools-located/.

National Archives and Records Administration. 1995. "Records of the National Institute of Education [NIE]." *Guide to Federal Records.* Washington, DC: National Archives. Available at https://www.archives.gov/research/guide-fed-records/groups/419.html.

National Association of Manufacturers. 2019. "N.A.M. Manufacturers Outlook Survey, First Quarter 2019." 5 March. Washington, DC: National Association of Manufacturers. Available at https://www.nam.org/wp-content/uploads/2019/04/Q1-2019-Outlook-page-text.pdf.

———. 2020. "N.A.M. Manufacturers Outlook Survey, Second Quarter 2020." 28 May. Washington, DC: National Association of Manufacturers. Available at https://www.nam.org/wp-content/uploads/2020/05/NAM-2020-Q2-Outlook-Survey.pdf.

National Center for Academic Transformation. N.d. "A Brief History of the National Center for Academic Transformation." Orlando: University of Central Florida. Available at https://www.thencat.org/NCATHistory.html.

National Center for Education Statistics. 1997. *NAEP 1996 Mathematics: Report Card for the Nation and the States.* Washington, DC: U.S. Department of Education.

———. 2000. *NAEP 1996 Trends in Academic Progress.* Washington, DC: U.S. Department of Education.

———. 2014. *Projections of Education Statistics to 2022,* forty-first edition. Washington, DC: U.S. Department of Education.

———. 2015. *School Composition and the Black-White Achievement Gap.* Washington, DC: U.S. Department of Education.

———. 2016a. *The Condition of Education: 2016.* Washington, DC: U.S. Department of Education.

———. 2016b. *Projections of Education Statistics to 2023,* forty-second edition. Washington, DC: U.S. Department of Education.

———. 2016c. *Projections of Education Statistics to 2024,* forty-third edition. Washington, DC: U.S. Department of Education.

———. 2017a. *Projections of Education Statistics to 2025,* forty-fourth edition. Washington, DC: U.S. Department of Education.

———. 2017b. *Table 4.7: States with Voucher Programs, by State: 2017.* Washington, DC: U.S. Department of Education. Available at https://nces.ed.gov/programs/statereform/tab4_7.asp.

———. 2019a. "Fast Facts: Public and Private School Comparison." Washington, DC: U.S. Department of Education. Available at https://nces.ed.gov/fastfacts/display.asp?id=55.

———. 2019b. *Status and Trends in the Education of Racial and Ethnic Groups 2018.* Washington, DC: U.S. Department of Education.

———. 2020a. *The Condition of Education: 2020.* Washington, DC: U.S. Department of Education.

———. 2020b. *Projections of Education Statistics to 2028,* forty-seventh edition. Washington, DC: U.S. Department of Education.

———. 2020c. *Table 221.10. Average National Assessment of Educational Progress (NAEP) Reading Scale Score, by Sex, Race/Ethnicity, and Grade: Selected Years, 1992 through 2019.* Washington, DC: U.S. Department of Education. Available at https://nces.ed.gov/programs/digest/d20/tables/dt20_221.10.asp.

———. 2020d. *Table 221.10. Average National Assessment of Educational Progress (NAEP) Mathematics Scale Score, by Sex, Race/Ethnicity, and Grade: Selected Years, 1990 through 2019.* Washington, DC: U.S. Department of Education. Available at https://nces.ed.gov/programs/digest/d20/tables/dt20_222.10.asp.

———. 2021a. *Table 222.85. Average National Assessment of Educational Progress (NAEP) Mathematics Scale Score, by Age and Selected Student Characteristics: Selected Years, 1973 through 2020.* Washington, DC: U.S. Department of Education. Available at https://nces.ed.gov/programs/digest/d21/tables/dt21_222.85.asp.

———. 2021b. *Table 221.85. Average National Assessment of Educational Progress (NAEP) Reading Scale Score, by Age and Selected Student Characteristics: Selected Years, 1971 through 2020.* Washington, DC: U.S. Department of Education. Available at https://nces.ed.gov/programs/digest/d21/tables/dt21_221.85.asp.

———. 2021c. *Table 105.30. Enrollment in Elementary, Secondary, and Degree-Granting Postsecondary Institutions, by Level and Control of Institution: Selected Years, 1869–70 through Fall 2030.* Washington, DC: U.S. Department of Education. Available at https://nces.ed.gov/programs/digest/d21/tables/dt21_105.30.asp.

———. 2022a. *Public Charter School Enrollment.* Washington, DC: U.S. Department of Education. Available at https://nces.ed.gov/programs/coe/indicator/cgb.

———. 2022b. *Table 104.20. Percentage of Persons 25 to 29 Years Old with Selected Levels of Educational Attainment, by Race/Ethnicity and Sex: Selected Years, 1920 through 2021.* Washington, DC: U.S. Department of Education. Available at https://nces.ed.gov/programs/digest/d21/tables/dt21_104.20.asp.

———. 2022c. *Table 105.20. Enrollment in Elementary, Secondary, and Degree-Granting Postsecondary Institutions, by Level and Control of Institution, Enrollment Level, and Attendance Status and Sex of Student: Selected Years, Fall 1990 through Fall 2030.* Washington, DC: U.S. Department of Education. Available at https://nces.ed.gov/programs/digest/d21/tables/dt21_105.20.asp.

———. 2022d. *Table 219.10. High School Graduates, by Sex and Control of School; Public High School Averaged Freshman Graduation Rate (AFGR); and Total Graduates as a Ratio of 17-Year-Old Population: Selected Years, 1869–70 through 2029–30.* Washington, DC: U.S. Department of Education. Available at https://nces.ed.gov/programs/digest/d20/tables/dt20_219.10.asp?current=yes.

National Center for Higher Education Management Systems. 2022. "Our History." Boulder, CO: National Center for Higher Education Managements Systems. Available at https://nchems.org/our-history/.

National Center for Public Policy and Higher Education. N.d. "National Center for Public Policy and Higher Education." San Jose, CA: National Center for Public Policy and Higher Education. Internet Archive, 18 October 2015. Available at https://web.archive.org/web/20151018013525/http://www.highereducation.org/reports/wellman/wellman11.shtml.

National Center on Education and the Economy. 1990. *America's Choice: High Skills or Low Wages!* Rochester, NY: National Center on Education and the Economy.

———. 2008. *Tough Choices or Tough Times: The Report of the New Commission on the Skills of the American Workforce,* revised and expanded edition. San Francisco: Jossey-Bass.

———. 2020. "Funders." Washington, DC: National Center on Education and the Economy. Internet Archive, 11 April. Available at https://web.archive.org/web/20200411140934/http://ncee.org/who-we-are/funders/.

National Commission on Excellence in Education. 1983. *A Nation at Risk: The Imperative for Educational Reform; A Report to the Nation and the Secretary of Education.* Washington, DC: U.S. Department of Education.

National Commission on Mathematics and Science Teaching for the 21st Century. 2000. *Before It's Too Late: A Report to the Nation from the National Commission on Mathematics and Science Teaching for the 21st Century.* Washington, DC: U.S. Department of Education.

National Council on Teacher Quality. 2007. "Our Funders." Washington, DC: National Council on Teacher Quality. Internet Archive, 21 January. Available at https://web.archive.org/web/20070121232529/http://www.nctq.org/nctq/about/our_funders.html.

National Institute of Education. 1984. *Involvement in Learning: Realizing the Potential of Higher Education.* Washington, DC: U.S. Department of Education.

Nejstgaard, Camilla H., Lisa Bero, Asbjorn Hrobjartsson, Anders W. Jorgensen, Karsten J. Jorgensen, Mary Le, and Andreas Lundh. 2020. "Association between Conflicts of Interest and Favourable Recommendations in Clinical Guidelines, Advisory Committee Reports, Opinion Pieces, and Narrative Reviews: Systematic Review." *British Medical Journal* 371:m4234.

Nestle, Marion. 2013. *Food Politics: How the Food Industry Influences Nutrition and Health,* revised and expanded edition. Berkeley, CA: University of California Press.

———. 2018. *Unsavory Truth: How Food Companies Skew the Science of What We Eat.* New York: Basic Books.

New America. 2019. "Our Funding." Washington, DC: New America. Available at https://www.newamerica.org/our-funding/2019/.

New Commission on the Skills of the American Workforce. 2011a. "Commission Report Staff." Washington, DC: National Center on Education and the Economy. Internet Archive, 19 September. Available at https://web.archive.org/web/20110919022639/http://www.skillscommission.org/?page_id=127.

———. 2011b. "Our Partners." Washington, DC: National Center on Education and the Economy. Internet Archive, 28 July. Available at https://web.archive .org/web/20110728031523/http://www.skillscommission.org/?page_id=133.

Newfield, Christopher. 2008. *Unmaking the Public University: The Forty-Year Assault on the Middle Class*. Cambridge, MA: Harvard University Press.

———. 2016. *The Great Mistake: How We Wrecked Public Universities and How We Can Fix Them*. Baltimore: Johns Hopkins University Press.

Newsweek. 1981. "Why Public Schools Are Flunking." 20 April.

New York Times. 1999. "Excerpts from Bush's Speech on Improving Education." 3 September.

———. 2018. "Medicine's Financial Contamination." Editorial Board. 14 September.

Office of the Registrar General and Census Commissioner, India. 2011. "Literates and Literacy Rate." In *Primary Census Data Highlights—India*. New Delhi: Ministry of Home Affairs. Internet Archive, 19 July 2018. Available at https:// web.archive.org/web/20180719110150/https://www.censusindia.gov.in/2011 census/PCA/PCA_Highlights/pca_highlights_file/India/Chapter-3.pdf.

Office of Science and Technology. 2018. "President Donald J. Trump Is Working to Ensure All Americans Have Access to STEM Education." Washington, DC: White House. Internet Archive, 6 December. Available at https://web.archive .org/web/20181206015836/https://www.whitehouse.gov/briefings-statements /president-donald-j-trump-is-working-to-ensure-all-americans-have-access-to -stem-education/.

Opportunity Insights. 2019. "Opportunity Insights." Cambridge, MA: Harvard University. Available at https://opportunityinsights.org/wp-content/uploads/2019 /11/Opportunity-Insights-Fact-Sheet.pdf.

Organization for Economic Cooperation and Development. 2019. *Family Database*, November. Paris: Organization for Economic Cooperation and Development. Internet Archive, 12 February 2020. Available at https://web.archive.org /web/20200212014231/https://www.oecd.org/els/CO_2_2_Child_Poverty.pdf.

Osborne, Michael A. 2021. *Curriculum Vitae*. Oxford: University of Oxford. Available at https://www.robots.ox.ac.uk/~mosb/public/pdf/MAOsborne.pdf.

Owens, Deborah Duncan. 2015. *The Origins of the Common Core: How the Free Market Became Public Education Policy*. New York: Palgrave Macmillan.

Painter, Kristen Leigh. 2019. "Richard Knowlton, Who Led Hormel through Turbulent Strike and Transformation, Dies at 86." *Star Tribune*, 7 February.

Paul, Annie Murphy. 2020. "Diane Ravitch Declares the Education Reform Movement Dead." *New York Times Book Review*, 21 January.

Pew Research Center. 2017. "Sharp Partisan Divisions in Views of National Institutions." 10 July. Washington, DC: Pew Research Center. Available at http:// www.people-press.org/2017/07/10/sharp-partisan-divisions-in-views-of-nation al-institutions/.

Philanthropy Roundtable. 2014. "2005: National Alliance for Public Charter Schools." Washington, DC: Philanthropy Roundtable. Internet Archive, 29 November. Available at https://web.archive.org/web/20141129054031/https://www .philanthropyroundtable.org/almanac/education/2005_national_alliance_for _public_charter_schools.

Piché, Dianne. 2007. "Basically a Good Model." *Education Next*, Fall, 57–59.

Piehler, Christopher. 2014. "Report: Testing and Assessment Products Are Now the Biggest Category of Ed Tech Sales." *The Journal*, 1 December. Available at

https://thejournal.com/articles/2014/12/01/report-assessment-now-the-biggest
-category-of-ed-tech-sales.aspx.

Piketty, Thomas. 2014. *Capital in the 21st Century*. Cambridge, MA: Belknap Press of Harvard University Press.

Piketty, Thomas, and Emmanuel Saez. 2003. "Income Inequality in the United States: 1913–1998." *Quarterly Journal of Economics* 118 (1): 1–39.

Pillow, Travis, and Paul Hill. 2018. "Funding a Nimble System." In *Thinking Forward: New Ideas for a New Era of Public Education*, edited by Robin J. Lake, 77–88. Seattle: University of Washington, Center on Reinventing Public Education. Available at https://www.crpe.org/sites/default/files/crpe-thinking-forward-new-ideas-new-era-public-education.pdf.

Pitsch, Mark. 1991. "School-College Links Seen as Fundamental to Education Reform." *Education Week*, 11 September.

Porter, Theodore. 1995. *Trust in Numbers: The Pursuit of Objectivity in Science and Public Life*. Princeton, NJ: Princeton University Press.

Postsecondary Value Commission. 2019. "Resources." Washington, DC: Institute for Higher Education Policy. Internet Archive, 4 August 2020. Available at https:// web.archive.org/web/20200804142432/https://www.postsecondaryvalue.org /resources/.

———. 2021. *Equitable Value: Promoting Economic Mobility and Social Justice through Postsecondary Education*. Washington, DC: Institute for Higher Education Policy. Available at https://www.postsecondaryvalue.org/wp-content /uploads/2021/05/PVC-Final-Report-FINAL.pdf.

President's Private Sector Survey on Cost Control. 1984. Washington: Ronald Reagan Administration.

Putnam, Robert D. 2015. *Our Kids: The American Dream in Crisis*. New York: Simon and Schuster.

Quart, Alissa. 2018. *Squeezed: Why Our Families Can't Afford America*. New York: Ecco.

Ravitch, Diane. 2010. *The Death and Life of the Great American School System: How Testing and Choice Are Undermining Education*. New York: Basic Books.

———. 2013. *Reign of Error: The Hoax of the Privatization Movement and the Danger to America's Public Schools*. New York: Knopf.

———. 2020. *Slaying Goliath: The Passionate Resistance to Privatization and the Fight to Save America's Public Schools*. New York: Knopf.

Reckhow, Sarah. 2013. *Follow the Money: How Foundation Dollars Change Public School Politics*. New York: Oxford University Press.

Redden, Elizabeth. 2020. "41% of Recent Grads Work in Jobs Not Requiring a Degree." *Inside Higher Ed*, 18 February. Available at https://www.insidehighered .com/quicktakes/2020/02/18/41-recent-grads-work-jobs-not-requiring-degree.

Reich, Rob. 2018. *Just Giving: Why Philanthropy Is Failing Democracy and How It Can Do Better*. Princeton, NJ: Princeton University Press.

Repp, Drew. 2020. "A New Understanding of a Job, Skills Series: Part One." 5 February. Moscow, ID: Emsi. Available at https://www.economicmodeling.com /2020/02/05/skills-a-new-understanding-of-a-job/.

Reuters. 2008. "Big US Student Loan Guarantor Files for Bankruptcy." 7 April. Available at https://www.reuters.com/article/educationresources-bankruptcy /big-us-student-loan-guarantor-files-for-bankruptcy-idINN0729399920080407.

Rhodes, Jesse H. 2012. *An Education in Politics: The Origins and Evolution of No Child Left Behind.* Ithaca, NY: Cornell University Press.

Riesman, David. 1972. "The Business of 'Business as Usual.'" In *Inside Academe: Culture in Crisis*, from the editors of *Change* 111–119. New Rochelle, NY: Change Magazine.

Ripley, Amanda. 2014. *The Smartest Kids in the World: And How They Got That Way.* New York: Simon and Schuster.

Robelen, Erik W. 1999. "Civil Rights Group Decries Implementation of Title I." *Education Week*, 22 September.

Ronald Reagan Presidential Library and Museum. 1988. "Statement on the Worker Adjustment and Retraining Notification Act." 2 August. Simi Valley, CA: Ronald Reagan Presidential Library and Museum. Available at https://www.reagan library.gov/archives/speech/statement-worker-adjustment-and-retraining-noti fication-act.

Rose, Charlie. 2015. "Interview with Tim Cook." *Sixty Minutes*, 20 December. New York: CBS. Available at https://www.cbsnews.com/news/60-minutes-apple -tim-cook-charlie-rose/.

Rose, Lowell C., and Alec M. Gallup. 2005. "The 37th Annual Phi Delta Kappa/ Gallup Poll of the Public Attitudes toward the Public Schools." *Phi Delta Kappa International* 87, no. 1 (September): 41–57.

Rose, Stephen J. 2017. *Mismatch: How Many Workers with a Bachelor's Degree Are Overqualified for Their Jobs?* Washington, DC: Urban Institute.

Roska, Josipa, and Richard Arum. 2011. "The State of Undergraduate Learning." *Change: The Magazine of Higher Learning* 43 (2): 35–38.

Rothstein, Richard. 2004. *Class and Schools: Using Social, Economic, and Educational Reform to Close the Black-White Achievement Gap.* New York: Teachers College Press and Economic Policy Institute.

Rottenberg, Dan. 1991. "Foundation for the Future: The Pew Charitable Trusts." *Town and Country*, December, 138.

Rudalevige, Andrew. 2003. "No Child Left Behind: Forging a Congressional Compromise." In *No Child Left Behind? The Politics and Practice of School Accountability*, edited by Paul E. Peterson and Martin R. West, 23–54. Washington, DC: Brookings Institution Press.

Ruiz, Neil G. 2017. "Key Facts about the US H-1B Visa Program." *Pew Research Center*, 27 April. Washington, DC: Pew Research Center. Available at https:// www.pewresearch.org/fact-tank/2017/04/27/key-facts-about-the-u-s-h-1b-visa -program/.

Ruppel Shell, Ellen. 2018. *The Job: Work and Its Future in a Time of Radical Change.* New York: Currency.

Ryan, Camille L., and Kurt Bauman. 2016. "Educational Attainment in the United States: 2015." *Current Population Reports*, 29 March, 1–11. Washington, DC: U.S. Department of Commerce.

Sah, Sunita, and Adriane Fugh-Berman. 2013. "Physicians under the Influence: Social Psychology and Industry Marketing Strategies." *Journal of Law, Medicine, and Ethics* 41 (3): 665–672.

Salzman, Hal. 2016. "The Impact of High-Skill Guestworker Programs and the STEM Workforce." Hearing on "The Impact of High-Skilled Immigration on U.S. Workers." Committee on the Judiciary, U.S. Senate, 25 February.

Salzman, Hal, and Lindsey Lowell. 2008. "Making the Grade." *Nature* 453, no. 1 (May): 28–30.

Sampson, Robert J. 2012. *Great American City: Chicago and the Enduring Neighborhood Effect.* Chicago: University of Chicago Press.

Sandia National Laboratories, U.S. Department of Energy. 1993. "Perspectives on Education in America." *Journal of Educational Research* 86 (5): 258–310.

Schemo, Diane Jean. 2003. "Questions on Data Cloud Luster of Houston Schools." *New York Times*, 11 July.

Schneider, Jack. 2017. *Beyond Test Scores: A Better Way to Measure School Quality.* Cambridge, MA: Harvard University Press.

Schneider, Jack, and Jennifer Berkshire. 2020. *A Wolf at the Schoolhouse Door: The Dismantling of Public Education and the Future of School.* New York: New Press.

Schneider, Joe, and Paul Houston. 1993. *Exploding the Myths: Another Round in the Education Debate.* Katy, TX: American Association of Educational Service Agencies.

School Choice Demonstration Project. 2022. "School Choice Demonstration Project." Fayetteville, AR: University of Arkansas, Department of Education Reform. Available at https://scdp.uark.edu/.

Schwartz, Robert B. 2011. *Curriculum Vitae.* Cambridge, MA: Harvard Graduate School of Education. Available at https://www.gse.harvard.edu/sites/default/files/faculty/documents/robert-schwartz-170.pdf.

Secretary of Education's Commission on the Future of Higher Education. 2006. *A Test of Leadership: Charting the Future of Higher Education.* Washington, DC: U.S. Department of Education.

Seltzer, Rick. 2016. "The High School Graduate Plateau." *Inside Higher Ed*, 6 December. Available at https://www.insidehighered.com/news/2016/12/06/high-school-graduates-drop-number-and-be-increasingly-diverse.

Shanker, Albert. 1988. "National Press Club Speech." 31 March. Washington, DC: National Press Club; Detroit, MI: Wayne State University.

Shelton, Jon. 2023. *The Education Myth: How Human Capital Trumped Social Democracy.* Ithaca, NY: Cornell University Press.

Sherman, Susan W. 1983. *Education for Tomorrow's Jobs.* Washington, DC: National Academy Press.

Simon, Stephanie. 2015. "No Profit Left Behind: In the High-Stakes World of American Education, Pearson Makes Money Even When Its Results Don't Measure Up." *Politico*, 10 February. Available at https://www.politico.com/story/2015/02/pearson-education-115026.

Singletary, Michelle. 2020. "Is College Still Worth It? Read This Study." *Washington Post*, 11 January.

Sismondo, Sergio. 2013. "Key Opinion Leaders and the Corruption of Medical Knowledge: What the Sunshine Act Will and Won't Cast Light On." *Journal of Law, Medicine, and Ethics* 41 (3): 635–643.

Slaughter, Sheila, and Gary Rhoades. 2004. *Academic Capitalism and the New Economy: Markets, State, and Higher Education.* Baltimore: Johns Hopkins University Press.

Smith, Jeff. 2005. "Foundation Identified as Donor: Siloam Springs Group Gives $10 Million to Study Reforming Education." *Morning News* (Springdale, AR), 27 January, 3A.

Smith Richardson Foundation. 2022. *Domestic Public Policy*. Westport, CT: Smith Richardson Foundation. Available at https://www.srf.org/programs/domestic -public-policy/.

Snow, Page. 2019. "The Tax Benefits of Creating a Private Foundation." *Forbes*, 8 April.

Song, Xi, Catherine G. Massey, Karen A. Rolf, Joseph P. Ferried, Jonathan L. Rothbaume, and Yu Xie. 2020. "Long-Term Decline in Intergenerational Mobility in the United States since the 1850s." *Proceedings of the National Academy of Sciences* 117 (1): 251–258.

Sprague, Shawn. 2017. "Below Trend: The U.S. Productivity Slowdown since the Great Recession." *Beyond the Numbers* 6, no. 2 (January). Washington, DC: U.S. Department of Labor, Bureau of Labor Statistics. Available at https://www .bls.gov/opub/btn/volume-6/below-trend-the-us-productivity-slowdown-since -the-great-recession.htm.

Starr, Evan, Justin Frake, and Rajshree Agarwal. 2019. "Mobility Constraint Externalities." *Organization Science* 30 (5): 961–980.

State Higher Education Executive Officers Association. 2022a. "SHEEO Job Posting: Policy Analyst." Boulder, CO: State Higher Education Officers Association. Available at https://sheeo.org/sheeo-job-posting-state-finance-policy-analyst/.

———. 2022b. "The State Higher Education Policy Center (SHEPC): Home to WICHE, NCHEMS, SHEEO." Boulder, CO: Western Interstate Commission for Higher Education. Available at https://www.wiche.edu/about-us/shepc/.

Stedman, Lawrence. 1993. "The Sandia Report and U.S. Achievement: An Assessment." *Journal of Educational Research* 87 (3): 133–146.

Stevens, Darlene Gavron. 1990. "Our Future: Katherine Haycock Helps Kids Make the Grade." *Chicago Tribune*, 9 September, 6, 3.

Stewart, Thomas, and Patrick J. Wolf. 2014. *The School Choice Journey: School Vouchers and the Empowerment of Urban Families*. New York: Palgrave Macmillan.

Strada Center for Education Consumer Insights. N.d. "Carol D'Amico, Ed.D.: Executive Vice President, Learning and Policy." Indianapolis, IN: Strada Center for Education Consumer Insights. Available at https://cci.stradaeducation.org /author/carol-damico/.

Strada Education Network. 2018. "Labor Market Advisory Group Emsi to Join Strada Education Network." Indianapolis, IN: Strada Education Network. Available at https://stradaeducation.org/press-release/labor-market-advisory-group -emsi-to-join-strada-education-network/.

———. 2019. *Form 990: 2019*. Indianapolis, IN: Strada Education Network.

———. 2021. "Our Network." Indianapolis, IN: Strada Education Network. Internet Archive, 17 January. Available at https://web.archive.org/web/2021011 7055237/https://www.stradaeducation.org/network/.

Strauss, Valerie. 2014. "Major Charter Researcher Causes Stir with Comments about Market-Based School Reform." *Washington Post*, 12 December.

Stuesse, Angela. 2016. *Scratching Out a Living: Latinos, Race, and Work in the Deep South*. Berkeley: University of California Press.

Suleiman, Ezra. 2003. *Dismantling Democratic States*. Princeton, NJ: Princeton University Press.

Summit Public Schools. 2022. "Summit Public Schools." Redwood City, CA: Summit Public Schools. Available at https://summitps.org/.

Swoboda, Frank. 1990. "Students of Labor Force Projections Have Been Working without a 'Net.'" *Washington Post*, 6 November. Available at https://www.wash ingtonpost.com/archive/politics/1990/11/06/students-of-labor-force-projections -have-been-working-without-a-net/7906eedd-6ba4-4837-988d-20bb832e81ec/.

Tavenner, Diane. 2019. *Prepared: What Kids Need for a Fulfilled Life*. New York: Currency.

Taylor, William L., and Crystal Rosario. 2007. *Fresh Ideas in Teacher Bargaining: How New Agreements Help Kids*. Washington, DC: Citizens' Commission on Civil Rights. Internet Archive, 14 July 2010. Available at https://web.archive .org/web/20100714052141/http://www.cccr.org/downloads/FreshIdeas.pdf.

———. 2009. *National Teachers' Unions and the Struggle over School Reform*. Washington, DC: Citizens Commission on Civil Rights.

Teachers College, Columbia University. N.d. "Thomas Bailey: The 11th President of Teacher's College." New York: Columbia University. Available at https://www .tc.columbia.edu/president/.

Teitelbaum, Michael. 2014a. *Falling Behind? Boom, Bust, and the Global Race for Scientific Talent*. Princeton, NJ: Princeton University Press.

———. 2014b. "The Myth of the Science and Engineering Shortage." *The Atlantic*, 19 March. Available at https://www.theatlantic.com/education/archive/2014 /03/the-myth-of-the-science-and-engineering-shortage/284359/.

Thomas B. Fordham Institute. 2001. "Closing the Deal, Citizens' Commission on Civil Rights." 30 May. Washington, DC: Thomas B. Fordham Institute. Available at https://fordhaminstitute.org/national/commentary/closing-deal-citizens -commission-civil-rights.

Time. 1980. "Help! Teacher Can't Teach!" 16 June, 54–63.

Tompkins-Stange, Megan E. 2016. *Policy Patrons: Philanthropy, Education Reform, and the Politics of Influence*. Cambridge, MA: Harvard Education Press.

Trump, Donald J. 2017. "Inaugural Address." 20 January. Washington, DC.

Tucker, Marc. 2007. "Reckless and Wildly Exaggerated? We Don't Think So! A Response to Mishel and Rothstein." *Phi Delta Kappan* 89, no. 1 (September): 52–54.

———, ed. 2011. *Surpassing Shanghai: An Agenda for American Education Built on the World's Leading Systems*. Cambridge, MA: Harvard Education Press.

Tyson, Laura, and Michael Spence. 2017. "Exploring the Effects of Technology on Income and Wealth Inequality." In *After Piketty: The Agenda for Economics and Inequality*, edited by Heather Boushey, J. Bradford DeLong, and Marshall Stenbaum, 170–208. Cambridge, MA: Harvard University Press.

United Nations Development Programme. 2019. *Latest Human Development Index Ranking*. New York: United Nations. Available at http://hdr.undp.org/en /content/latest-human-development-index-ranking.

University of Arkansas, Department of Education Reform. 2022. "Education Reform." Fayetteville, AR: University of Arkansas. Available at https://edre.uark.edu/.

University of Dayton, Public Relations Department. 1966. "The University of Dayton Is Awarded a Capital Grant by the Esso Education Foundation." Dayton, OH: University of Dayton, eCommons. Available at https://ecommons.udayton .edu/cgi/viewcontent.cgi?article=4090&context=news_rls.

———. 1969. "The University of Dayton Receives ESSO Education Foundation Grant." Dayton, OH: University of Dayton, eCommons. Available at https:// ecommons.udayton.edu/cgi/viewcontent.cgi?article=4579&context=news_rls

#:~:text=DAYTON%2C%20Ohio%2C%20December%209%2C,of%20seven %20ESSO%20Foundation%20programs.

U.S. Census Bureau. 2014. "Census Bureau Reports Majority of STEM College Graduates Do Not Work in STEM Occupations." 10 July. Washington, DC: U.S. Department of Commerce. Internet Archive, 16 July. Available at https:// web.archive.org/web/20140716031918/http://www.census.gov/newsroom/releas es/archives/employment_occupations/cb14-130.html.

———. 2015. "Facts for Features: Hurricane Katrina 10th Anniversary." 29 July. Washington, DC: U.S. Department of Commerce. Available at https://www.cen sus.gov/newsroom/facts-for-features/2015/cb15-ff16.html#:~:text=The%20city's %20population%20was%20494%2C294,to%20230%2C172%20one%20year %20later.

———. 2019. *Income and Poverty in the United States: 2018. Income Inequality:* "Table A4: Selected Measures of Household Income Dispersion, 1967–2018." Washington, DC: U.S. Department of Commerce. Available at https://www .census.gov/library/publications/2019/demo/p60-266.html.

———. 2020. "Historical Income Tables: Income Inequality; Table H-3. Mean Household Income Received by Each Fifth and Top 5 Percent." Washington, DC: U.S. Commerce Department. Internet Archive, 21 October. Available at https://web.archive.org/web/20201021020229/https://www2.census.gov/pro grams-surveys/cps/tables/time-series/historical-income-households/h03ar.xlsx.

———. 2022. "Census Bureau Releases New Educational Attainment Data." 24 February. Washington, DC: U.S. Department of Commerce. Available at https:// www.census.gov/newsroom/press-releases/2022/educational-attainment.html #:~:text=In%202021%2C%2029.4%25%20of%20men,women%20and%2046.9 %25%20were%20men.

U.S. Centers for Medicare and Medicaid Services. 2022. "Open Payments: About." Washington, DC: U.S. Centers for Medicare and Medicaid Services. Available at https://openpaymentsdata.cms.gov/about.

U.S. Chamber of Commerce. 2020. "Donohue: Skills Gap and Worker Shortages an 'Urgent Priority' across the Country." 9 January. Washington, DC: U.S. Cham ber of Commerce. Available at https://www.uschamber.com/press-release/dono hue-skills-gap-and-worker-shortages-urgent-priority-across-the-country.

U.S. Chamber of Commerce Foundation. 2022. "Robert T. Jones, President, Educa tion Workforce Policy, LLP." Washington, DC: U.S. Chamber of Commerce Foun dation. Available at https://www.uschamberfoundation.org/bio/robert-t-jones.

U.S. Citizenship and Immigration Services. 2017. *Characteristics of H-1B Specialty Occupation Workers: Fiscal Year 2016 Annual Report to Congress October 1, 2015–September 30, 2016.* Washington, DC: U.S. Department of Homeland Security.

U.S. Department of Education. N.d. "Academic Performance and Outcomes for English Learners." Washington, DC: U.S. Department of Education. Available at https://www2.ed.gov/datastory/el-outcomes/index.html#two.

U.S. Department of Health and Human Services. 2016. *Poverty in the United States: 50-Year Trends and Safety Net Impacts.* Washington, DC: U.S. Department of Health and Human Services.

U.S. Department of the Treasury. 2016. *Non-compete Contracts: Economic Ef fects and Policy.* Washington, DC: U.S. Department of the Treasury, Office of Economic Policy.

U.S. General Accounting Office. 1992. *The Changing Workforce: Demographic Issues Facing the Federal Government.* Washington, DC: U.S. General Accounting Office.

U.S. Government Accountability Office. 2012. *Higher Education: A Small Percentage of Families Save in 529 Plans.* Report to the chairman, Committee on Finance, U.S. Senate, December.

———. 2018. *Department of Education: Resource and Achievement Trends.* Report to the Committee on Homeland Security and Governmental Affairs, U.S. Senate, February.

———. 2019. *Workforce Automation: Better Data Needed to Assess and Plan for Effects of Advanced Technologies on Jobs.* GAO-19-257, March. Washington, DC: U.S. Government Accountability Office.

Verougstraete, Remie. 2020. "A Skill-Based Approach to Creating Work-Relevant Credentials." 23 September. Moscow, ID: Emsi. Available at https://www.economicmodeling.com/2020/09/23/skills-and-microcredentials/.

Waddington, R. Joseph, and Mark Berends. 2018. "Impact of the Indiana Choice Scholarship Program: Achievement Effects for Students in Upper Elementary and Middle School." *Journal of Policy Analysis and Management* 37 (4): 783–808.

Wagner, Tony. 2008. *The Global Achievement Gap: Why Even Our Best Schools Don't Teach the New Survival Skills Our Children Need—and What We Can Do about It.* New York: Basic.

———. 2012. *Creating Innovators: The Making of Young People Who Will Change the World.* New York: Scribner.

Waldron, Hillary. 2013. "Mortality Differentials by Lifetime Earnings Decile: Implications for Evaluations of Proposed Social Security Law Changes." *Social Security Bulletin* 73 (1): 1–37.

W. Allen Wallis Institute of Political Economy. 2022. "About Us: W. Allen Wallis." Rochester, NY: University of Rochester. Available at https://www.wallis.rochester.edu/about/wallis.html.

Walsh, Mark. 1993. "Singing up the Public." *Education Week*, 7 April.

Walton Family Foundation. 2022. "K–12 Education." Bentonville, AR: Walton Family Foundation. Available at https://www.waltonfamilyfoundation.org/strategy2025#k12-education.

Washington Examiner. 2011. "The Three-Minute Interview: Kenneth R. Weinstein." 7 November. Available at https://www.washingtonexaminer.com/the-3-minute-interview-kenneth-r-weinstein.

Washington Monthly. 2020. *Washington Monthly 2019 College Rankings.* Washington, DC: Washington Monthly. Internet Archive. 4 August. Available at https://web.archive.org/web/20200804145307/https://washingtonmonthly.com/2019college-guide.

Washington Post. 2000. "Text: George W. Bush's Speech to the NAACP." On Politics. 10 July.

———. 2012. Obituary for Roger B. Semerad. 23 October.

Weaver, Andrew, and Paul Osterman. 2017. "Skill Demands and Mismatch in U.S. Manufacturing." *ILR Review* 70, no. 2 (March): 275–307.

Webber, Douglas. 2018. "Higher Ed, Lower Spending: As States Cut Back, Where Has the Money Gone?" *Education Next* 18, no. 3 (Summer): 50–56. Internet Archive. Available at https://web.archive.org/web/20190109104905/https://www.educationnext.org/files/ednext_xviii_3_webber.pdf.

Wentzel, Michael. 1999. "UR Sets Up School-Policy Center." *Democrat and Chronicle* (Rochester, NY), 8 June, B1.

Wermund, Benjamin. 2016. "Vouchers Have Been a Tough Sell When Put to a Vote." With Caitlin Emma and Kimberly Hefling. *Politico: Morning Edition*, 2 December. Available at https://www.politico.com/tipsheets/morning-education/2016/12/vouchers-have-been-a-tough-sell-when-put-to-a-vote-217673.

Western, Bruce, and Jake Rosenfeld. 2011. "Unions, Norms, and the Rise in U.S. Wage Inequality." *American Sociological Review* 76 (4): 513–537.

Western Association of Schools and Colleges. 2012. "Public Statement regarding Patton University." Alameda, CA: Western Association of Schools and Colleges, Senior College and University Commission. Internet Archive, 6 February 2013. Available at https://web.archive.org/web/20130206225009/http://wascsenior.org/publicstatements/public-statement-regarding-patten-university.

Western Interstate Commission for Higher Education. 2003. *Knocking at the College Door: Projections of High School Graduates by State and Race/Ethnicity, 1998–2018*. Boulder, CO: Western Interstate Commission for Higher Education.

———. 2008. *Knocking at the College Door: Projections of High School Graduates by State and Race/Ethnicity, 1992–2022*. Boulder, CO: Western Interstate Commission for Higher Education.

———. 2012. *Knocking at the College Door: Projections of High School Graduates by State and Race/Ethnicity*. Boulder, CO: Western Interstate Commission for Higher Education.

———. 2016. *Knocking at the College Door: Projections of High School Graduates*. Boulder, CO: Western Interstate Commission for Higher Education.

———. 2019. *Annual Report: FY 2019*. Boulder, CO: Western Interstate Commission for Higher Education. Available at https://www.wiche.edu/wp-content/uploads/2020/07/AnnualReport2019.pdf.

———. 2020. *Knocking at the College Door: Projections of High School Graduates*. Boulder, CO: Western Interstate Commission for Higher Education.

———. 2022. "About WICHE." Boulder, CO: Western Interstate Commission for Higher Education. Available at https://www.wiche.edu/about-us/.

Western Interstate Commission for Higher Education and the College Board. 1991. *The Road to College: Educational Progress by Race and Ethnicity*. Boulder, CO: Western Interstate Commission on Higher Education.

———. 1998. *Knocking at the College Door: Projections of High School Graduates by State and Race/Ethnicity, 1986–2012*. Boulder, CO: Western Interstate Commission for Higher Education.

Western Interstate Commission for Higher Education Cooperative for Educational Technologies. 2022. "Mission, Vision, and Values." Boulder, CO: Western Interstate Commission for Higher Education Cooperative for Educational Technologies. Available at https://wcet.wiche.edu/about/mission-vision-values/.

White, Charlene. 1992. "Good Work: Charlene White's Personal Perspective on Forty Years at the A.A.H.E." *A.A.H.E. Bulletin* 45, no. 1 (September): 11–13.

White, Eileen. 1982. "The Reagan Administration and N.I.E: Uncertain Future and New Priorities." *Education Week*, 22 December.

White, Jenny, and Lisa A. Bero. 2010. "Symposium: Academic Integrity; Corporate Manipulation of Research: Strategies Are Similar across Five Industries." *Stanford Law and Policy Review* 21 (105): 105–133.

White, Karl R. 1982. "The Relation between Socioeconomic Status and Academic Achievement." *Psychological Bulletin* 91 (3): 461–481.

Williams, Roger M. 1991. "From Inside Right to Out Front." *Foundation News*, May/June, 20–25.

Wilson, William Julius. 1987. *The Truly Disadvantaged: The Inner City, the Underclass, and Public Policy.* Chicago: University of Chicago Press.

Windgate Foundation. 2017. "About Us." Siloam Springs, AR: Windgate Foundation. Internet Archive, 25 June. Available at https://web.archive.org/web/2017 0625044508/http://www.windgatefoundation.org/about-us.html.

Wolf, Barbara, William Evans, and Teresa E. Seeman, eds. 2012. *The Biological Consequences of Socioeconomic Inequalities.* New York: Russell Sage.

Wolf, Patrick J., and Anna J. Egalite. 2016. *Pursuing Innovation: How Can Educational Choice Transform K–12 Education in the U.S.?* Indianapolis, IN: Friedman Foundation for Educational Choice. Available at https://www.edchoice .org/wp-content/uploads/2016/04/2016-4-Pursuing-Innovation-WEB-2.pdf.

Wolf, Patrick J., Babette Gutmann, Michael Puma, Brian Kisida, Lou Rizzo, Nada Eissa, and Matthew Carr. 2010. *Evaluation of the DC Opportunity Scholarship Program: Final Report* (NCEE 2010-4018). Washington, DC: National Center for Education Evaluation and Regional Assistance, Institute of Education Sciences, U.S. Department of Education.

Wolf, Patrick J., Jonathan N. Mills, Yujie Sude, Heidi H. Erickson, and Matthew L. Lee. 2019. "How Has the Louisiana Scholarship Program Affected Students? A Comprehensive Summary of Effects after Four Years." Louisiana Scholarship Program Evaluation Policy Brief School Choice Demonstration Project, updated 24 April.

Xie, Yu, and Alexandra A. Killewald. 2012. *Is American Science in Decline?* Cambridge, MA: Harvard University Press.

Yaphe, John, Richard Edman, Barry Knishkowy, and Joseph Herman. 2001. "The Association between Funding by Commercial Interests and Study Outcome in Randomized Controlled Drug Trials." *Family Practice* 18 (6): 565–568.

Yu, Corrine, and William L. Taylor, eds. 1999a. *The Test of Our Progress: The Clinton Record on Civil Rights.* Washington, DC: Citizens Commission on Civil Rights.

———, eds. 1999b. *Title I in Alabama: The Struggle to Meet Basic Needs.* Washington, DC: Citizens Commission on Civil Rights.

———, eds. 1999c. *Title I in Midstream: The Fight to Improve Schools for Poor Kids.* Washington, DC: Citizens Commission on Civil Rights.

Zamudio-Suarez, Fernanda. 2017. "Missouri Lawmaker Who Wants to Eliminate Tenure Says It's 'Un-American.'" *Chronicle of Higher Education*, 12 January.

Index

Neil Kraus is Professor of Political Science at the University of Wisconsin, River Falls. He is the author of *Majoritarian Cities: Policy Making and Inequality in Urban Politics* and *Race, Neighborhoods, and Community Power: Buffalo Politics, 1934–1997*.